Mentoring, Coaching, and Collaboration

Mentoring, Coaching, and Collaboration

Edited by Corwin Press

CORWIN
PRESS
A SAGE Company

For information:

Corwin Press
A SAGE Company
2455 Teller Road
Thousand Oaks, California 91320
www.corwinpress.com

SAGE Ltd.
1 Oliver's Yard
55 City Road
London EC1Y 1SP
United Kingdom

SAGE India Pvt. Ltd.
B 1/I 1 Mohan Cooperative
    Industrial Area
Mathura Road, New Delhi 110 044
India

SAGE Asia-Pacific Pte. Ltd.
33 Pekin Street #02-01
Far East Square
Singapore 048763

Printed in the United States of America

ISBN: 978-1-4129-6969-7

This book is printed on acid-free paper.

08   09   10   11   12   10   9   8   7   6   5   4   3   2   1

Acquisitions Editor:	Dan Alpert
Editorial Assistant:	Tatiana Richards
Production Editor:	Melanie Birdsall
Typesetter:	C&M Digitals (P) Ltd.
Indexer:	Sheila Bodell
Cover Designer:	Anthony Paular

Contents

Preface

Mentoring and coaching are critical aspects of teacher leadership. Mentors play a vital role in the teaching profession by providing support, training, and collegiality, alleviating the isolation so often experienced by beginning teachers. Similarly, coaches perform a variety of important roles and responsibilities including those of mentor, resource provider, curriculum specialist, learning facilitator, and change agent. Recent years have brought an explosion of interest in both mentoring and coaching as ways to support teachers in meeting today's accountability challenges.

Mentoring, Coaching, and Collaboration is a compilation of book excerpts that presents voices of leading-edge scholars and practitioners of K–12 professional development. Most of the readings on coaching are drawn from an upcoming Corwin Press title, *Coaching: Approaches and Perspectives* (2009), by Jim Knight of the University of Kansas Center for Research on Learning. Knight brought together a team of leaders in the field of coaching and gave them a mandate to present an overview of their particular visions of coaching. The pieces selected include introductions to differentiated coaching (Kise), instructional coaching (Knight), content coaching (West), and cognitive coaching (Ellison & Hayes). The chapters on mentoring were derived from Kathleen Jonson's *Being an Effective Mentor* (Corwin Press, 2008). Jonson, who is a professor at the University of San Francisco, introduces readers to the complex process of guidance, assistance, and support to promote growth and success for beginning teachers. Additional chapters on intergenerational considerations (from *Generations at School: Building an Age-Friendly Learning Community* by Suzette Lovely and Austin G. Buffum, Corwin Press, 2007) and personality types (from *Teachers Working Together for School Success* by Mario Martinez, Corwin Press, 2004) have also been selected as introductions to these important topics.

The editors of this book have deliberately preserved the physical design of the original source materials to underscore the fact that it is a collection of individual voices from the field. We hope you enjoy the journey.

Introduction to Coaching

Approaches and Perspectives

Jim Knight

In the past decade, there has been an explosion of interest in the form of professional learning loosely described as *coaching*. The magnitude of this explosion can be measured by comparing conference programs from the nation's leading professional learning organization, the National Staff Development Council (NSDC). In the 1997 NSDC conference program, the word *coach* (or variations such as *coaching* and *coaches*) occurs 19 times. Ten years, later, in the 2007 program, the word *coach* or its variation is used 193 times. People are talking and learning about coaching, and school districts and states are implementing coaching on a grand scale.

WHY HAS INTEREST IN COACHING GROWN SO DRAMATICALLY?

Until recently, one of the most common forms of professional learning in schools was the traditional one-shot workshops offered on professional development days. Unfortunately, traditional one-shot professional development sessions are not effective for fostering professional learning. When there is no follow-up to workshops, the best educational leaders can hope for is about 10 percent implementation (Bush, 1984). What's more, traditional one-shot training sessions involve complex interactions that can actually decrease teachers' interest in growth and development and increase an anti-learning culture in schools.

After the No Child Left Behind Act (Public Law 107–110) became law on January 8, 2002, educational leaders' questions about the effectiveness of traditional professional development became more frequent, and many came to see that moving schools forward requires a variety of approaches to professional learning. One of the most promising approaches appeared to be coaching.

What coaching offers is authentic learning that provides differentiated support for professional learning. Coaching is not a quick fix; it is an approach that offers time and support for teachers to reflect, converse about, explore, and practice new ways of thinking about and doing this remarkably important and complex act called teaching. Perhaps most important, coaching puts teachers' needs at the heart of professional learning by individualizing their learning and by positioning teachers as professionals.

WHAT IS COACHING?

Although many schools and districts have been quick to recognize the potential effectiveness of coaching, leaders have been understandably less clear on what kind of coaching they are actually adopting. Today, schools employ instructional coaches or cognitive coaches or leadership coaches or differentiated coaches or reading or literacy coaches or data coaches or math coaches or content coaches—to name but a few. As my friend and colleague Candace Bixler, a leader of professional developers in Austin, Texas, has commented, "What we are doing right now in education is like bringing together successful coaches from varied sports—basketball, gymnastics, football, tennis, and swimming—to develop a winning team when we haven't even determined the sport or the playing field." With so many different approaches, leaders are excused if they are just a little confused about what coaching is and what coaching offers their school, teachers, and students.

This book has been created to (we hope) undo some of the confusion. The authors are among the leaders in the field of coaching, and their mandate has been to present an overview of their ideas about a particular approach to coaching, or their thoughts on what coaching is and what it can be. However, this book is a starting point. We hope the book helps readers better understand coaching's potential so that they will be able to make better decisions about what kind of coaching best fits their schools,' teachers,' and students' needs.

REFERENCE

Bush, R. N. (1984). Effective staff development. In *Making our schools more effective: Proceedings of three state conferences* (pp. 223–228). San Francisco: Far West Laboratories.

1

Passing the Torch

Kathleen Feeney Jonson

Those having torches will pass them on to others.

—Plato, *The Republic*

Twenty second graders stand in line inside the door to Room 3D at Lincoln Elementary School. "Kyle cut!" Cameron insists, gripping his folder and lunch box. Ms. Blackwell glances at the boys, but Kyle denies the accusation. The clock ticks to 2:40 p.m., and the bell rings. With a weary smile, Ms. Blackwell waves good-bye and watches as the children scurry out, the two boys still arguing. Feeling a sense of relief, she turns back into the classroom. Too late, she discovers that Caitlin has forgotten to put her chair up on her table again, and Danny hasn't picked up his pencil from the floor as she asked him to do. She must work on better follow-through.

Ms. Blackwell kneels to pick up Danny's pencil, lifts up Caitlin's chair, and returns to her desk. Sighing, she looks at the pile of spelling papers on her desk, the large, dark letters carefully—or not so carefully—printed on wide lines. With a glance, she can tell that most of the words on the top paper are misspelled. She had been so sure that her new study-in-buddies idea would work, but apparently it hadn't. At least not for everyone.

Reprinted from Jonson, K. F. (2008). *Being an effective mentor: How to help beginning teachers succeed* (2nd ed.). Thousand Oaks, CA: Corwin Press. Copyright © 2008 by Corwin Press, www.corwinpress .com. All rights reserved.

Ms. Blackwell sets aside the papers, too disheartened to review them. Her eyes burn as she reflects on her day. Again today, Maggie complained that James was chasing her on the playground. The experiment Ms. Blackwell had planned for the unit on rocks was too difficult. And her throat is burning—but she can't take time off and leave her class with a substitute. She looks at her desk. Oh, and there's that form she was supposed to have returned to the office yesterday. She should take care of that now—except that she doesn't really understand it. Besides, she needs to get to a teachers' meeting by 3:00. She was late to the last one. Better be on time for this one. Don't want to appear unable to manage.

Ms. Blackwell plants the late form in the middle of her desk so she will be sure to see it first thing when she returns, gathers her papers for the meeting, grabs a tissue for her runny nose, and heads out into the hall. She wonders if any of the other new teachers have these problems or if it's just her.

She had done so well at the university, had loved student teaching with Mr. Beverly. What had happened? Would it ever get easier? She had worked so hard last August to set up her classroom perfectly, tacking up colorful wall coverings and organizing things as discussed in her university classes. Everyone—her professors and friends and the people at Mr. Beverly's school—had assured her that she would make a great teacher. But she doesn't seem to be doing so well now. She tries to think about how Mr. Beverly might handle James. But the boys in Mr. Beverly's fourth grade hadn't chased the girls. Seems that few of the problems she faces now came up when she student-taught with Mr. Beverly. If only she had a Mr. Beverly to turn to now.

The anxieties and frustrations that Ms. Blackwell feels are typical of first-year teachers—and sometimes of teachers in general. No matter how well prepared a beginning teacher may be on entering the profession—no matter how positive her preservice experience—the early years are always difficult. Issues of classroom and time management commonly cause significant stress. The tasks to be completed seem endless, and when a problem arises, the teacher, alone in the classroom, cannot turn to a coworker for immediate support as another professional in another field might do. Too often during their first years of on-the-job training, teachers throughout history have had to master their craft by trial and error, in an isolated environment, with little feedback.

The first two years of teaching are particularly critical. During this time, the teacher builds the foundation for what could be a satisfying and productive career. But these first two years are also considered by many to be the hardest. In this profession, unlike in others, the beginning teacher has the same workload and responsibilities as the veteran. Teachers are expected to be experts ready to tackle the biggest challenges on the first day they enter a school (Alliance for Excellent Education, 2004, p. 2). There is no period for adjustment. What might seem to be the simple mechanics of running a real-world classroom from day to day prove to be surprisingly distressing and stressful.

The result? Often during this "induction" period, beginning teachers become frustrated and eager to leave. Far too many report lying awake, unable to sleep at night, fretting about their students and school responsibilities. According to a survey of stress in various professions, teachers (followed by nurses, accountants, and newspaper reporters) are the people most likely to report losing sleep over work-related worries ("Losing Sleep," 2001). This beginning teacher sheds some light on the problem:

> Stress! You're teaching classes all day long. You're keeping students on task, you're testing, you're trying to follow all the rules—every principle and guideline that's set out for you. You're adhering to a schedule: you must teach all the things in the course of study by the end of the year. After school you go home and take your job with you. Then you must face kids who have homework and a husband who has had a tough day, too (quoted in Gordon & Maxey, 2000, p. 66).

To many in their first year of teaching, then, figuring out how to control students whose first instincts are anything but cooperative makes just surviving a real accomplishment. Without assistance and support, these beginning teachers burn out early at a high rate. Some, overwhelmed by all the "juggling" they have to do, leave the teaching profession altogether. Nationwide, 30% of beginning teachers leave the profession within two years, another 10% leave after three years, and more than half leave within five to seven years (Alliance for Excellent Education, 2004, p. 1; Ingersoll, 2001, p. 514; Pearson & Honig, 1992, p. 5). In urban districts, attrition occurs even faster: Half the new teachers are gone within three years (Haberman, 1987; Zimpher & Grossman, 1992, p. 141). According to the Alliance for Excellent Education (2004), the current "rate of attrition among beginning teachers is astronomical."

And this rate of attrition affects everyone: the community that must continue to recruit and train new teachers, the teachers who find themselves leaving a career they had spent years preparing for, and the children. The National Commission on Teaching and America's Future (NCTAF) has gathered information on teacher preparation since the early 1990s and has published many reports on the relationship between teacher quality and student success. In a 2003 report, *No Dream Denied: A Pledge to America's School Children*, the commission states,

> Schools pay a price as high turnover rates force an annual scramble to replace those who leave. Teachers pay a price as their frustrations lead to short-circuited careers. But students pay the highest prices of all: diminished learning and dreams denied (p. 11).

Particularly disturbing is research indicating that the most academically proficient teachers are also the ones who are most likely to leave the field (Schlechty & Vance, 1983; Smith, 1993, p. 6). In a study of beginning teachers in San Diego County, California, a teacher leaving the profession after her first year had received one of only six National Education Outstanding Student Teacher Awards (Mathison, 1996, p. 15). The loss of such a potentially exceptional teacher clearly indicates that something is wrong. And according to First Lady Laura Bush's *Ready to Read, Ready to Learn* initiative, "teachers with higher standardized test scores leave teaching at much higher rates than those with lower scores" (2001, p. 11).

Why would someone who had spent four to six years preparing for a profession leave the career within a year or two? What is it that makes beginning teacher after beginning teacher feel as if his years of study have left him unprepared for the world of teaching? And how can this situation be changed to benefit the children in U.S. classrooms?

ENTER THE MENTOR

Throughout the United States, educational systems began to realize in the early 1980s that a serious problem existed: Teachers need assistance and guidance, especially during their early years in the profession. According to *No Dream Denied*, teacher retention relates strongly not only to adequate preparation (background in subject matter and teaching methods) but also to meaningful induction and mentoring programs (NCTAF, 2003). No matter how well prepared, a teacher such as Ms. Blackwell needs someone to turn to with the inevitable questions and problems that arise as she begins her profession in the classroom.

With this recognition, more than 30 states now mandate support for beginning teachers as part of their teacher induction programs (Portner, 1998, p. 3). Increasingly, school districts are arranging for experienced teachers (*mentors*) to guide beginning teachers (*mentees* or *protégés*) through the difficult early years and to help them develop as professionals. And although this book focuses on support for beginning teachers, it is important to note that teachers new to a system also often need assistance (Smith, 1993, p. 7). In some locations, mentors have been recruited to work not only with beginning teachers but also with teachers new to the district or even with experienced teachers having difficulty. Both of the two latter groups of teachers need practical assistance with tasks such as making schedules for breaks and for lunch, hall, and yard duties, and they need information about where to get supplies and materials, about required forms and meetings, and so on. Like newcomers to the profession, veterans moving to a different location need a realistic view of their new school to help them "understand the challenges that inevitably surface when people experience the transition from one job to another" (Gordon & Maxey, 2000, p. 84). Mentors can help the newcomer understand the culture and philosophy of the school and can provide the emotional and intellectual support needed in the early days and months of adjustment.

The idea of a mentor helping a beginner is nothing new. The term *mentor* itself dates back to the eighth or ninth century BCE, specifically to Homer's *Odyssey*. In his epic poem, Homer describes his hero, Odysseus, as Odysseus prepares to set out on a 10-year voyage. Odysseus must leave behind his son, Telemachus, and asks his trusted friend Mentor to guide and counsel Telemachus in his absence. While the father is gone, Mentor serves as a sage adviser to the younger man, helping him grow intellectually, emotionally, and socially. From this ancient literary figure, *mentor* has come to refer to a wise and faithful counselor who helps guide a protégé through a developmental process. This could be the process of transition from youth to adulthood, as in the case of Telemachus, or from student to professional, as with a first-year teacher.

Modern-day mentors are found in many segments of society. The Big Brother and Big Sister programs are based on the mentor concept: Responsible adults are paired with children; they build a trusting relationship with those children and share with them a variety of activities, guiding them as they grow into young adults. Athletic or drama coaches could also be considered mentors, directing novices in their field. In the professional arena, doctors and lawyers have long been mentored through internship programs, and plumbers, printers, and other skilled tradespeople serve in apprenticeships, another variation of mentorships.

As these examples illustrate, the skills involved, age groups, and degree of formality vary widely among mentoring programs. The common thread, though, is that all such programs are based on a trusting relationship between an experienced adult and a novice. In each case, the organization or business that wants to retain and develop its members provides some sort of mentor support. The idea is not for the mentor to evaluate or judge the protégé, but rather for the mentee to receive guidance. The mentor is defined more by the relationship with a beginner than by a position or title.

Some such relationships happen spontaneously. For example, a new employee asks advice of a more experienced colleague, who sees potential in the beginner and continues to offer support. Other pairings result from a considered design. Large corporations, for example, sometimes match senior managers to ambitious, talented junior employees. Mentors in this situation may help newer employees with such issues as balancing personal and business lives, as well as working within the corporate environment. The mentees learn that their concerns are not unique—that other employees have experienced the same problems—and this knowledge helps them grow professionally.

According to several studies, mentors have played an important role in the career development of many highly successful people in business. In one study, researchers found that businesspeople who had mentors earned more money at a younger age and were more satisfied with their work and career advancement than were those without mentors (Bolton, 1980; Odell, 1990, p. 5; Roche, 1979). Mentoring programs in business were found to help the protégé with personal adjustment, satisfaction, and professional achievement (Bova, 1987; Cohen, 1995, p. 4; Kram, 1985; Marsick, 1987; Zey, 1984). In both university and business settings, protégés of mentors learned risk-taking behaviors, communication skills, political skills, and specific skills that helped them in their professions (Bova & Phillips, 1983; Odell, 1990, p. 6). Even in government, mentors have helped employees develop their careers and prepare for senior positions (Cohen, 1995, p. 4; Murray, 1991).

Mentoring would seem to be a natural progression in the teaching profession, too, where experienced teachers have traditionally passed on their expertise and wisdom to new colleagues. For a beginning teacher, the benefits of working closely with a mentor are great, no matter how extensive the preservice education. Beginning teachers are faced by and accountable for (or to—it is not always clear which) an array of unknown students, teaching colleagues, administrators, and parents. As Ms. Blackwell discovered, even routine paperwork can be overwhelming when the teacher does not understand it and does not know where to look for help. In addition, school and community environments have norms and rituals that are probably new and obscure to a newcomer. The large number of actual and procedural unknowns can send the beginning teacher into a state of shock wherein it becomes impossible to transfer previously mastered concepts and skills from the university to the K–12 classroom. Ms. Blackwell could have benefited greatly from the help of a veteran teacher familiar with her grade level and school site.

So far in education, relatively little hard research has been conducted on the effects of mentoring. Many descriptive studies and program evaluations clearly conclude, however, that a good mentor-mentee relationship significantly benefits the beginning teacher, not only during the difficult first year but also in years to come. Through an examination of the literature and many research studies on beginning teachers, Varah, Theune, and Parker (1986) have concluded that "collaborative teacher induction programs are effective means of strengthening beginning teacher performance" (quoted in Smith, 1993, p. 6). Other studies have also indicated that mentors and induction programs are overwhelmingly successful, increasing the retention of beginning teachers and ameliorating first-year difficulties (Bey, 1992, p. 114; Smith, 1993).

Despite this seemingly natural form of assistance, teachers have had no formal system like those used in businesses through which to receive guidance once they entered their first professional classroom—until recently. Not until the early 1980s did those in the teaching profession begin to take up the mentoring torch. Now the trend is gaining momentum, however. In 1997, the U.S. Secretary of Education included in his initiatives, published in *The Seven Priorities of the U.S. Department of Education*, "special efforts to retain beginning teachers in their first few years of teaching"

(U.S. Department of Education, 1997). That same year, in his *Call to Action for American Education in the 21st Century*, then-President Bill Clinton announced that school districts must "make sure that beginning teachers get support and mentoring from experienced teachers" (*President Clinton's Call*, 1997).

With rising student enrollment, teacher attrition ranging from 35% to 50% nationwide during the first five years, class size reduction in some states, and many teachers approaching retirement, the need for new teachers continues. The U.S. Department of Education projected that more than 2 million new teachers would be needed within the first decade of the 21st century (Moir & Gless, n.d., p. 1). Although President George W. Bush has focused more recently on standards and testing, it is increasingly important to guide and retain those who enter the profession if children in the classrooms are to learn.

Teachers themselves support the idea of teacher-mentors. Teachers have reported that they get their best innovative ideas regarding teaching from other teachers (Sergiovanni, 1992, p. 86). In one large national study funded by Public Agenda, many administrators and new teachers expressed a belief that mentoring programs could significantly improve teacher quality (Farkas, Johnson, & Foleno, 2000, p. 29). In another national sample, this one looking at 1,007 beginning teachers, 46% said an experienced teacher assigned to advise and assist them would have been most helpful in preparing them to become more effective as first-year teachers (Bey, 1992, p. 111; Lou Harris & Associates, 1991).

THE ROLE OF THE TEACHER-MENTOR

In the field of teaching, the mentor plays a vital and unique role in the development and training of someone new to the profession. An effective mentor provides support and collegiality, alleviating the isolation so often experienced by the beginning teacher. What makes mentors different from others who may help is that they develop a relationship of trust with beginning teachers over an extended period of time and remain with the mentees as they evolve and as issues develop. One California mentor notes that this trust is particularly important: "My mentee and I have a trusting relationship in that he can be open and honest with his needs." In contrast, a principal, for example, may be available to help with a specific, one-time problem on a practical level, but does not necessarily provide ongoing, daily help with a range of emotional, curricular, and instructional questions.

For a variety of reasons, an experienced colleague is particularly suited to the mentor role. According to Acheson and Gall, "The most available source of expertise is teachers themselves: to analyze their own teaching on the basis of objective data, to observe others' classrooms and record data teachers cannot record themselves, to help one another analyze these data and make decisions about alternative strategies" (as quoted in Heller, 2004, p. 194).

A colleague who is close at hand is available when the mentee needs guidance, in both formal and informal contexts. If both parties work in the same setting and with similar goals, they can often relate to each other's experiences; Ms. Blackwell, for example, might have found help from a mentor who had shared her problems with the students at her school. Because integrity and trust are vital to a good mentor-mentee relationship, many experienced mentors feel strongly that mentors should not be involved in evaluating their mentees. If this is the case, mentees are more likely to share experiences, fears, and concerns without the anxiety of being judged. Those same beginning teachers might be reluctant to share these feelings or problems with their principal, for example, who will later evaluate them and help make decisions about the future of their careers.

The primary task of the mentor, then, is to establish a relationship with the beginning teacher based on mutual trust, respect, and collegiality. Through the sharing of frustrations and successes, the beginning teacher learns that problems are normal, and this helps build confidence. One California mentor believes that important contributions for a mentee might include "validating the challenges of teaching; taking [the mentees'] ideas and feelings seriously; helping them to trust their own judgment." Another points out the value of "discussing problems realistically and letting them know I have the same problems sometimes; just letting them vent."

Support and encouragement from an effective mentor can thus greatly benefit the beginning teacher: In most beginner assistance programs, however, the mentor also directly assists beginning teachers, helping them learn quickly as they are immersed in the complex art and science of teaching. "When I first visited my mentee," one California mentor recalls, "his classroom was completely out of control. Afterward I gave him feedback and five simple, concrete policy suggestions. Immediate implementation led to immediate results." Yet another mentor tells about helping with a specific lesson. "My mentee was having trouble organizing a weather unit," this one said. "So we took a couple of hours and we went through my whole weather file and we made a schedule and lesson plan for the new unit."

Among the mentor's goals, then, should be to help beginning teachers develop and enhance the following attributes:

- Competence: mastery of the knowledge, skills, and applications that effective teaching requires
- Self-confidence: belief in one's ability to make good decisions, to be responsible, and to be in control
- Self-direction: the assurance and ability to take charge of one's personal, professional, and career development

- Professionalism: an understanding and assumption of the responsibilities and ethics of the profession

THE GOOD MENTOR: WHAT DOES IT TAKE?

The task of mentoring is complex and requires the skills of a teacher, counselor, friend, role model, guide, sponsor, coach, resource, and colleague. Through the years, mentors have also gone by the names of *host, supporter, adviser, positive role model, confidant, guru, master teacher, teacher adviser, teacher specialist, colleague teacher, peer teacher,* and *support teacher.*

Under any name, though, the idea is the same: An experienced and expert professional develops a relationship with a trained but inexperienced protégé. The mentor may incorporate a variety of strategies and activities to help the protégé grow and develop in professional competence, attitudes, and behaviors—but regardless of the specific activities and goals, the qualitative nature of the relationship determines the overall effectiveness of the mentor.

So what makes a good mentor? Is it just a matter of being a highly accomplished teacher? Certainly that's a good starting point, but it's not enough. Commitment to promoting excellence in the teaching profession? That's important, too. But even more is required. Mentors are special people. Good ones have qualities and responsibilities that include but go beyond those of a good teacher. For teachers, a good mentor

- is a skilled teacher,
- has a thorough command of the curriculum being taught,
- is able to transmit effective teaching strategies,
- can communicate openly and effectively with the beginning teacher,
- is a good listener,
- is able to transmit effective teaching strategies,
- has strong interpersonal skills,
- has credibility with peers and administrators,
- is sensitive to the needs of the beginning teacher,
- understands that teachers may be effective using a variety of styles,
- is not overly judgmental,
- demonstrates an eagerness to learn, and
- demonstrates a commitment to improving the academic achievement of all students.

Studies show that other desirable qualities in a mentor include wisdom, caring, humor, nurturing, and commitment to the profession (Hardcastle, 1988; Kay, 1990; Odell, 1990, p. 11). If the job were to be posted, an announcement might read something like that in Box 1.1.

BOX 1.1

Job Announcement

Teacher-Mentor

Description

Experienced teachers who have mastered their craft and who are dedicated to promoting excellence in the teaching profession are sought as mentors for beginning teachers just starting their careers. Mentors must play several roles, including guide, role model, sponsor, counselor, coach, resource, and colleague.

Responsibilities

As a mentor, you will be responsible for

- Meeting regularly with your protégé, both formally and informally
- Guiding your protégé through the daily operation of the school
- Arranging for your protégé to visit different teachers' classes
- Demonstrating lessons for your protégé
- Observing your protégé's teaching and providing feedback
- Being a role model in all aspects of professionalism
- Developing your skills as a mentor as well as a teacher
- Supporting and counseling your protégé, providing perspective when needed

Qualifications

It takes a special person to be a good mentor. Maturity, self-assurance, patience, and confidence in your knowledge and ability are prerequisites for this important undertaking. More specifically, a good mentor is a teacher who

- Is a skillful teacher
- Is able to transmit effective teaching strategies
- Has a thorough command of the curriculum being taught
- Is a good listener
- Can communicate openly with the beginning teacher
- Is sensitive to the needs of the beginning teacher
- Understands that teachers may be effective using a variety of styles
- Is careful not to be overly judgmental

Conditions of Employment

Extra time, effort, and commitment are required. Increased contact with colleagues, professional stimulation, and sense of accomplishment are likely. Tangible compensation—never enough; intangible rewards—priceless.

Mentors needed every year! Apply now!

Requirements for mentoring go even beyond these general characteristics and qualities. Good mentors understand the needs of beginning teachers and of teachers building professionalism. They are armed with effective instructional coaching strategies appropriate for the adult learner. Problem-solving skills and the ability to think critically and reflectively are also prerequisites.

Mentoring requires commitment and a willingness to extend oneself for another person. Good mentors must be conscious that their own professional development serves as a model for the beginning teacher and that lifelong learning is as much an attitude as it is an activity; for true professionals, learning is a way of life. With an effective program, the rewards include not only the satisfaction of helping a beginning teacher succeed but also personal and professional growth for the mentor.

> Being a mentor keeps me current. When I have to answer my mentee's questions, it makes me ask, "Why am I doing what I'm doing?" In discussing philosophy, problems, or techniques with this new teacher, I find out what I really believe. That makes me a stronger person and a better teacher.
>
> —A mentor (quoted in Gordon & Maxey, 2000, p. 66)

REFERENCES

Acheson, J., & Gall, M. (1980). *Techniques in the clinical supervision of teachers.* New York: Longman.

Alliance for Excellent Education. (2004, June 23). *Tapping into potential: Retaining and developing high-quality new teachers.* Washington, DC: Author.

Bey, T. M. (1992). Mentoring in teacher education: Diversifying support for teachers. In T. M. Bey & C. T. Holmes (Eds.), *Mentoring: Contemporary principles and issues* (pp. 111–120). Reston, VA: Association of Teacher Educators.

Bolton, E. (1980). A conceptual analysis of the mentor relationship in the career development of women. *Adult Education, 30,* 195–297.

Bova, B. (1987). Mentoring as a learning experience. In V. J. Marsick (Ed.), *Learning in the workplace.* London: Croom Helm.

Bova, B. M., & Phillips, R. R. (1983). Mentoring as a learning experience for adults. *Journal of Teacher Education, 35*(3), 16–20.

Bush, L. (2001). *Ready to read, ready to learn: An education initiative.* Retrieved January 8, 2007, from www.whitehouse.gov/firstlady/initiatives/readyto readoverview.pdf

Cohen, N. H. (1995). *Mentoring adult learners: A guide for educators and trainers.* Malabar, FL: Krieger.

Farkas, S., Johnson, J., & Foleno, T. (2000). *A sense of calling: Who teaches and why.* New York: Public Agenda.

Gordon, S. P., & Maxey, S. (2000). *How to help beginning teachers succeed.* Alexandria, VA: Association for Supervision and Curriculum Development.

Haberman, M. (1987). *Recruiting and selecting teachers for urban schools.* Reston, VA: Association of Teacher Educators and ERIC Clearinghouse on Urban Education.

Hardcastle, B. (1988). Spiritual connections: Protégés' reflections on significant mentorships. *Theory Into Practice, 27,* 201–208.

Heller, D. A. (2004). *Teachers wanted: Attracting and retaining good teachers.* Alexandria, VA: Association for Supervision and Curriculum Development.

Ingersoll, R. (2001). Teacher turnover and teacher shortages: An organizational analysis. *American Educational Research Journal, 38*(3), 499–534.

Kay, R. S. (1990). Mentoring: Definition, principles, and applications. In T. M. Bey & C. T. Holmes (Eds.), *Mentoring: Developing successful new teachers.* Reston, VA: Association of Teacher Educators.

Kram, K. E. (1985). *Mentoring at work.* Glenview, IL: Scott Foresman.

Losing sleep. (2001, January 23). *Contra Costa Times,* sec. D.

Lou Harris & Associates. (1991). *The Metropolitan Life Survey of the American Teacher, 1991. The first year: New teachers' expectations and ideals.* New York: Author.

Marsick, V. J. (Ed.). (1987). *Learning in the workplace.* New York: Croom Helm.

Mathison, C. (1996). The challenges of beginning middle and secondary urban school teachers. *Issues in Teacher Education, 5*(1), 5–18.

Moir, E., & Gless, J. *Quality induction: An investment in teachers. Santa Cruz New Teacher Center.* Retrieved September 21, 2006, from www.newteachercenter.org/article1.php

Murray, M. (1991). *Beyond the myths and magic of mentoring.* San Francisco: Jossey-Bass.

National Commission on Teaching and America's Future. (2003). *No dream denied: A pledge to America's school children.* Washington, DC.

Odell, S. J. (1990). Support for new teachers. In T. M. Bey & C. T. Holmes (Eds.), *Mentoring: Developing successful new teachers* (pp. 3–23). Reston, VA: Association of Teacher Educators.

Pearson, M. J., & Honig, B. (1992). Problems confronting beginning teachers. In *Success for beginning teachers: The California New Teacher Project* (pp. 5–14). Sacramento: California Department of Education, California Commission on Teacher Credentialing.

Portner, H. (1998). *Mentoring new teachers.* Thousand Oaks, CA: Corwin.

President Clinton's Call to Action for American Education in the 21st Century. (1997). Retrieved February 8, 2002, from www.ed.gov/updates/PresEDPlan

Roche, G. R. (1979). Much ado about mentors. *Harvard Business Review, 57*(1), 14–16, 20, 24–27.

Schlechty, P. C., & Vance, V. S. (1983). Recruitment, selection, and retention: The shape of the teaching force. *Elementary School Journal, 83,* 469–487.

Sergiovanni, T. J. (1992). Collegiality as a professional virtue. In *Moral leadership: Getting to the heart of school improvement.* San Francisco: Jossey-Bass.

Shanker, A. (1995, February 22). *Sink or swim.* Retrieved February 8, 2002, from www.aft.org/stand/previous/1995/012295.html

Smith, R. D. (1993). Mentoring new teachers: Strategies, structures, and successes. *Teacher Education Quarterly, 20*(4), 5–18.

U.S. Department of Education. (1997). *Seven priorities of the U.S. Department of Education* (Working document). Retrieved February 8, 2002, from www.ed.gov/updates/7priorities

Varah, L. J., Theune, W. S., & Parker, L. (1986). Beginning teachers: Sink or swim? *Journal of Teacher Education, 37*(1), 30–33.

Zey, M. G. (1984). *The mentor connection.* Homewood, IL: Dow Jones-Irwin.

Zimpher, N. L., & Grossman, J. E. (1992). Collegial support by teacher mentors and peer consultants. In C. D. Glickman (Ed.), *Supervision in transition: 1992 yearbook of the Association for Supervision and Curriculum Development* (pp. 141–154). Alexandria, VA: Association for Supervision and Curriculum Development.

2

Coaches' Roles, Responsibilities, and Reach

Joellen Killion

Improving student academic success is hard work and the challenge grows each day. School and district leaders have initiated reforms that range from curriculum alignment; common assessment; new curricular programs; increased expectations for students, teachers, and principals; and improved instruction. Each of these initiatives has the potential to add value to the educational system. The potential impact of these and other reform initiatives increases exponentially if school-based implementation support is added into the mix.

Implementation support provides crucial school- and classroom-based support that facilitates the use of, rather than knowledge about, the reform efforts. Increasingly schools and districts are employing coaches to assume some of the responsibilities related to implementation support. Coaches are master teachers who participate in explicit professional development about coaching to become skilful. In professional development they examine their fundamental beliefs about student learning, teaching, and coaching; acquire deep knowledge about adult development and change; and acquire skillfulness with a broad range of strategies to use in their new role. Called by many different titles, teacher leaders in this role are primarily school-based professional development specialists who work with individuals and teams to design and facilitate appropriate learning experiences, provide feedback and support, and assist with implementation challenges. Their work centers on refining and honing teaching, and their indicator of success is student academic success.

This chapter focuses on the work coaches do when they interact with individuals and teams. First, it describes the variation in coaches' work by identifying the 10 most common forms of assistance coaches provide to teachers and some of the challenges coaches face in each role. Second, it examines variables that influence coaches' decisions regarding the support they provide teachers. Last, this chapter explores the concepts of coaching heavy and coaching light—ways to think about the intensity and impact of coaching and how the roles and coaches' beliefs influence their decisions about how they allocate their time and services to support teachers.

TEN ROLES OF COACHES

In our book, *Taking the Lead: New Roles for Teacher Leaders and School-Based Coaches,* my colleague Cindy Harrison and I (Killion & Harrison, 2006) describe 10 different roles coaches fill in their work. Some coaches serve in all 10 roles. Others have a narrower focus and may serve in only a few roles. By narrowing the range of roles, coaches focus their work more intensely on those roles that have the greatest potential for impact on teaching and student learning. However, determining which roles have the greatest leverage on improving teaching and learning depends on several factors. This section first describes the roles and second examines factors that influence the allocation of time and effort to each role.

Without a clear framework for their day, coaches find that their time is fragmented. When coaches' work is so expansive, the potential exists that coaches will take on too many roles and, as a result, dilute the impact of their work.

The roles described here constitute a range of support coaches provide teachers. Each role requires a specific set of knowledge and skills. Each role has a distinctive set of challenges. Each meets a specific teacher need.

Data Coach

A data coach assists individual teachers or teams of teachers to examine student achievement data and to use these data to design instruction that addresses student learning needs. School improvement planning teams usually begin the data analysis process in a school by analyzing state and district achievement data to identify school improvement goals. Coaches take this work a step further. Their data work concentrates on facilitating teachers' understanding of grade-level, team, and classroom data, helping teachers use these data to make instructional and curricular decisions. Through fine analysis guided by coaches, teachers determine which students will benefit from moving on, reteaching, additional practice, or extension. Coaches assist teachers in using a wide variety of classroom data to monitor progress on academic goals. One of the most significant challenges coaches have as data coaches is creating a safe, blame-free environment for ruthless analysis of data.

Resource Provider

Teachers turn to their coach for resources that are not immediately available to them. Sometimes, the request for resources includes accessing supplies, leveled books, and additional resources for students to use in the classroom that would meet the needs of students with different learning preferences, academic ability, or interest. Sometimes, the requests for resources are teacher resources such as lesson or unit plans, assignments, or references to help teachers develop instructional plans. Occasionally, the resource requests are for services outside the school or district such as a guest speaker. Teachers expect coaches to be knowledgeable about what is available within the school and district and even within the community. This resourcefulness does not go unnoticed. Their challenge as resource providers, many coaches find, is that this role constitutes a good deal of their time.

Mentor

Coaches serve the needs of new teachers or new-to-the-school teachers. When working with this particular client group, coaches may find that they are engaging in all 10 of the roles simultaneously. The role of mentor is distinguished as a distinct role for coaches because the teacher client is unique and requires coaches to have specific knowledge about stages of teacher development and coaching skills specific to novice teachers. As a mentor, the coach's primary responsibility is acclimatizing the new teacher to the school's professional norms, practices, and policies. With support, the new-to-the-school teacher or novice teacher more quickly feels comfortable and adjusts to the expectations and routines of the school. Mentors frequently provide other support particular to new teachers that includes the roles of curriculum specialist, instructional specialist, and classroom supporter. A challenge coaches encounter as mentors is balancing support with building professional capacity. The struggle between dependence and independence looms in coaches' daily interactions with novice teachers. Coaches balance providing advice with developing novice teachers' capacity to make decisions.

Curriculum Specialist

The coach serving as a curriculum specialist focuses on the *what* of teaching rather than the *how*. A coach in this role helps a teacher understand and use the district's adopted curriculum, know how to break concepts into attributes, use the pacing guide, and understand the scope of concepts taught. In this role, coaches might find that they are deepening teachers' understanding of the concepts they teach. Teachers, with the support of their coach, use a deep understanding of the curriculum to engage in planning the sequence of concepts within instructional units that have both rigor and relevance. Teachers with support of their coaches develop a clear understanding of what successful learning looks like to guide the development of student assessments. Assessments of student learning align with the curriculum and developmental and academic needs of students, engage students in critical and creative thinking, and provide students multiple ways to demonstrate their learning. Coaches responsible for supporting teachers in grades beyond their teaching experience or content area may feel inadequate and, as a result, may find it challenging to provide schoolwide support to *all* teachers.

Instructional Specialist

Once teachers know *what* to teach and what successful learning looks like, they turn their attention to *how* to teach it. Coaches help teachers choose appropriate instructional methodologies and differentiate instruction to meet students' different learning preferences and academic readiness levels. Matching instructional approaches with curriculum requires that teachers have a broad repertoire of strategies as well as assessment methodology to reach all students. Coaches also support teachers in creating safe and productive learning environments that enhance learning for all students, including English language learners, special needs learners, and gifted students. Coaches help teachers think about how to manage grouping within their classrooms, integrate resource staff when appropriate, hold students responsible for their learning, and establish classroom routines that facilitate students' independence and responsibility. A significant challenge that coaches in this role face is that they may not know enough about instructional methodology to reach *all* students.

Classroom Supporter

This is often called the *big* role for coaches. Typically, when people talk about coaching they hold an image of this role in which the coach works side by side with the teacher inside the teacher's classroom engaged in modeling effective teaching practices, coteaching, and/or observing and giving feedback. What is unique to this role is the location of the coaches' work. They work inside the classroom with one or more teachers while teaching and student learning are occurring. No other role takes place in the same way. All others are done outside the classroom or in the classroom when students are elsewhere. Yet for some coaches this role constitutes only a small portion of their work. This role requires a broad range of skills including coplanning, coteaching, observing, crafting feedback, and engaging in thoughtful, reflective conversation about teaching and learning. In this role, coaches may face resistance from teachers because of the intrusiveness required to fulfill the role.

Learning Facilitator

Learning facilitators organize, coordinate, support, design, or facilitate learning among adults within the school. Some might call this role *professional development*, however, coaching is professional development. A learning facilitator enhances or enriches teachers' instructional repertoire, deepens teachers' content knowledge, and expands their understanding of how students learn. In this role, coaches may lead a book study, coordinate action research teams, hold a workshop on new instructional strategies, engage a team in lesson study, facilitate a faculty meeting in which teachers examine student work using the Tuning Protocol or Critical Friends Process, or engage a department in scoring common assessments. In each of these roles, the coach starts with student achievement data. From these data, working together coaches and teachers determine the teacher learning needs. Then coaches create their instructional plan driven by explicit outcomes for teachers and procedures that are respectful and appropriate for the adult learners and the content. Meeting the diverse learning needs of *all* teachers is a challenge coaches in this role face, yet by employing more collaborative, team-based designs for professional learning, coaches build communities of learners who learn with and from one another.

School Leader

As school leaders, coaches contribute to schoolwide reform initiatives. Those in the role of coach have a difficult time avoiding this role. They are perceived as leaders both by their peers and by the school's administrators. In this role, coaches lead reform within their schools and classrooms. Coaches advocate for school and district initiatives and assist teachers in fully implementing the reform behaviors. Coaches may lead task forces, facilitate school improvement teams, chair schoolwide committees, and represent their school on districtwide committees. Coaches lead most importantly with their attitude and integrity. They model salient behaviors of education professionals and work to create a healthy, collaborative community of learners among adults in their schools. Yet, coaches walk a delicate line between administration and teachers. They are neither really. Coaches have no supervisory responsibilities and so their allegiance rests most often with teachers. Occasionally, however, they are asked to engage in administrative responsibilities that confuse their identity within a school.

Catalyst for Change

Beyond serving as school leader, coaches frequently initiate change. In the role of catalyst for change, coaches demonstrate dissatisfaction with the status quo and question routines with inquiry. By making observations, stating their point of view, and inquiring into practice, coaches erode stagnant practice and unchallenged routines to spark analysis, reflection, and appropriate change. In this role, a coach is not about change for change sake, but rather for continuous improvement and fine tuning to meet clearly articulated goals. In his landmark research of schools in Georgia, Carl Glickman (1993) notes that schools that had the greatest improvements in student achievement were those in which the staff expressed dissatisfaction with their work, and that schools with limited improvement in student achievement had staff who were satisfied with their work. Coaches have the capacity to question and instill curiosity and doubt, thereby generating dissonance essential to promote change. As one coach reported, finding the delicate balance between sufficient dissonance and disruptive dissonance is tricky. She said it is hard to know if she goes too far until she arrives there.

Learner

The last of the 10 roles of coaches is that of learner. As a learner, a coach engages in his or her own continuous development, searching for ideas, resources, and strategies to strengthen coaching practices, and to reflect on his or her work as a coach. Coaches, as learners, attend conferences and workshops on topics related to their school's reform efforts and coaching skills. They read widely both in education and outside. Together with other coaches, they network and problem solve in their own community of practice. They write to develop deep understanding of their experiences and to identify both their strengths and their areas for improvement. Their journals or logs serve as a source of reflective analysis about their work as a coach. Using the data from their logs, they ask whether they have engaged in the most appropriate roles with a particular group of teachers and if they are balancing their time among their many roles and responsibilities. Coaches as learners model learning for their peers by talking about what they are learning and reading, their mistakes, their insights, and their discoveries. They talk too about how they learn and explore multiple learning approaches. Their challenge in this role, coaches report, is devoting time to their own learning.

BALANCING THE ROLES

While most coaches recognize these roles as the work they do, they also wonder how to balance the roles. This curiosity represents a significant programmatic issue that many coaching programs fail to address in the earliest stages. Sadly, too many coaching programs have been launched with an insufficient program framework designed to maximize the impact of coaching on teaching and student learning. Multiple factors influence the balance among the roles. They include coaches' job descriptions, their role expectations, the goals of the coaching program, the goals of a school's improvement plan, the context in which they work, the time of the school year, the experience of the coach, and the experience of the teacher. The influence of some of these factors may seem obvious; others may not. Knowing how to allocate time during the workday is difficult when any of these factors is fuzzy.

Job Descriptions and Role Expectations

When asking the question about balancing the roles, coaches first look to their clear job descriptions and role expectations. Some job descriptions make coaches' work explicit. In the School District of Philadelphia, for example, the school growth teachers have three explicit roles—mentor, data coach, and learning facilitator. Literacy and numeracy coaches fill the roles of instructional and curriculum specialist and classroom supporter and work in tandem with school growth teachers. Working as a team, these resource personnel provide comprehensive support to teachers. In Fairfax County (Virginia) Public Schools, cluster-based instructional coaches are responsible for improving reading and math achievement, closing the achievement gap, and creating a culture of collaboration. Their primary roles are data coach, instructional specialist, curriculum specialist, classroom supporter, and learning facilitator. Because they spend 60% of their time working with teams of teachers and 40% with individuals, they are able to focus on more roles. In Walla Walla (Washington) Public Schools, coaches are responsible for increasing math and literacy achievement. They do this mostly in the roles of data coach, classroom supporter, curriculum specialist, instructional specialist, and learning facilitator.

Role expectations are defined in the performance standards for the role of coach. Many school districts with coaches attempt to use teacher performance standards when evaluating coaches. This does a disservice to coaches. Their new role as a coach has new expectations, new responsibilities, and therefore requires new standards of performance. Missing even more frequently than job descriptions in coaching programs are performance standards specifically for the role of coaches. When the job description and performance standards give clear direction and focus, coaches and their supervisors can make decisions about how coaches allocate their time.

Goals

The goals of the coaching program are another source of information that helps coaches know how to structure their workday. Some coaching programs have unspecific goals such as *supporting teachers*. Other goals are clearer such as *improving reading and math achievement in the lowest perform-ing schools by 15%* or *creating a collaborative culture in which teachers work together to improve teaching and student learning.* The clearer the goals of the coaching program, the easier it is for coaches to prioritize the many requests they receive for services and to say *no* to what isn't related to the goal and *yes* to what is.

Both district and school personnel have a responsibility to make the goals of the coaching program clear. Primary responsibility for this deci-sion rests with the individuals or team overseeing coaching in a school or district. These individuals or team usually include those responsible both for financing coaching and for supervising coaches. The bottom line is this: the clearer the program's goals and coaches' role expectations, often defined in a set of performance standards, the easier it is for a coach to know how to allocate time and which services to provide during that time.

Context

Another factor influencing coaches' work is the context in which they work. Several considerations arise in this arena. Time of the school year, experience of the coach and teachers, the role of the principal, and the cul-ture of the school are a few influencing factors.

Time of the School Year

The sequence of the school year influences how coaches allocate time. Early in the year, coaches may spend more time on data coaching, facili-tating learning, and providing resources. As the year evolves and the beginning-of-the-year routines are in place, teachers and coaches can turn their attention to instruction and curriculum. Coaches facilitate meetings of teacher teams to plan instruction, analyze classroom data, and monitor implementation of the approved curriculum. In individual, team, and schoolwide meetings, coaches guide decision making about adjustments in their pace and instruction to meet student learning needs. Coaches share in new strategies, resources, or information to help teachers address topics and problems related to their classrooms. In these meetings coaches serve as curriculum specialists, instructional specialists, classroom sup-porters, and learning facilitators. As the year moves on, attention turns to schoolwide initiatives, changing the status quo, and becoming a commu-nity of adult learners. In these situations, the coach serves as school leader, catalyst for change, and learner.

New to School

If a coach is new to a school or the school is new to coaching, coaches strive first to establish a trusting, safe relationship with their colleagues. Some roles are more conducive to this. Resource provider is one. In this role, coaches demonstrate their resourcefulness, their commitment to help, and their ability to meet the needs of teachers without an expectation for change. They provide materials and resources teachers may request or find helpful. They do it in a timely manner. They provide resources that are tailored to the requestor. They keep their promises. Yet in this role, there is little intrusiveness in classroom practices or even expectation that the resources will be used appropriately. Once relationships are established and the coach has proven his or her trustworthiness, then conversations begin about how to use the resources and their impact on teaching and student learning.

Coaches' Experience Level

If a coach is new to coaching, he or she may tread lightly until relationships are developed. Novice coaches, especially those with thorough preparation for their new role, want to be useful, yet not intrusive. So, they wait patiently until someone extends an invitation for assistance. Coaches sometimes call this "getting used" and they speak of it with great pride. Once teachers recognize that the coach brings a wealth of knowledge and skills, the floodgate of requests for assistance opens. Most novice coaches want to be accepted and to demonstrate the value they add to the school. As a result, they may *overpromise* and *underdeliver,* a dangerous situation for a coach. Novice coaches feel more comfortable in roles that open doors, build their own competence and their acceptance in this new role of coach, and demonstrate their skills as a coach. The two roles they take on most often are resource provider and the model teaching aspect of classroom supporter.

As coaches grow more competent, confident, and even courageous in their work, they are willing to take on the roles that are more complex, require more focus on teaching and learning, and hold a greater expectation for change in teacher behavior. Some of these roles are data coach; classroom supporter, specifically observing and giving feedback; school leader; and catalyst for change. Coaches, when they have established their commitment to teacher and student success, have more leeway and permission to step into classrooms and interact about teaching practices and the impact of those practices on student learning.

Experience Level of Teachers

Teachers' years of experience may influence how coaches allocate time among the roles. When teachers are less experienced, coaches (a) may serve as mentors helping teachers feel comfortable; (b) have the right resources including curriculum guides, student texts, classroom supplies, and handbooks; (c) know procedures for situations, such as discipline; and (d) provide emotional and work-related support, especially to teachers who are new to the profession. Discussion and support may focus on classroom routines, behavior management systems, and curriculum expectations. As the year proceeds, coaches assist with lesson and unit planning, common assessments, and using data. These responsibilities include the roles of curriculum specialist, instructional specialist, and data coach.

Among more veteran teachers, coaches may experience some resistance. However, most experienced teachers are open to any support available to help them improve their instructional practices. They describe more precisely what help they want, how that help is best delivered, and whether the help is useful. They tend to want assistance and to define the parameters of that assistance. While more experienced teachers may benefit from observation and feedback or coteaching, they may want resources instead of the instructional support from which they might benefit most. Skillful coaches are flexible and know how to provide a variety services to accomplish similar outcomes.

Role of the Principal

How principals view coaching influences the roles coaches fill. When principals view themselves as the sole instructional leader in the school, coaches may assume roles that have less impact on teaching and student learning because they are respectfully deferring to principals. If principals abdicate their responsibility for instructional leadership to coaches, coaches have little hope of making a difference because teachers will believe that continuous improvement is unimportant. When principals engage coaches as co-instructional leaders, coaches will approach their work with heightened responsibility for students' academic success.

Principals are essential to the success of coaches within a school. Principals' actions as instructional leaders help coaches focus their daily work with teachers on teaching and learning by

- creating structures and schedules that allow teachers to interact with coaches individually and in teams;
- meeting frequently with coaches to review their work plans and the impact of their work;
- being visible in classrooms and monitoring curriculum implementation;
- protecting coaches' time from interruptions that distract their attention from the most crucial work with teachers;
- examining with coaches data about their work;
- holding coaches accountable for meeting their role expectations;
- upholding the parameters of the school's or district's coaching program;
- interacting with teachers about the importance of coaching to support continuous improvement.

School Culture

A school's culture—the invisible, yet powerful structure of a school—influences how a coach allocates time in each role. Culture includes the school's history with deep change. The relationship and trust among teachers and the relationship between the teachers and the principal are contributors to a school's culture. How a school faculty communicates, whether openly and honestly in meetings and other forums or secretly in the parking lot, influences a coach's potential for impact. The longevity and stability of the school's administration and the staff contribute to the culture. How a staff solves problems, whether it shares or hordes resources, and how it handles conflict are other factors.

In essence, culture exists on a continuum. There are schools with healthy cultures and a few, unfortunately, with weak or divisive cultures. There are many along the continuum. A coach is better able to influence improvements in teaching and student learning in a school with a healthy culture. The same work in a school with an unhealthy culture may be futile. Coaches assess the culture, check perceptions, and adjust their work depending on the culture in which they work. This topic alone is sufficient for its own book. What we know is that some coaching roles work better in one school than in another school. The factor is frequently the culture of the school, not the coach.

ASSESSING ROLE ALLOCATION

In *Taking the Lead: New Roles for Teacher Leaders and School-Based Coaches* (Killion & Harrison, 2006), the authors make this statement: "When school-based coaches appear to be everywhere doing everything all the time within a school, it is possible that that image is accurate" (p. 30). This may be the image, yet the question now is this: "Is this effective?" Perhaps not. Assessing the allocation of time among the roles helps coaches hone their skills and their impact.

To assess the allocation of time among the roles, coaches consult data. They analyze their logs and solicit feedback from teachers and their supervisor. As a part of the evaluation of the National Staff Development Council's Coaches Academy, funded by the Wachovia Foundation's Teachers and Teaching Initiative, coaches logged the nature of their interactions with teacher clients. Logs such as these provide useful information to the coach primarily to assess his or her decisions related to services provided. They can provide data for conversations with supervisors that allow the coach and supervisor together to draw inferences about the relationship between the work provided and its impact.

The interaction log chart of a coach whose primary responsibility is to provide curriculum and instructional support appears in Table 2.1. This chart confirms that the coach allocated more of his time to interactions that align with those roles. The large percentage of time devoted to planning, curriculum, and instructional assistance are consistent with the roles of instructional and curriculum specialists.

Table 2.2 shows the aggregated interactions for one elementary coach for five months: September, October, November, January, and February.

Table 2.1   Coach and Client Interactions: 2006–2007 Summary for a Coach Responsible for Curriculum and Instructional Support

| Type of Interaction | Percentage of Total Interactions by Type | | | | | |
	Sept.	Oct.	Nov.	Dec.	Jan.	Feb.
Classroom management assist	11	10	5	0	24	9
Curricular assist	25	10	8	80	9	19
Instruct assist	6	37	22	0	20	39
Planning assist	44	39	31	7	24	18
Resource assist	13	2	21	0	17	8
Data related	0	0	0	3	5	1
Facilitate groups	0	0	0	0	0	0
Teach/model/demo	0	0	7	10	0	2
Workshop/training	0	0	0	0	0	2
Other	0	2	5	0	1	3

SOURCE: Adapted from Taylor (2007), p. 34.

Table 2.2   Coach and Client Interactions: 2006–2007 Summary 1 School, K–5, 23 Clients

| Type of Interaction | Percentage of Total Interactions by Type | | | | |
	Sept.	Oct.	Nov.	Jan.	Feb.
Classroom management assist	30	55	56	17	27
Curricular assist	10	3	0	9	2
Instruct assist	8	9	6	2	7
Planning assist	0	9	5	49	42
Resource assist	4	0	6	4	2
Data related	44	0	17	0	7
Facilitate groups	0	9	0	11	0
Teach/model/demo	4	15	9	8	13
Workshop/training	0	0	2	0	0
Other	0	0	0	0	0

SOURCE: Adapted from Taylor (2007), p. 37.

This table indicates that the coach used seven different types of interactions. She devoted considerable time to assistance with classroom management. The coach focused on data more in September than any other months. Fewer demonstration teaching occurred in September than in any other month. January and February included substantial time

Table 2.3   Coach and Client Interactions: 2006–2007 Summary for a Coach Returning to Teaching

Type of Interaction	*Percentage of Total Interactions by Type*					
	Sept.	*Oct.*	*Nov.*	*Dec.*	*Jan.*	*Feb.*
Classroom management assist	1	7	6	3	4	14
Curricular assist	24	20	11	10	15	19
Instruct assist	10	11	16	17	8	17
Planning assist	10	1	5	12	21	7
Resource assist	24	15	15	20	8	14
Data related	0	10	9	0	7	6
Facilitate groups	13	4	6	7	3	6
Teach/model/demo	0	3	2	0	14	9
Workshop/training	9	3	0	0	7	0
Other	7	25	31	31	14	8

SOURCE: Adapted from Taylor (2007), p. 36.

focused on planning. More team facilitation occurred in January than in any other month. The chart does not provide information on whether the allocation of support is appropriate; however, by using these data as a base, coaches and their supervisors can engage in inquiry about whether the allocation is appropriate for this school.

By comparison, Table 2.3 is an aggregated interaction log for a coach who is returning to the classroom next year. The principal expressed dissatisfaction with the skill level of the coach. It is interesting to notice the differences between Table 2.2 and Table 2.3 and how the two coaches spent their time.

The most notable differences between Tables 2.2 and 2.3 are evident in percentage of "Other" interactions and in the number of different kinds of interactions. This comparison raises a question about whether streamlining or narrowing the coaches' responsibilities allows coaches to develop greater competence in a few roles rather than to work with fewer skills in many roles.

Examining data about how coaches allocate their time in terms of services and teacher clients helps both the coach and the coach's supervisor analyze the coach's work. Some questions coaches may use in their reflective analysis about these data are as follows:

- To whom am I providing services?
- Is the distribution of time to individuals or groups appropriate at this point in time (recognizing that there may be a teacher, a grade level, team, or department that needs more intensive services for some length of time)?

- What kind of services do teachers request most often?
- How might I work teacher X toward more strategic use of my time?
- How does the nature of services provided change from month to month and during the course of a year?
- Are the changes appropriate? Do I want to play a more active role in directing the changes?
- How have my interactions with teachers changed as I have gained experience/trust/expertise?
- Is there a "typical" interaction curve from inductee to competent experience professional (e.g., are there different types of interactions with new vs. experienced teachers)? Are there activities/interactions I would like to use more?
- What skills do I need to work on (e.g., strategies or services that are not requested—why not? Is it because they don't know I can do this for them, or is it that I haven't had good success with it, or is it that I'm simply not good at it?)? (Killion & Harrison, 2006, Tool 17.8)

COACHING HEAVY AND COACHING LIGHT

As coaches and their supervisors analyze coaches' work with the intention to strengthen both the work and its impact, they examine how coaches allocate their time among the 10 roles. As is visible in Tables 2.1–2.3, coaches who have specific role expectations devote more time to those clearly defined roles. Table 2.3 suggests a potential problem that might arise when coaches do not have clear role expectations. They might not spend enough time in any one role to develop and refine the skills of coaching. They may not know how to assess teachers' needs and then prioritize their work to align with those needs. Or, they may regard all of their work as equally important. Without strong supervision and adequate skills, coaches fall into traps that may lead to ineffectiveness. For the promise of coaching to have the greatest impact on teaching and student learning, it is essential that coaches make choices about how to allocate their time that are driven by a clear intention to have the greatest impact on the results they seek from coaching—improving student learning.

From my perspective, the hope of coaching rests with coaches providing teachers foundational support that can make a significant impact on teacher practice and student learning. The Tennessee Value-Added studies conducted by William Sanders and his colleagues (Sanders, Saxton, & Horn, 1997) and others (Resnick, 2004; Rowan, Correnti, & Miller, 2002), demonstrate that the quality of teaching and the policies related to "teacher hiring, placement, and training make a difference for academic achievement" (Resnick, 2004, p. 4). If the goal of a coaching program is to improve student academic performance, then coaches who focus their services on strengthening the quality of teaching and learning will likely make a greater contribution to achieving that goal. If any of the providers of the coaching program—the school, the district, or the coach—is unclear about the intended results of coaching, then coaches will struggle to keep a laser-like focus on doing what matters.

I assert that there are two kinds of coaching—coaching *light* and coaching *heavy.* The difference essentially is in the coaches' perspective, beliefs, role decisions, and goals, rather than in what coaches do. The difference is magnified in the results achieved. It is possible to have two coaches working side by side, one coaching light and the other coaching heavy, and have their overt behavior strongly resemble each other. As a result, the distinction between coaching light and coaching heavy is not easy to see in practice. It is, rather, evident in how coaches talk about their work, their motivation, their purpose, and the results they achieve.

Coaching light results in coaches being accepted, appreciated, and even liked by their peers. When coaches' work is driven by the goal of being appreciated, coaches tend to say "yes" to services that they believe will ingratiate them with staff members, particularly those who may exhibit some reluctance to working with a coach. Coaches who coach light are valued, although they may not be needed.

Coaching light occurs when coaches want to build and maintain relationships *more* than they want to improve teaching and learning. From this perspective, coaches act to increase their perceived value to teachers by providing resources *and* avoiding challenging conversations. They may provide demonstration lessons, curriculum materials, or facilitate learning without holding an expectation that the learning will be applied in classrooms. While each of these services has value and contributes to improving teaching and learning, they can also be acts of avoidance. When budget cuts are inevitable, coaching programs or even coaches that focus mostly on coaching light may find themselves on the "cut list" because, while they are valued, they may not be needed.

From the perspective of the teacher, coaching light feels supportive. Teachers appreciate the resources and ideas, yet they simultaneously wonder if it wouldn't be better if the coach were working directly with students. Teachers feel as if they have an advocate in the coach, someone who understands the complexity of their work and who will empathize with them. They may request resources or support from the coach that they might ask from a classroom aide, if they had one. Teachers acknowledge that they have received strategies and ideas from the coach that are useful and that they may even try some in their classrooms. Coaches who lack confidence and courage may tread lightly in their interactions with teachers and limit the focus of their interactions to praise or to questions that merely ask teachers to recall or describe their actions.

To build relationships and establish their credibility, coaches may compromise their influence by engaging in tasks that have limited potential for impact on teaching and learning. This is coaching light. Identifying examples of coaching light is not easy since the key distinguishing factor is the coaches' intention and results. Some coaching services that tend toward the light side include testing students, gathering leveled books for teachers to use, doing repeated demonstration lessons, finding Web sites for students to use, or sharing with teachers professional publications or information about workshops or conferences. Coaching light might include providing feedback to teachers that focuses on their behavior rather than on student learning.

Coaches may be saying, "Yes, but the services you describe as coaching *light* have the potential to build trusting relationships, establish my credibility, convey to teachers that we are serious when we say, 'We are here to help you.'" I agree that coaching light achieves these goals; however, I also believe that there are other ways to build trusting, professionally respectful relationships and establish credibility grounded in tackling the difficult issues by addressing what has previously been "undiscussable" in schools—the relationship between teaching and student learning.

Coaching heavy, on the other hand, includes high-stakes interactions between coaches and teachers, such as curriculum analysis, data analysis, instruction, assessment, and personal and professional beliefs and how they influence practice. It is driven by a coach's deep commitment to improve teaching and learning, even if that commitment means risking being liked. Coaching heavy focuses on planning powerful instruction, implementing and analyzing frequent formative assessments, holding high expectations for teachers' performance, and delivering a rigorous curriculum. Coaching heavy requires coaches to say "no" to trivial requests for support and to turn their attention to those high-leverage services that have the greatest potential for improving teaching and learning. Coaching heavy requires coaches to work with *all* teachers in a school, not just those who volunteer for coaching services. Coaching heavy requires coaches to seek and use data about their work and regularly analyze their decisions about time allocation, services, and impact. When coaching heavy, coaches work outside their comfort zone and stretch their coaching skills, content knowledge, leadership skills, relationship skills, and instructional skills. They are increasingly aware of the beliefs that drive their actions and reexamine them frequently. Coaching heavy is not being heavy handed, but rather having significant impact.

From a teacher's perspective, just as coaching light feels light, coaching heavy feels heavy—in the sense that each coach shares equally with teachers the collective responsibility and commitment for the success of every student. To teachers, coaching heavy causes them to feel on edge, questioning their actions and decisions. This does not mean that teachers feel fear, anxiety, or dread. Rather, teachers feel a heightened sense of professionalism, excitement, increased efficacy, and satisfaction with teaching. Coaching heavy holds all adults responsible for student success and engages them as members of collaborative learning teams to learn, plan, reflect, analyze, and revise their daily teaching practices based on student learning results.

Coaching heavy occurs when coaches ask thought-provoking questions, uncover assumptions, have fierce or difficult conversations, and engage teachers in dialogue about their beliefs and goals rather than their knowledge and skills. For example, rather than talking about what a teacher decides to do in a lesson, the coach asks the teacher to describe his of her belief about teaching, student learning, and student capacity to learn. These differences are not just subtle shifts in the way questions are worded, but rather tied directly to the coach's desire to engage teachers in examining their mental models and how those beliefs drive their decisions and resulting behaviors. For example, rather than asking, "What did you think about when the students were unable to respond to your questions?" the coach asks, "What do you believe is the role of teacher questions in the learning process? What intentions do you hold when asking questions in your lessons?" The purpose of interaction at the belief and goal level rather than at the knowledge and skills level is to facilitate teachers' exploration of who they are as teachers as much or more than what they do as teachers. It is at this level where deep reform can occur.

I presented the concept of coaching heavy and coaching light to coaches in Walla Walla Public Schools. This conversation was as enlightening as the conversations with coaches in Fairfax County Public Schools. Where I have visualized coaching heavy and light as two ends of a seesaw with the light end in the air and the heavy end on the ground, they see an image that is more of a spiral with each revolution focusing more narrowly on the target—student learning. Coaches, they said, use a blend of coaching heavy and light and with each turn they narrow their focus.

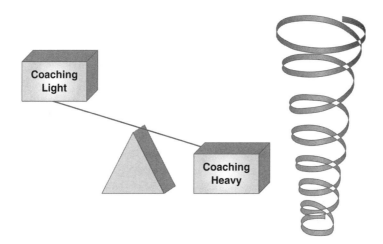

The views of these coaches helped me clarify my own understanding of these concepts. My perspective shifted as a result of listening to their thinking. I recognize that coaches may use both coaching heavy and light in their repertoire of strategies. Yet I believe that, beyond a few introductory weeks of coaching light, coaches must shift to coaching heavy and stay there. In this way, coaches increase the potential to significantly impact teaching practices and student learning. I will grant coaches a short period of time at the beginning of a new coaching program—when they are new to a school or when coaching is new to the school—to coach light. During this time, coaches assess the culture, context, and conditions in which they work. However, the shift to coaching heavy cannot wait long because students cannot wait for the best teaching possible.

When I talked with a team of coaches in Fairfax County Public Schools about the concepts of coaching heavy and coaching light, I expressed my uncertainty about using the words *heavy* and *light*. I worry, I said, that heavy connotes that coaching heavy focuses on corrective action or conveys a supervisory or evaluative orientation to coaching. This is not coaching heavy. Rather the orientation is one of laser-like focus on the work of improving teaching and student learning. Like a laser, a coach focuses intense energy into a small space. That small space is the interaction that occurs between teachers and students. Coaching heavy is not heavy-handed or directive, but rather focused like a laser, a narrow ban of intense energy.

These insightful coaches suggested another way to describe coaching heavy and coaching light. They suggested coaching *shallow* and coaching *deep*. I have thought about their metaphor and share it with my own embellishments. In shallow water, both the coach and teacher feel safe. They can touch bottom. They have a limited perspective of what it means to swim because they can still stand.

In deep water, however, both the coach and the teacher, unless they are competent swimmers, are outside their comfort zone. Depending on their skills, both the coach and the teacher may experience anxiety or even fear. Coaches can provide flotation devices to reduce teachers' anxiety if necessary, yet coaches must be competent swimmers and be ready to rescue a teacher who may struggle, tire, or need to refine his or her strokes. When coaches and teachers need a break from the intensity of navigating deep water, they can resort to the shallow water to rest and renew. Coaches help teachers improve the strength and accuracy of their strokes so they become as competent and confident in deep water as they are in shallow water. Eventually, nonswimmers develop a view of themselves as master of both elementary and advanced swim strokes and, when they demonstrate that they have become swimmers, they navigate easily and eagerly and even for distances. Coaching heavy builds teachers' competence, capabilities, and courage to accomplish goals beyond what they may think possible.

Coaching heavy demands that coaches shift their drivers from being liked and appreciated to making a difference. To know which orientation to coaching they are using, coaches examine their goals and the beliefs they hold about who they are as a coach, the role of coaching in the school, and about change. These beliefs drive who they are as coaches.

Coaching heavy requires that coaches move to the edge of or beyond their comfort zone and perhaps their competence to encourage teachers to move beyond theirs as well. For some coaches, this notion produces tremendous anxiety. When coaches opt to stay in their own or in teachers' comfort zones too long, they limit the impact of their work and even waste their precious time and the resource of coaching. When coaches decide to stay in their comfort zone, their practice conveys their belief that the primary goal of coaching is to help teachers feel good or to make coaches feel valued. It is by operating outside their comfort zone, moving from coaching light to coaching heavy, that coaches improve teaching and student learning.

Some beliefs that may interfere with a coach's ability to accept responsibility to coach heavy are identified in Table 2.4, along with possible side effects.

Table 2.4   Beliefs and Possible Side Effects

Belief	Side Effects
1. Being accepted gives me more leverage to work with teachers.	Working on being accepted may delay conversations on what matters most—teaching and learning.
2. Being viewed as credible is essential to being a coach.	Credibility emerges from the alignment between one's actions and one's words. Acting on what matters immediately builds credibility.
3. The work of coaches is to support teachers.	Saying that a coach's role is to support teachers misleads teachers. A coach's primary responsibility is to improve student learning.
4. Teachers are resistant to change.	As professionals, teachers seek continuous improvement. Teachers are motivated to change when they see proven results in terms of student success. When that success can be evident in their own classrooms, they become change enthusiasts.
5. Coaches can't impose on teachers since they have no supervisory responsibilities.	Coaches can't afford not to impose on what teachers believe and how that impacts their actions. Their work is too important and without conversations about beliefs, deep change is unlikely.
6. Helping teachers to know *about* or learn *how* to implement new instructional strategies is a coach's primary responsibility.	Coaches' primary responsibility is student learning often mediated by teachers' application of effective practices rather than knowing *about* or knowing *how* to use those practices.
7. Coaches are not responsible for what teachers do.	Coaches are responsible for helping teachers explore the beliefs that drive their actions. In dialogue, through reflective questioning, and by presenting data, coaches can influence what a teacher thinks and does.

CONCLUSION

Coaches' work is complex and challenging. What coaches do each day influences what teachers do and that, in turn, influences what students know and do. When coaches choose to allocate their time to services that hold the greatest potential for deep change in teaching and student learning within their schools, students, teachers, and principals will benefit. The benefits might include the following:

- Every student succeeds as a result of high-quality teaching.
- Every teacher succeeds as a result of coaching *heavy.*
- No teacher ever faces an instructional challenge alone.
- Every school community engages in ongoing, ruthless analysis of data, and continuous cycles of improvement that allow its members to measure results in a matter of weeks, not months or years.

Coaches support teachers as they work together to grapple problems of practice and to make smarter, collaborative decisions that are enriched by the shared practice of the entire community. When coaches choose roles and allocate their time and services to those that have the greatest potential for impacting teaching and student learning, the value of coaching and coaches will be unquestioned, even when budgets are tight and other competing priorities emerge.

REFERENCES

Glickman, C. (1993). *Renewing America's schools.* San Francisco: Jossey-Bass.

Killion, J., & Harrison, C. (2006). *Taking the lead: New roles for teacher leaders and school-based coaches.* Oxford, OH: National Staff Development Council.

Resnick, L. (Ed.). (2004, Summer). Teachers matter: Evidence of valued-added assessments. *Research Points, 2*(2), 1–4.

Rowan, B., Correnti, R., & Miller, R. (2002). What large-scale research tells us about teacher effects on student achievement: "Insights from the prospects" study of elementary schools. *Teachers College Record, 104*(8), 1525–1567.

Sanders, W., Saxton, A., & Horn, B. (1997). The Tennessee value-added assessment system: A quantitative outcomes-based approach to educational assessment. In J. Millman (Ed.), *Grading teachers, grading schools: Is achievement a valid measure?* Thousand Oaks, CA: Corwin Press.

Taylor, M. (2007). *National Staff Development Council's Coaches Academy Annual Report.* Littleton, CO: MJT Associates, Inc.

3

Working as a Partner With the Adult Learner

Kathleen Feeney Jonson

Teaching was the fulfillment of a lifelong dream for Sherie, 40, a first-year elementary school teacher. When Sherie was an intern, her site principal noticed her strong teaching abilities, outgoing personality, and unusual dedication. He took a personal interest in her teaching career, offered her advice during her internship, and encouraged her to stay at his school site during her first official year of teaching.

As the teacher of a first- and second-grade combination class with students from many language backgrounds, Sherie worked diligently at maintaining each learner's ethnic integrity. In Saturday seminars, she participated in learning activities based on the *California Standards for the Teaching Profession* (California Commission on Teacher Credentialing and the California Department of Education, 1997). Sherie used the standards to assess her own teaching, and she developed a classroom-research questionnaire to foster her professional growth: "How can I develop teaching strategies that address different student learning styles?" Over the year, she compiled student work and evidence of her teaching practices into a teaching portfolio (WestEd, 1997).

During her first year of teaching, Sherie had two mentors: her principal and her mentor in the Beginning Educators' Seminars on Teaching (BEST) program. Each held regular conversations with her, observed her teaching, listened to her concerns, and offered advice when she asked for it. They provided different perspectives, two backdrops from which she could view teaching as her chosen profession. Latisha, her BEST mentor, conducted four formal, standards-based observations of Sherie's teaching as it related to her research questions. She offered Sherie emotional support and suggestions for classroom management, curriculum planning, assessment, and educational materials. Latisha helped Sherie understand how to meet state and district curriculum standards while individualizing instruction of her culturally diverse students. She reinforced the BEST seminars' emphasis on the importance of reflective conversations and writing. Sherie completed her first year of teaching with a deeper understanding of school and a greater trust in administration than are usually present in novice teachers.

—Scherer (1999, pp. 116–117)

———————— ⇒◆⇐ ————————

A good teacher of children is not necessarily a good mentor of another teacher. Needed above and beyond expertise in teaching is the ability to facilitate the learning of adults. Good mentors stray from the traditional "authoritarian teacher/supplicant learner" archetype. They work on establishing a collaborative learning partnership with their mentee, grounded in knowledge about adult learning.

Adult learning, or *andragogy*, is rooted in principles delineated by Malcolm Knowles (1980) in *The Modern Practice of Adult Education: From Pedagogy to Andragogy.* Knowles points out that adult learners bring their own history of experience to a learning relationship. They learn best when they are engaged as active partners, not when they serve as passive receivers. A good mentor seldom acts as an authority figure, but more often serves as a facilitator, a "guide on the side," rather than a "sage" on or off a stage. Adult mentees—even those initially unsure of themselves and needing extensive support—require as adults as much self-direction as possible, with involvement in diagnosing, planning, implementing, and evaluating their own learning. Portner notes that they also tend to be goal oriented, constantly looking for relevance in learning (2006, p. 14), and that many adults struggle with self-esteem issues and bring with them memories of bad experiences in traditional education as well as a preoccupation with events outside the classroom (p. 15).

Effective mentors of adult learners understand that their role is mainly one of facilitation. In a dynamic facilitative process, a mentor-mentee learning partnership evolves over time as the developing teacher becomes more and more comfortable and self-directed. Facilitation involves

- encouraging beginning teachers to set their own learning objectives,
- involving beginning teachers in planning how they will learn,
- encouraging beginning teachers to use a wide variety of resources to get to their objectives, and
- helping beginning teachers implement and evaluate their learning.

Beginning teachers want to be treated as equals to their colleagues, and it is extremely important when mentoring to treat the mentee as a partner, an equal in the learning process. "The legitimate recognition that [beginning teachers] should be actively involved as both planners and participants in their own learning continues to have a deservedly important impact on the theory and practice of adult education and, by extension, of adult mentoring," writes Cohen (1995, p. 10). A mentee will not necessarily grow in ability or in desire to improve simply because a mentor has discussed a topic or a goal. Rather, the mentor and mentee need to work through ideas together, both fully participating in the process. Experienced mentors report a "balancing act," in which they carefully adjust their mentoring behaviors so as not to tilt the relationship into either inappropriate control or an unrealistic "hands-off" position. Adult learning requires time for trial and error, reflection, and self-correction. Effective mentors respect their mentees' singular learning curves. They watch for appropriate timing, keeping in mind that the new, often overwhelmed teacher must be ready to grow from the process before any "teaching" can occur. The mentor, in other words, must present suggestions at a time when the mentee is ready to absorb them.

BELIEFS ABOUT SUPERVISION AND MENTORING

Methods of supervising teachers are changing radically from those used in the 1980s, when school administrators observed teachers in their classrooms to see how they were doing. "The pattern of the 1980s—when principals were encouraged to be 'instructional leaders' and teacher evaluation and staff development programs were built on 'effective teaching' research—is being challenged," writes John O'Neil (1993, p. 1). "So is the appropriateness of principals' serving dual roles, supervising teachers in the administrative sense (evaluating their performance, for example) while also trying to help them improve their instruction." As a result, experts say, traditional forms of supervision are being questioned. New avenues to teacher growth are more peer oriented and less likely to fit comfortably under the mantle of supervision.

Whereas supervision in the 1980s was based on the evaluation model, most mentoring today is based more closely on some combination of clinical supervision and cognitive coaching models. A quick summary of these models reveals some of their important differences and provides a background for further discussion.

The Evaluation Model. In the traditional evaluation model, the board of trustees and the state or province initiate an evaluation, and only personnel holding an administrative credential are authorized to evaluate. Districts set up policies and deadlines for evaluation of teachers as a way of meeting contractual requirements and controlling quality. Commonly, an evaluator rates the teacher based on standards developed, negotiated, adopted, and made public. Performance behaviors to be evaluated might include punctuality, willingness to participate in extracurricular and professional activities, personal characteristics, professional attitudes and growth, and so on. The evaluator observes the teacher based on the criteria established by the district and enters ratings on a preprinted form. Copies of the evaluation go to the teacher, to the teacher's personnel file, and to the building principal. Teachers receive ratings such as outstanding, adequate, or needs to improve (Costa & Garmston, 1994, p. 14).

Clinical Supervision. Under this model, an administrator or another supervisor trained in the techniques of clinical supervision works with the teacher to determine objectives, concepts, techniques, materials, and assessment methods. The supervisor then observes in-class instruction, analyzes the data to determine patterns of behavior and critical incidents of teaching and learning, and confers with the new teacher to share the data. The cycle continues, with more planning to determine future directions for growth (Glatthorn, 1984, pp. 7–8). Clinical supervision "is an intensive process designed to improve instruction by conferring with the teacher on lesson planning, observing the lesson, analyzing the observational data, and giving the teacher feedback about the observation" (Glatthorn, 1984, p. 7).

Cognitive Coaching. In the cognitive coaching model, new teachers allow themselves to be coached by someone who is respected for being helpful and having good leadership qualities. The coach may be a department chair or a peer. Coaching begins on the new teacher's first day on the job and can continue throughout the year. Under this model, new teachers determine criteria relating to student and teacher behavior for the coach to observe. Such behaviors might include classroom interaction, instruction, student learning, student performance, curriculum adherence, individual student behavior, teacher behavior and skills, and so on. New teachers let the mentor-coach know what they would like the coach to look for and what feedback would be helpful. After observation, the coach shares any information collected with the new teachers, who self-evaluate based on the criteria established in a planning period. The goal is to improve instruction, curriculum, and student learning (Costa & Garmston, 1994, p. 14).

Costa and Garmston (1994) outline the following steps in the cognitive coaching cycle:

1. The planning conference (Costa & Garmston, 1994, pp. 18–20): The initial conference is a period for building trust. During this conference, coaches focus attention on new teachers' goals. As the new teachers

discuss their lessons, they refine their strategies, discover potential problems, and essentially "rehearse" (mentally work through) their upcoming lesson. They also establish the parameters for a reflecting conference to follow the observation and set the agenda for that meeting. The planning conference forces new teachers to think about their instruction plans and promote future self-coaching.

2. Observation of the lesson (Costa & Garmston, 1994, p. 21): During this step, the coach collects data as requested by the teacher and discussed in the planning conference. The idea is for the new teachers to experiment with their own strategies and techniques, with the coach gathering data.

3. The reflecting conference (Costa & Garmston, 1994, pp. 21–22): This follow-up conference, according to Costa and Garmston, is best if delayed somewhat after the observation to allow time for the teacher to reflect and analyze and for the coach to organize data and plan the reflective coaching strategy. To begin this conference, the new teachers share their impressions of the lesson and specific examples supporting those impressions. They are asked to compare what occurred during the lesson with what was planned. Ideally, the coach helps beginning teachers draw conclusions regarding relationships between their actions and student outcomes. Finally, the new teachers are encouraged to project how new insights will affect future lessons and also to reflect on the coaching process itself.

The Mentor. The traditional mentoring role, then, is based on the model of clinical supervision, with mentoring strategies often following the model of cognitive coaching. The mentee takes an active role, suggesting topics to be addressed; the mentor observes and collects data; and the two meet to reflect, learn, and grow. This formal process can greatly enhance a teacher's ability to apply what is learned to the classroom. According to researchers Joyce and Showers (Albert, Blondino, & McGrath, 1990), in fact, beginning teachers are most likely to use what they know if coaching is built into the staff development process (see Table 3.1).

Table 3.1   Effectiveness of Training Components

	Knowledge	Workshop Application	Classroom Use
Theory	100%	5%	5%
Theory plus demonstration	100%	5%	5%
Theory, demonstration, and practice with feedback	100%	85–90%	5–10%
Theory, demonstration, and practice with feedback and coaching	100%	85–90%	75–85%

SOURCE: From the research of Joyce & Showers, as cited in Albert, Blondino, & McGrath (1990).

Glickman (1985) presents a self-assessment for supervisors interested in discovering their own orientation in supervision. Although Glickman uses the term "supervision," much of what he says applies to mentoring as well.

PHASES IN THE MENTORING RELATIONSHIP: THREE MODELS

The core of mentoring . . . is the focus on collaborative participation and mutual critical thinking and reflection about the process, value, and results of jointly derived learning goals established for the mentee.

—Norman H. Cohen (1995, p. 14)

Mentors and their mentees go through predictable phases in their relationship as it develops and matures over time. Where they are in these phases will determine strategies to be used by the mentor. Cohen (1995, pp. 15–16) describes the following four phases:

1. The early phase: In the beginning, the mentor-mentee pair focuses primarily on building a trusting relationship. Mentees must feel comfortable with their mentor and trust that they will not be judged when they seek help.

2. The middle phase: Once the mentee is comfortable, the partners exchange information. The mentor accumulates knowledge about the mentee in an effort to understand the mentee's goals and concerns.

3. The later phase: The mentor explores the interests and beliefs of the mentee and attempts to learn the reasons for the mentee's decisions. This might include inviting the mentee to self-appraise.

4. The last phase: The mentor motivates mentees to reflect on their goals, to pursue challenges, and to follow through on their own personal, educational, and career path.

How quickly a mentee is ready to move from one of these phases to the next varies considerably, depending on the individual. A perceptive mentor will be aware of the mentee's readiness to move on and will let that readiness guide the progression of the relationship.

The Association for Supervision and Curriculum Development (ASCD, 1999a) presents a different model of mentee learning, also breaking the mentor-mentee relationship into four phases. Like Cohen, ASCD's (1999a) *Mentoring to Improve Schools* emphasizes the need for the mentor to be aware of the mentee's progression and to time interventions accordingly. "Be a good listener and ask questions to continually assess the developmental needs of the protégé, the state of mentoring, and the most appropriate mentoring response," ASCD advises.

The four phases of this model (ASCD, 1999a, pp. 103, 105) are as follows:

1. In the beginning, mentors and mentees start to develop their relationship, with the mentors taking primary responsibility for leadership. The new teachers are just beginning their careers and may well move quickly from excited anticipation of their job into a period of stress and survival. They are most likely to ask basic questions with only one correct answer (e.g., "How do I let the office know how many kids are absent?"). In this phase, mentors provide information as needed and model for the mentees and then move on to help the mentees set priorities and direction (e.g., how to conduct a class meeting, prepare for a parent conference, or set up a grade book).

2. Later, mentees and mentors build a partnership. Often new teachers by this time are disillusioned with their jobs and question the way things are (e.g., "Help! Got any ideas for dealing with this unruly student behavior?"). Mentors offer assistance (e.g., providing samples of classroom discipline policies), but at the same time seek suggestions from the mentee. They attempt to let the mentee take more responsibility for the relationship.

3. As the mentor-mentee relationship becomes strong, the two enjoy working together, sharing ideas, analyzing, and making decisions together (e.g., "Why do we have so many assemblies? It's hard to get the kids focused back on classwork afterward. I'm losing too much valuable class time!"). The mentor helps with prioritizing but defers to the mentee's judgment whenever possible. The mentee is in a period of rejuvenation.

4. The mentor begins to withdraw from the relationship, encouraging the mentee to become independent. The mentor now uses questions to encourage analysis and reflection from the mentee (e.g., asks the new teacher how a new strategy might affect student learning; listens as the new teacher discusses an assessment of examples of student work; engages the new teacher in a reflective conversation about an issue or concern). The mentor defers to the mentee's judgment and affirms the mentee's abilities and understanding. By this time, the mentee is often headed back into a period of anticipation and is ready for self-growth (see Figure 3.1).

Figure 3.1   Dynamics within the mentoring process

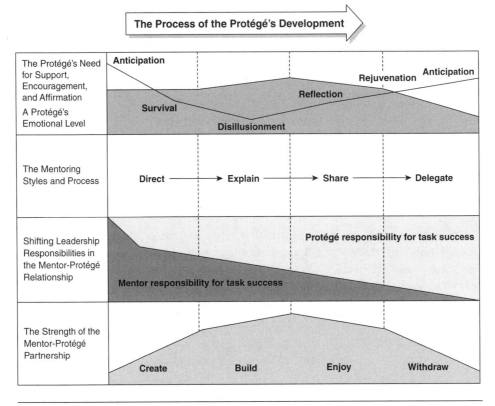

SOURCE: From Association for Supervision and Curriculum Development. (1999). *Mentoring to improve schools: Facilitator's guide* (p. 105). Alexandria, VA: ASCD. Used with permission. The Association for Supervision and Curriculum Development is a worldwide community of educators advocating sound policies and sharing best practices to achieve the success of each learner. To learn more, visit ASCD at www.ascd.org.

Joyce and Showers (1982, 1983) and Showers (1985) characterize the process of coaching or mentoring as a similar phased-in approach. They describe five functions:

1. *Providing companionship.* The first function of mentoring is to "provide interchange with another human being over a difficult process" (Joyce & Showers, 1983, p. 19). The mentoring relationship involves mutual reflection, the checking of perceptions, the sharing of frustrations and successes, and the informal thinking through of problems. When one person watches another try a new model of teaching for the first time, for instance, the two will find much to talk about. Companionship provides reassurance that problems are normal. It not only makes the new teacher's learning process technically easier but also enhances the quality of the experience. "It is more pleasurable to share a new thing than to do it in

isolation. The lonely business of teaching has sorely lacked the companionship that we envision for our coaching teams" (Joyce & Showers, 1983, p. 19). Companionship also helps overcome the tendency to avoid the awkwardness of practicing a new strategy.

2. *Giving technical feedback.* In the course of their relationship, the team will reach the stage where the mentor will provide feedback based on observations of the mentee's teaching. This technical feedback is not to be confused with general evaluation. Feedback does not imply judgment about the overall quality of teaching, but is confined to information about the execution of specific skills. The mentor might point out omissions, examine how materials are arranged, check to see whether all parts of a teaching strategy have been brought together, and so on. Technical feedback keeps the mind of the developing teacher on the business of perfecting skills, polishing them, and working through problem areas. Whether the mentee is trying a new model of teaching, implementing a new curriculum, or setting up a classroom management system, feedback must be accurate, specific, and nonjudgmental.

3. *Analyzing application and extending executive control.* As the new teacher's skills develop and solidify, mentoring moves into a more complex stage: mutual examination of the appropriate use of new strategies:

> The cognitive aspects of transferring new behaviors into effective classroom practice are more difficult than the interactive moves of teaching. While all teachers can develop skill in performing a new teaching strategy fairly readily, the harder tasks come as the skill is applied in the classroom (Showers, 1985, p. 14).

One of the important things a new teacher learns is when to use a new model appropriately and what will be achieved by doing so. Selecting the right occasions to use a teaching strategy is not as easy as it sounds. For instance, the new teacher may have learned in college about inductive teaching strategies, such as concept attainment, and may have had little difficulty learning the pattern of the models and discussing the models with materials provided. But it is a different task for beginning teachers to select concepts to teach in their own classrooms, reorganize materials from the standard textbook, teach students to respond to the new strategy, and create lessons they have never seen demonstrated directly. In this phase, these tasks become the substance of conversations between the new and the experienced teachers. The new teacher is developing what Joyce and Showers (1982, 1983) call executive control—that is, a "meta understanding" about how the strategy works, how it can be fitted into their instructional repertoire, and how to modify or create instructional materials for its use. Executive control comes with the new teacher's growing judgment and competence.

4. *Adapting to the students.* New teachers expend much energy trying to figure out how best to apply new teaching strategies to their particular group of students. Successful teaching means that students are responding successfully. Mentors can help new teachers adapt strategies to fit the needs of their students and can suggest ways of acquainting students with what is expected of them:

> One of the major functions of the coach is to help [the mentee] to "read" the responses of the students to make decisions about skill training and how to adapt the model. This is especially important in the early stages of practice when teachers are concerned with their own behavior and it is difficult to worry about the students as well (Joyce & Showers, 1982, p. 7).

5. *Facilitating.* Successfully implementing any new teaching method requires practice. Mentors should expect that a new teacher's early tries will not come close to reaching standards. With this in mind, Joyce and Showers (1982) point out that a major job of mentors is to help their mentees feel good about themselves during these early trials. "Teachers' lack of interpersonal support and close contact with others in the context of teaching is a tragedy. Coaching reduces this isolation and increases support" (p. 7).

In his book, *Mentor: Guiding the Journey of Adult Learners,* Laurent Daloz (1999) explains facilitation this way:

> It is very important to watch for the growing edge, like a coach photographing their forward movement and replaying it for them. This may mean being very explicit about what [mentees] have done well. It is generally more effective to show people when they are on track than to tell them where they should go or to criticize when they have strayed. Emphasize positive movement, underline it, restate it, praise it. By spending undue time on the negative, we run the risk of helping our [mentees] construct a vision of the impossible, whereas our job is to help them imagine the possible and then move toward it. Always we are guides, encouraging movement (pp. 123–124).

All three of these mentoring models move along a continuum to a more facilitative approach. The goal is autonomy for the beginning teacher to self-assess and self-prescribe. The mentor assumes different support and assessment roles at different stages of the continuum of the relationship. In the early stages, information tends to flow from mentor to the beginning teacher, with the mentor offering suggestions and solutions. As the beginning teacher develops increasing autonomy, the relationship becomes more collaborative, with the beginning teacher and the mentor reflecting and co-constructing solutions. See Chapter 7, Stages in Teacher Development, for more on specific developmental patterns within the profession.

GETTING TO TRUST

Trust: assured reliance on the character, ability, strength, or truth of someone or something.

—*Merriam Webster's Collegiate Dictionary*, 10th ed.

In each of the mentoring sequences just described, the pattern of an evolving relationship is built on a foundation of trust. Feelings of jitteriness, tension, fear, and nervousness have no place in the relationship. Trust is a vital aspect of school life that influences basic patterns of interpersonal and group behavior. From the beginning, mentors need to establish trust between themselves and the new teachers with whom they work. Trust is a fundamental feature of mentoring and pervades all successful mentor-protégé relationships (see Box 3.1). As one San Francisco mentor put it, "You must get to trust, or you get nowhere" (Jonson, 1999).

BOX 3.1

Trust

- Trust is built by focusing directly on it.
- Taking risks is necessary to build trust.
- Getting supported for taking risks builds trust.
- Allowing yourself to be vulnerable increases others' trust of you.
- Caring about each other is necessary to establish trust.
- Letting go of negative incidents in the past is critical to trust building.

To establish trust, a mentor must demonstrate openness, honesty, and candor. Such openness breeds confidence and trust: A person who seeks to conceal nothing does not, in all likelihood, seek to harm others. Effective mentors are willing to be treated as human beings and do not tend to hide behind the cloak of bureaucratic power and seniority. Such candor and authenticity promote a climate of trust and intimacy. In a trusting relationship, beginning teachers believe that they can depend on the mentor in difficult situations, that they can rely on the integrity of this new colleague, and that confidentiality will not be broken. In contrast, a mentor displaying inauthentic behavior has been characterized as "playing the role," "manipulating and using people and the system," "passing the buck," and "blaming others for his own mistakes and shortfalls." See Box 3.2 for a list of ways to build trust.

BOX 3.2

A Menu of Trust Builders

- Ensure—and keep—confidentiality.
- Hold regular team meetings, with both task and trust issues on the agenda.
- Clarify expectations.
- Discuss expectations.
- Negotiate expectations.
- Be congruent. Walk the talk.
- Create multidirectional communications.
- Respect, honor, and celebrate each individual's style.
- Confront directly with caring.
- Focus on gains, not losses.
- Describe, don't evaluate.
- Delegate power and authority.
- Admit your own mistakes and vulnerability.
- Be a risk taker when it comes to trusting others.
- Create interactions.
- Share feelings as well as thoughts.
- Accept that we all get frustrated and angry at times.
- Encourage balance and renewal for the team and for each individual.
- Celebrate—even mistakes.
- Practice openness.
- Play, laugh, and use humor with love and respect.
- Listen actively.

Strange as it may sound, simply listening—with concern—is one of the best ways to build trust. "Just listening" can build a relationship. This concept is difficult for many mentors who understand the myriad tasks confronting their new teachers and want very much to tell them what works, to analyze, to question, to support. Often the new teacher needs encouragement, but in many cases these other kinds of help are not helpful at all.

"As a mentor project, I have held meetings for the new teachers at my school," one San Francisco mentor says (Jonson, 1999). "Partly we focus on school activities such as an all-school writing test, but mostly the meetings are open-ended so the teachers can bring concerns and questions as well as stories of successes."

Ineffective mentors often have one or two styles of responses for most situations. Following are some typical ineffective ways of responding to problems.

Judging. The mentor might judge the mentee's thoughts or behaviors in some way. This judgment might be favorable (e.g., "That's a good idea," "You're on the right track now") or unfavorable (e.g., "An attitude like that won't get you anywhere"). In either case, the implication is that the mentor is superior and can pass judgment on the speaker's thoughts or actions. Furthermore, judgmental language is likely to make the beginning teacher defensive. This type of response might put the beginning teacher on guard and, in so doing, end the conversation and the possibility of help. "My mentee and I have a trusting relationship in that he can be open and honest when he needs to," one San Francisco mentor says (Jonson, 1999). "He does not fear my judgment." (On the other hand, a mentor can help the beginning teacher evaluate and reflect on a situation in a nonjudgmental way.)

Analyzing. The analyzer's response suggests that the mentor understands the mentee better than the mentee does: "What's bothering you is . . ." or "What you really think is . . ." Two problems are associated with this sort of analyzing. First, the mentor's interpretation may not be correct, in which case the new teacher may become even more confused by accepting it. Second, even if the mentor's analysis is accurate, sharing it might not be useful to the mentee. It may make the mentee defensive (because analyzing implies superiority), or the beginning teacher may not be able to understand the mentor's view of the problem. Analyzing can be a way to help beginning teachers see the "blind parts" of themselves or a situation, but many mentors use this style of response too often and too early.

Questioning. Although questioning often helps mentors understand the unclear parts of a mentee's statements, it can also be used to direct the beginning teacher's thoughts. All beginning teachers have likely had the experience of being questioned by a parent, a teacher, or another authority figure who seemed to be trying to trap them. Used in this way, questioning implies that the person doing the asking already has some idea of what direction the discussion should take. The careful mentor will instead choose open-ended questions and will avoid questions that begin with "Why?"

Supporting. Sometimes the beginning teacher just needs encouragement, and a supportive response is the best thing in these cases. In many cases, however, this kind of response is not really much help. Telling an obviously upset beginning teacher that "everything is all right" or joking about a problem can communicate that the mentor does not accept the mentee's feelings or that the mentee's feelings are not justified.

Good intentions are not always enough. All of these responses may be helpful at times, but they often confuse those asking for help, making them feel defensive or worse than before they shared their problems. The mentor may be right about what caused the mentee's problem and how the mentee could solve the problem, but if beginning teachers do not discover the answer for themselves, it may not be useful to them. As one overzealous mentor commented, "[My mentee] often ignores the truth, even when it's so obvious you'd think she would trip over it."

Another way of responding can often be much more helpful. This style of response is simply active listening. With active listening, mentors maintain eye contact, ask questions to clarify, and otherwise help beginning teachers make clear their feelings. Mentors paraphrase beginning teachers' statements to check their understanding of what they hear, usually beginning by saying something like, "What I hear you telling me is . . ." In these kinds of conversations, it is important that mentors feed back only what they have heard the beginning teacher say without making any judgment or offering an interpretation. In building trust, the mentors' job is simply to understand, not to analyze or judge. Also, they should use their own language in checking back with the beginning teacher and not just parrot the original words.

To understand how listening can be so worthwhile, mentors need to realize that their role is really not to solve all their mentees' problems for them. Mentors can, however, help beginning teachers work things out for themselves. This is a difficult lesson for many mentors to learn. When someone they care for and are charged with supporting is in trouble and feeling bad, their first tendency is to try to make things better—to answer questions, soothe hurts, fix whatever is bothersome. Even in cases when mentors are sure they know what is right for the person, however, it is generally necessary to let that person discover the solution for him- or herself. Active listening is easy to implement, but its importance cannot be over-emphasized in the development of mentor-mentee trust.

ADULT LIVES, ADULT LEARNING STYLES

> I need to understand Jean's whole life; I need to be able to see all the pressures on her. . . . I think we can work with the whole framework, the holistic approach, so that the chances of success are going to be greater than if we don't focus on the whole picture of the adult.
>
> —Laurent A. Daloz (1999, p. 110)

As mentors work with beginning teachers, they must keep in mind the whole of the beginning teacher's life. The temptation to "steer them into courses you know would be good for them without regard for their capacity to handle the work, given the rest of the forces in their lives" (Daloz, 1999, p. 110) is often great. Many of these beginning teachers are caught between duties at home/family relationships and the responsibilities of school/students' needs. They struggle to define new personal and professional lives. They are "learning to swim" in the give-and-take of whirling new roles. "It's a journey with a lot of potholes and trees across the road, and thunderstorms, and needing to take detours," one mentor explains. "Last term she really had to take a detour, and maybe she's had to fill in a couple of potholes this year, but she's underway again, still moving ahead" (Daloz, 1999, p. 109).

So what's a mentor to do? When facing difficult real-life challenges with her mentee, one mentor responded,

> Maybe just trying to be there with the flashlight and keeping the door at various places of the journey open when she wants or feels that she is able to make it in . . . helping her find balance, looking at the different piles of stuff in her life with the old flashlight and saying, "Where are you going to put this chunk called school?" (Daloz, 1999, p. 109).

Mentors must see themselves as facilitators of learning, all the while "listening, empowering, coaching, challenging, teaching, collaborating, aiding, assisting, supporting, expediting, easing, simplifying, advancing, and encouraging" (Zachary, 2000, p. 23). "Facilitators of learning see themselves as resources for learning rather than didactic instructors who have all the answers" (Brookfield, 1986, p. 63).

According to Brookfield (1986), "One important element in facilitating adult learning is helping learners become aware of their own idiosyncratic learning styles" (p. 64). Just as children have different learning preferences, patterns, or styles, so do adults. For some, learning through verbal modes is an easy and efficient method. These mentees learn best through their ears, picking up ideas more completely when they get or work with them auditorily. Others seem to grasp ideas more easily if they can see a diagram or a visual representation of what is being discussed. They are at their best when input comes through their eyes. For some, touch is especially important in their thinking and learning. Still others are kinesthetic learners and thinkers; motion and action are significant factors in how they interface with ideas. One mentor described her frustration working with a new teacher until the two of them began their conferences on the middle school playfield. Several times each week, they met on the playfield for a brisk walk around and around, with the young man pouring out his concerns as they pounded the track side by side. Only when the mentee was moving could he really express himself. Just as a child, then, so might the adult mentee benefit from learning strategies that take into account adult learning styles. Knowledge of these different learning styles, as well as of supervision models and stages in teacher development, can help mentors be more effective in their efforts.

Honoring specific learning styles helps facilitate learning. In her book, *The Mentor's Guide: Facilitating Effective Learning Relationships*, Lois Zachary (2000, pp. 24–25) offers further general guidelines that relate to adult learning styles or patterns of preferred responses:

- *Pace the learning.* The pace of learning varies and is often interrupted by individual need. Sometimes learners withdraw or become avoidant when they are uncomfortable. This self-declared time-out is part of the learning process as well and needs to be acknowledged.

- *Time the developmental intervention.* Mentors need to understand where their mentees are developmentally. They cannot assume readiness.
- *Keep the focus on learning.* Mentoring is not a chemistry contest. The partners should not get hung up on personality issues. Stick with the main attraction: learning.
- *Build the relationship first.* The learning will follow. Too often, mentors and mentees do not make the time to create the appropriate climate for learning.
- *Structure the process.* Sharing the responsibility for structuring the learning relationship (even in an informal learning relationship) improves the quality of the interaction.

In addition, it is always important that the mentor and mentee celebrate successes if the mentee is to remain engaged and enthusiastic. Success invites more success.

THE IMPORTANCE OF REFLECTION

Reflection is the fulcrum of learning that lasts. Without it, I doubt if protégés could sustain the changes we attempt to implement. Reflection provides distance so a protégé can look back at what has happened. The word reflection brings a mirror to mind. When we hold up a mirror, we can examine images in detail. Without it, we could have a distorted view or no view at all.

—Jane Fraser (1998, p. 55)

Whether it's student behavior or student writing, classroom relationships or classroom logistics, information from parents or information from administrators, the many issues that a teacher deals with throughout the day provide plenty of substance for reflection. To reflect, as *Merriam Webster's Collegiate Dictionary* (10th ed.) defines it, is "to think seriously; contemplate; ponder." Without such reflection, past events and occurrences disappear into history. Whether they have been dealt with well or not, they are done. With reflection on past events, though, they become stepping-stones to improvement, opportunities for growth. When teachers think about what they have learned from an experience, they can consolidate their knowledge and skills, evaluate their own performance, recognize successes, and develop strategies for improvement. For these reasons, reflecting on specific teaching problems as well as on larger professional and career development issues is important.

"In teaching, as in life, maximizing meaning from experiences requires reflection," write Costa and Kallick (2000).

The act of reflection, particularly with a group of teaching colleagues, provides an opportunity for the following:

- Amplifying the meaning of one's work through the insights of others
- Applying meaning beyond the situation in which it was learned
- Making a commitment to modifications, plans, and experimentation
- Documenting learning and providing a rich base of shared knowledge (Costa & Kallick, 2000, p. 60)

While reflection may seem to be a natural process, however, in fact, it is not. In a study of 42 preservice teachers at a Midwestern university, researchers found that those who received specific training in reflecting had significantly higher levels of reflection than did those in a control group. Notably, some who did not receive training improved their reflection skills anyway through repeated reflective exercises (Galvez-Martin, Bowman, & Morrison, 1999, p. 4). This study illustrates the need to work on the skill of reflection and to practice reflection regularly to realize its benefits.

Reflecting is at its most powerful when teachers collaborate in an active, honest search for answers. Perhaps the best way to reflect—the most productive—is out loud, talking with a mentor or a peer. Mentoring, in fact, is really just one teacher facilitating the growth of another. An active listener can be an important source of information for a beginning teacher, can provide emotional support, and often helps the beginning teacher grow and gain strength as a professional. Reflection should be a part of many of the teaching strategies discussed in Chapter 8: notably, demonstration teaching, observation and feedback, informal contact, and assistance with an action plan for professional growth.

Following interviews with 22 teacher-mentors in Southern California, Shulman and Colbert reported that the mentors "suggested that teaching teachers how to reflect on their own teaching is what mentoring should ultimately include, because it will engender teachers with a mode for life-long improvement and revitalization" (Shulman & Colbert, 1988, p. 9).

Life can only be understood backwards; but it must be lived forwards.

—Søren Kierkegaard (quoted in Costa & Kallick, 2000, p. 60)

CONCLUSION

A teacher talented in working with children may not necessarily have the skills to work well with teachers as adults. This chapter reviewed different aspects of working with adult teachers: models of supervision used through the years, phases in the developing mentor-mentee relationship, the need to build a trusting relationship, and the importance of reflection. In Chapter 7, Stages in Teacher Development, we look at phases of growth specific to teachers and how mentors can shape their guidance of new teachers with those stages in mind.

> I needed these two years of support, having the time to deal with problems and being able to see myself in the "stages of development" for a beginning teacher as I ride the roller coaster through the depths of despair in December and January and then go back uphill toward the end of the year.
>
> —Cathy, a beginning teacher ("Teacher Voices," 1996, p. 3)

REFERENCES

Albert, S., Blondino, C., & McGrath, J. (1990). *Peer coaching.* Seattle, WA: Puget Sound Educational Service District.

Association for Supervision and Curriculum Development. (1999a). *Mentoring to improve schools: Facilitator's guide.* Alexandria, VA: ASCD.

Association for Supervision and Curriculum Development. (1999b). *Mentoring to improve schools: Successful mentoring programs* [Videotape]. Alexandria, VA: ASCD.

Brookfield, S. D. (1986). *Understanding and facilitating adult learning.* San Francisco: Jossey-Bass.

California Department of Education. (2006, February). *Developing highly qualified teachers and administrators initiative.* California Department of Education.

Cohen, N. H. (1995). *Mentoring adult learners: A guide for educators and trainers.* Malabar, FL: Krieger.

Commission on Teacher Credentialing. (1991). "I was really nervous, but I learned a lot": New developments in the CNTP assessment component. *Teacher News, 3*(2), 1–7.

Costa, A. L., & Garmston, R. J. (1994). *Cognitive coaching: A foundation for renaissance schools.* Norwood, MA: Christopher-Gordon.

Costa, A. L., & Kallick, B. (2000). Getting into the habit of reflection. *Educational Leadership, 57*(7), 60–62.

Daloz, L. A. (1999). *Mentor: Guiding the journey of adult learners.* San Francisco: Jossey-Bass.

Fraser, J. (1998). *Teacher to teacher: A guidebook for effective mentoring.* Portsmouth, NH: Heinemann.

Galvez-Martin, M. E., Bowman, C., & Morrison, M. (1999). *ATE Newsletter, 32*(6), 4.

Glatthorn, A. A. (1984). *Differential supervision.* Alexandria, VA: Association for Supervision and Curriculum Development.

Glickman, C. D. (1985). *Supervision of instruction: A developmental approach.* Alexandria, VA: Association for Supervision and Curriculum Development.

Jonson, K. (1999). [Survey of 28 mentor-teachers in the San Francisco Unified School District]. Unpublished raw data.

Joyce, B., & Showers, B. (1982). The coaching of teaching. *Educational Leadership,* *40*(1), 4–12.

Joyce, B., & Showers, B. (1983). *Power in staff development through research on training.* Alexandria, VA: Association for Supervision and Curriculum Development.

Joyce, B., & Showers, B. (1995). *Student achievement through staff development.* White Plains, NY: Longman.

Knowles, M. S. (1980). *The modern practice of adult education: From pedagogy to andragogy.* River Grove, IL: Follett.

O'Neil, J. (1993). Supervision reappraised. *ASCD Update, 35*(6), 1, 3, 8.

Portner, H. (2006). *Workshops that really work: The ABC's of designing and delivering sensational presentations.* Thousand Oaks, CA: Corwin Press.

Scherer, M. (Ed.). (1999). *A better beginning.* Alexandria, VA: Association for Supervision and Curriculum Development.

Scherer, M. (2001). Making standards work. *Educational Leadership, 1*(1), 5.

Showers, B. (1985, April). Teachers coaching teachers. *Educational Leadership, 42*(7), 43–48.

Shulman, J. H., & Colbert, J. A. (Eds.). (1988). *The intern teacher casebook.* San Francisco: Far West Laboratory for Educational Research and Development.

Teacher voices: The beginning teacher project. (1996). *Newsletter of Beginning Teacher Induction Network, 1*(3), 3.

U.S. Department of Education. (1997). *Seven priorities of the U.S. Department of Education* (Working document). Retrieved February 8, 2002, from www.ed .gov/updates/7priorities

Zachary, L. J. (2000). *The mentor's guide: Facilitating effective learning relationships.* San Francisco, CA: Jossey-Bass.

The Generations at Work in Schools

Suzette Lovely and Austin G. Buffum

Every few hundred years in Western history . . . we cross a "divide." Within a few short years, society rearranges itself—its worldview, its basic values, its social and political structure, its arts, its key institutions.

—Peter Drucker

From bowties and brooches to tank tops and tattoos, the canvas of the modern schoolhouse is changing. And it's not just students who look and act differently nowadays. Teachers, administrators, and parents are morphing too. Enter a campus and you might find faculty members showing off their latest nose piercings, while their ponytailed principal cruises the corridors in his Dockers and polo shirt. As older employees huddle in the staff lounge lamenting about how "things ain't what they used to be," the 20-something parent volunteer making copies in the workroom hardly bats an eye.

According to the bestselling book *Generations at Work* (Zemke, Raines, & Filipczak, 2000), the American workforce has never been so diverse, yet so uniquely singular. No other country in the world can boast such a rich blend of race, gender, ethnicity, and age in its workplace. One of the most significant, and potentially problematic, effects of such diversity is the growing generational infusion that brings old, young, and in-betweens together in the same employment venue. Whether by choice or necessity, senior teachers are postponing retirement while those graduating from college are launching their careers. For school systems, a multigenerational workforce can be both a blessing and a curse.

THE PERFECT STORM

As the end of the 20th century drew near, teachers and administrators found themselves whirling inside the vortex of shifting ideology. Between 1992 and 1999, the educational community was tossed around from autonomy to accountability, from restructuring to reform, from socialization to standards, from teaching to testing, from menus to mandates, and from *every child happy* to *every child a reader.* No wonder educators cruised into the millennium feeling a bit dizzy.

Confusion in California, for example, puts the dilemma into perspective. In July 1996 the state legislature poured $771 million into schools to lower class size in grades K–3 (CSR Research Consortium, 2002). This massive reform was tied to 10 reading initiatives and 22 other programs all launched around the same time. Elementary teachers quickly became overwhelmed. Depending on their generational rank, these schoolhouse sailors either (a) decided "this too shall pass" and stayed below deck, (b) spent 12 hours a day in the eye of the storm trying to batten down their curriculum, or (c) jumped ship.

Although there is general consensus among the educational community that the shift from teaching to learning is a good thing, theories abound as to the best way to tackle such a lofty endeavor. Without looking more closely at the cross-age profile inside schools, it may be difficult to achieve and sustain coalescence—especially during the stormy seas ahead. Bridging the gap and managing the friction means employee wants, needs, hopes, and fears have to be noticed and appreciated.

Table 4.1 Who's Who? A Snapshot of Four Living Generations

Generation/Age Span	General Characteristics	Defining Moments/Cultural Icons
Veterans (born 1922–1943) 38 million Americans	Formed worldview during hard times of Depression and WWII Built much of the nation's infrastructure Believe in duty before pleasure Spend conservatively Embrace values that speak to family, home, patriotism	The Great Depression Bombing of Pearl Harbor The Golden Era of Radio Superman FDR, Patton, Eisenhower

Generation/Age Span	General Characteristics	Defining Moments/Cultural Icons
Baby Boomers (born 1944–1960) 64 million Americans	Grew up in optimistic times of economic expansion Think of themselves as "cool" and "stars of the show" Covet status and power; driven to succeed Are service oriented Tend to be competitive because of their group size Pursue own gratification, often at a price to themselves and their families	Vietnam War Assassinations Civil rights movement Women's lib The peace sign *Captain Kangaroo* The Beatles
Generation X (born 1960–1980) 39 million Americans	Raised in an era of soaring divorce rates, struggling economy, and fallen heroes Are self-reliant and skeptical of authority Seek sense of family through network of friends and work relationships Maintain nontraditional orientation of time and space Eschew being labeled in any way, shape, or form	Microwaves, computer games, VCRs Nixon resignation MTV AIDS Extreme sports *The Simpsons*
Millennials (born 1980–2000) 79 million Americans	Feel wanted and indulged by parents Lead busy, overplanned lives Embrace core values similar to Veterans—optimism, civic duty, confidence, morality Are well mannered and polite Able to use technology in unforeseen ways	9-11 Columbine The Internet X Games Reality TV The Olson twins

SOURCE: Adapted from U.S. Census Bureau, 2004; Zemke, Raines, & Filipczak, 2000.

WHO'S WHO? A SNAPSHOT OF FOUR LIVING GENERATIONS

The current public school workforce comprises four distinct groups: Veterans, Baby Boomers, Generation X, and Millennials (see Table 4.1). Although there are no hard-and-fast rules about where one generation ends and another begins, demographers such as Neil Howe and William Strauss, who have studied generations dating back to the colonial period, note that specific life events tie a group together through shared experiences, hardships, social norms, and turning points. These common threads create self-sustaining links that cause people of a given era to maintain similar attitudes, ambitions, and synergy. Consider the profile of Veteran superintendents as a case in point. In their minds, age correlates with rank and status in the organization. Employees move up the ladder one rung at a time through perseverance, loyalty, and hard work. Older leaders tend to be formal, steeped in tradition, and have difficulty with change or ambiguity.

Generation X, on the other hand, came of age in times of corporate downsizing, a struggling economy, and an explosion of technology that allowed work to be done differently. Self-reliance, an impatience for bureaucracy, and the ability to change directions on a dime can make them seem irreverent to a Veteran. Generation X is not interested in working around the clock or keeping score of who has paid their dues. While a Veteran might ask, "How did he become a superintendent at age 35? He's just a boy!" the 30-something superintendent is likely to respond, "Send me an e-mail if you have a concern. And, take a little time off if the pressure is getting to you."

Today's living generations span roughly 80 years. People born within the same general timeframe—about every 18 to 25 years—are referred to as a *cohort* (Zemke, Raines, & Filipczak, 2000). Key life experiences from entering school, reaching puberty, graduating from high school, starting work, getting married, and having children define the core beliefs among each cohort. Although every human being has his or her own unique personality, many people underestimate how similar they are to their generational counterparts. Despite one's race, gender, socioeconomic status, and moral or religious views, the music, politics, heroes, headlines, scandals, and world events shared by an age group cannot be weaned from one's system. No matter how different individuals may be in mind, body, or spirit, they are age-bound in perceptions, passions, and pleasures. Common exposure breeds common thoughts.

To get a glimpse of who's who, let's examine the generational landscape of today's workplace:

Veterans (born before 1943): Described by Tom Brokaw as "the greatest generation," this cohort won a world war, rebuilt the nation's economy after a debilitating Depression, sent a man to the moon, and coined the phrase *American values.* Veterans come from a mold of honor and dedication. If they commit to something, you can take their word to the bank.

Throughout their formative years, Veterans had to make do or go without. After decades of frugality, they've amassed a whopping 75 percent of the financial assets in the United States (Zemke, Raines, & Filipczak, 2000). Despite entering their golden years with money to burn, Matures—as they are sometimes called—think nothing of driving across town to save ten cents on a gallon of gasoline. If you remember VJ Day, you are probably a Veteran.

Largely responsible for creating the infrastructure of American schools, Veterans are convinced that students need to be taught in a disciplined, orderly, and standardized fashion. To them, the hierarchical nature of the military and manufacturing—with a strong leader in charge—made perfectly good sense in schools too. Careful spending is another Veteran trademark. If you don't believe it, check out the supply cabinet of your oldest teacher or peruse the end-of-year carryover of your most senior principal. After all, one never knows when eight staplers or thousands of unencumbered dollars might come in handy.

Baby Boomers (born 1944 to 1960): The post–WWII baby boom era marked a reversal in the declining population trend that had stymied American growth for decades. Baby Boomers were the first generation in which child rearing was considered a pleasure rather than an economic or biological reality. Not only were these babies wanted, Dr. Spock implored parents to love and cherish them. His book instructed adults to go light on punishment and heavy on reason, with the main objective to make children happy.

Such overindulgence likely explains Baby Boomer patterns of excess, self-absorption, and insistence on getting their way. As trendsetters, Baby Boomers have made turning 50 fashionable and transformed fitness, spirituality, and cosmetic surgery into billion dollar industries. From Bill Clinton, to Martha Stewart, to Madonna, their ability to reinvent themselves is legendary.

Because there were so many of them, Baby Boomers were the first group of school-aged children to be graded on cooperation and "shares materials with classmates" (Raines, 1997, p. 27). Hence, teamwork is in their blood. They also grew up being told, "Ask not what your country can do for you, but instead what you can do for your country." As a result, these overachievers devised the 60-hour workweek with the hope that a better life was just around the corner. Those who recall the day President Kennedy was shot are likely to be members of the Baby Boom generation.

Many school systems are managed by Baby Boomer principals and superintendents, which helps to explain why reforms and innovations never cease. This is the cohort that has a hard time saying no and can't quite grasp the concept that less is more. Baby Boomers remain the dominant force in education today, first, because of their sheer size and second, because they are not all that anxious to retire. Their influence over what happens in schools is expected to continue for several more years.

Generation X (born 1960 to 1980): Sometimes thought of as detached, morose, and unmotivated, Generation X has had a tough go of things. Conceived in the shadow of the Baby Boomers, this smaller cohort has struggled to compete. Consequently, their psyche is shaped by a survivor mentality. They survived the divorce of their parents. They survived joint custody and life as latchkey kids. They survived college on student loans and Top Ramen. They survived oil embargos, real estate plunges, and stock market crashes. And they continue to survive the roller coaster ride of dot.com meltdowns and outsourcing.

While the parents and grandparents of Generation X stuck with the same employer for most of their career, the average tenure for today's 25- to 34-year-old is 2.9 years (Bureau of Labor Statistics, 2004, September 21). At this rate, an "Xer" could change jobs as many as 10 times before retirement. Such overexposure to hard knocks puts their distrust of authority and disdain for bureaucracy into perspective. As a cohort, they have lower-than-average expectations of what work can offer and aren't motivated by rewards that require perseverance or longevity. If you watched the *Challenger* disaster on a classroom TV, odds are good you belong to Generation X—although you dislike being labeled or lumped in with any mainstream group whatsoever.

What Generation X lacks in loyalty, they more than make up for in technical savvy and talent. Left alone to hook up their Atari and manipulate the microwave, this is the ingenious generation of eBay founder Pierre Omidyar, Larry Page and Sergey Brin of Google fame, and Michael Dell of Dell Computers. Their nontraditional approach to solving problems is an asset, especially in places such as schools, where it took 20 years to move the overhead projector from the bowling alley into the classroom. Although they don't always buy into the teamwork manifesto of their Boomer bosses, they are able to work on teams if given the discretion to complete tasks, make decisions, and implement solutions their own way.

Millennials (born 1980 to 2000): Also referred to as Generation Y, Echo Boomers, and Nexters, Millennials are expected to surpass Baby Boomers in size and achievement. Unrivaled as a consumer group, they average $100 a week in disposable income and influence $50 billion in annual family purchases (Zemke, Raines, & Filipczak, 2000). In 1999, the *Wall Street Journal* reported that 11 percent of the nation's 12- to 17-year-olds owned their own stock (Howe & Strauss, 2000). With unbridled spending power, America's youth exude a level of sophistication and tenacity that is sure to set any workplace on fire.

Adults are often surprised to learn that Millennials tend to subscribe to a strict moral code in which abstinence and zero tolerance hold sway. Most American teens actually enjoy spending time with their family and have glommed on to many of the same civic values embraced by the Veteran generation. Children who have the Columbine shootings and the morning of September 11 firmly etched into their young memories are Millennials.

With unlimited technology connecting them to people and places around the globe, today's youth have done and seen more than their parents or grandparents did in an entire lifetime. Thought to be the most open-minded generation in modern history, Millennials embrace group dating, biracial friendships, and study-abroad programs with a nonchalance that makes them color blind.

As the oldest Millennials graduate from high school and complete college, they are blossoming at a time when jobs are fairly abundant. For 20-somethings arriving in our classrooms as the newest teachers, principals should be ready to satisfy their craving for ongoing learning experiences, include them in decisions, and assign them to supportive teams.

As with any label or generalization, not all peer groups fit into the same box. Certainly, stereotypes can interfere with performance and cause resentment. Therefore, a commonsense approach is necessary when hiring, mentoring, directing, or evaluating employees based on their generational coding. Knowing the underpinnings that bind colleagues together or set them apart is beneficial in establishing collaborative teams, building capacity, and bringing out the best in people.

Table 4.2, The Generational Footprint of a Workplace, depicts the manner in which the different age groups perform on the job, integrate into teams, and lead others. As the portrait of each cadre unfolds, school leaders can hone in on strengths, make weaknesses irrelevant, and foster greater appreciation for diversity. Without such awareness or sensitivity, it is impossible to cultivate professional learning communities that are results based and improvement driven.

Table 4.2 The Generational Footprint of a Workplace

Generation/ Age Span	How They Perform on the Job	How They Integrate on Teams	How They Lead Others
Veterans Age Span 63 and older	Driven by rules and order Strive to uphold culture and traditions Able to leave work at work Need more time for orientation Find technology intimidating	Are okay with the power of collective action, as long as a central leader is in charge Respect experience Want to know where they stand and what's expected of them Eager to conform to group roles	Value dedication and loyalty Equate age with status/power Impose top-down structures Make most decisions themselves Keep work and personal life separate View change as disruptive and undesirable
Baby Boomers Age Span 45 to 62	Have a strong need to prove themselves to others May manipulate rules to meet own needs	Enjoy and value teamwork Expect group to stick to the schedule and agenda	Shy away from conflict Tend to lead through consensus Generally apply a participatory

(Continued)

Table 4.2 (Continued)

Generation/ Age Span	How They Perform on the Job	How They Integrate on Teams	How They Lead Others
	Deferential to authority Focus on product outcomes Can become political animals if turf is threatened Work long hours	Willing to go the extra mile Good at building rapport and solving problems Embrace equity and equality Want credit and respect for accomplishments	approach, but may struggle with delegation and empathy Embrace leadership trends and personal development Expect people to put in their time Less flexible with change
Generation X Age Span 25 to 44	Strive for balance, freedom, and flexibility Strong dislike for corporate politics, fancy titles, or rigid structures Expect to have fun at work Prefer independence and minimal supervision Good at multitasking Value process over product	Like to work on teams with informal roles and freedom to complete tasks their own way Do well on projects calling for technical competence and creativity Work best with teammates of their own choosing Detest being taken advantage of Struggle to build rapport with other group members	Drawn to leadership for altruistic reasons—not power or prestige Casual and laid-back Try to create an environment that is functional and efficient May lack tact and diplomacy Able to create and support alternative workplace structures Willing to challenge higher-ups Adapt easily to change
Millennials Age Span 24 and younger	Anxious to fit in Respectful of authority, but unafraid to approach their boss with concerns Value continuing education Exceptional at multitasking Drawn to organizations with career ladders and standardized pay/benefits	Accepting of group diversity Determined to achieve team goals Respond well to mentoring Enjoy working with idealistic people Expect to be included in decisions Need a bit more supervision and structure than other groups	Open to new ideas Able to work with varying employee styles and needs Prefer flattened hierarchy Hopeful and resilient Display more decorum and professionalism than Xers Lack experience handling conflict and difficult people

SOURCE: Adapted from Lancaster & Stillman, 2002; Raines, 2003; Zemke, Raines, & Filipczak, 2000.

ROAD MAPS AND ASPIRATIONS

Although we share the same profession, our career road maps may differ significantly. For Veterans, and Baby Boomers to a lesser degree, the end of WWII and the GI Bill prompted large numbers of men to migrate into teaching. The idea was to find a district in which you could establish roots and, if desired, move up by becoming a principal or superintendent. Job security was determined by virtue of one's accomplishments and tenure. This thinking worked fine when schools were more insular and lifetime employment was an unconditional guarantee.

On the other side of the coin is career security, a work ideal more aligned with Generation X and Millennial thinking. The premise here is that you build up a bank of knowledge and experiences so that no matter what bad things might happen, you are able to bounce back. Limitations on the portability of service credit prevents teachers from job hopping to the same degree as contemporaries in the private sector; however, young teachers today are far more nomadic than their Boomer colleagues. Loyalty to a school district doesn't resonate with Generation X in particular because they aren't convinced the system is committed to looking out for them over the long haul. While Veteran educators focused on building a legacy, and Boomers aspired to build stellar careers, Generation X and Millennials replacing them are more interested in building portable and parallel careers (Lancaster & Stillman, 2002).

As generational variances are examined, the catalyst for turbulence in schools becomes obvious. A typical clash of occupational values versus workplace reality is featured in Table 4.3, Storyboard. The sagas of Doug and Evelyn demonstrate how cross-age dissent can bruise egos and wither relationships.

In Doug's case, he has used a communication style that is completely distasteful to the Generation X principal. Since this cohort sees things from a more cynical lens, clichés and hyperbole don't sit well with them.

A better strategy is for Doug to set expectations that define the right outcomes and then give the principal latitude in formulating steps to get there. Through weekly or biweekly conversations, Doug can offer constructive feedback that spotlights the principal's progress, rather than her failure. Members of Generation X often complain that their Boomer bosses are wishy-washy and give lip service to concepts such as *teamwork* and *empowerment* without practicing what they preach. So the most sensible way for Doug to guide the principal in laying out her plan is via a direct, yet individualistic, approach.

Taking a Veteran teacher like Evelyn by surprise is bad business. Maybe it's been convenient for this teacher to do her own thing because

Table 4.3   Storyboard

The Saga of Doug	The Saga of Evelyn
Doug, a 52-year-old assistant superintendent, is anxious to see test scores improve at an underperforming elementary school. Doug isn't convinced that the principal is doing all she can to push her staff and ratchet up the learning.	Evelyn, a 64-year-old English teacher, is asked to see the principal during her planning period on the last day of school. The Generation X principal matter-of-factly explains to Evelyn that declining enrollment has created a staffing surplus.
During a meeting, Doug tries to pump up the Generation X principal by urging her to "win one for the Gipper." The principal immediately scoffs at the metaphor. While Doug writes the principal off as uncooperative, the principal is convinced that everyone at the central office is self-righteous. It's obvious that Doug and the rest of his cronies don't have a clue about the challenges this overworked principal is facing!	Despite Evelyn's senior status, the principal believes her refusal to collaborate with colleagues is incompatible with the school's mission of working as a professional learning community. Thus, Evelyn is being transferred to a cross-town high school.
	Evelyn's response is laced with hurt and anger. "How can you do this to me?" she cries. "I opened this school in 1972 while you were still in diapers. This is my home!" Evelyn stomps out of the office and immediately contacts the union president. Her next step is to file a grievance.

no one has asked her to do otherwise. Before writing Evelyn off, the Generation X principal should slow down and look deeper into what is actually going on. She may be willing to contribute more and share her knowledge, but simply has never been asked. Outlining objectives that emphasize the experience and historical perspective of seasoned staff like Evelyn enables principals to pair them with younger faculty who see things through a different lens. Without checking up on Veteran faculty regularly and respectfully, administrators may unwittingly be permitting them to check out.

If leaders hope to load the big yellow bus with the right people and get the wrong people to move on, the career desires and distinctions of staff have to be considered. As aspirations are understood, forks can be drawn in the road to provide various routes for each employee. Asking teachers, "Where do you see yourself in five years?" "What kind of committees and projects do you prefer to work on?" "How would you like me to support you?" and "Is there anything that might get in your way of achieving these goals?" gives administrators insight into workplace ideals while also honoring age-based ambitions.

CONCLUSION: A CAUSE CÉLÈBRE

For the first time in the history of public education, four distinct age groups are working elbow to elbow. School systems require new tools for dealing with employees in age-sensitive ways. If intergenerational planning isn't embraced as a cause célèbre, the educational community may find itself on a demographic collision course. Consider why. First, schools are vulnerable to a mass exodus of employees entering their golden years. Yet, as Baby Boomers live longer, they aren't all that enamored with retirement. Older teachers and administrators, whose knowledge may not be as current as those coming straight out of the university, are inclined to have conflicting opinions about what's best for students.

Another cause for concern is that the working population between ages 25 and 54 will decline by 4.3 percent in the next five years, while the number of people age 55 and older will grow by 4.8 percent (Bureau of Labor Statistics, 2004, June). A shrinking pool of job prospects will necessitate an even more aggressive recruitment campaign of immigrant and minority workers. Such an influx of diversity in the workplace certainly hastens the potential for conflict. Employers must openly acknowledge that other ages, other cultures, and other voices have as much claim on the world as they do.

Finally, escalating demands from parents have created a growing chasm between what is expected of local schools and what teachers may be willing or able to give. Veteran parents like Ward and June Cleaver considered it taboo to question authority. But now they have been replaced by Boomer dads and Generation X moms who see their obligation to their offspring as all encompassing. Clearly, such opposing personalities can drive a wedge into the core mission of building and sustaining collaborative learning communities.

The generational force orbiting schools is both powerful and subtle. Unlike other diversity factors such as race, gender, or ethnicity, cross-age differences affect every school employee every day. Unresolved discord leads to biases, dysfunctional relationships, and toxic cultures—all of which stand as a huge impediment to achievement.

Unfortunately, public institutions lag behind private industry when it comes to initiating harmonious, student-centered work environments. Educators have been accused of supporting mediocrity, being behind the times, and failing to accept the evolving needs of constituents. Through an emphasis on job flexibility, respectful relations, and appreciation for generational differences, exceptional school districts are turning the corner. Leaders who focus on their human capital as the blueprint for success can bridge the gap by knowing what makes their employees tick.

REFERENCES

Bureau of Labor Statistics. (2004, June). *Tomorrow's jobs: Occupational outlook handbook, 2004–05 edition* (Bulletin 2540). Washington, DC: U.S. Department of Labor.

Bureau of Labor Statistics. (2004, September 21). *Employee tenure summary: Employee tenure in 2004: Current population survey.* Washington, DC: U.S. Department of Labor.

Bureau of Labor Statistics. (2004, Fall). *More education: Lower unemployment, higher pay: Occupational outlook quarterly.* Washington, DC: U.S. Department of Labor.

CSR Research Consortium (2002, June). *Evidence inconclusive that California's class size reduction program improves student achievement.* Retrieved April 22, 2005, from www.classize.org/press/index-02.htm

Howe, N., & Strauss, W. (2000). *Millennials rising: The next great generation.* New York: Vintage Books.

Lancaster, L., & Stillman, D. (2002). *When generations collide.* New York: HarperBusiness.

Raines, C. (1997). *Beyond generation X: A practical guide for managers.* Menlo Park, CA: Crisp Publications.

Zemke, R., Raines, C., & Filipczak, B. (2000). *Generations at work.* New York: American Management Association.

CHAPTER FIVE

Teacher to Teacher

Personality and Communication

Mario C. Martinez

School-related problems can often be traced to problems between people. One teacher may have a problem with the way another teacher communicates. Each teacher communicates differently because each has a different personality, and personality influences communication and the way we think, act, and behave. For example, a problem between two teachers may arise in a committee meeting while the group is discussing how to implement a new instructional practice. One teacher may believe that more discussion is needed and that the practice should be phased in, but another teacher thinks it should be implemented immediately. Each teacher requires a different level of detail about the new instructional practice and an individual idea of how fast it should be implemented. It is likely that these differences have a lot to do with each teacher's personality. Some people require a good deal of detail and feel it would be unwise to immediately implement a new instructional program without more information. Others may be more tolerant of taking a risk, so immediate implementation may seem like a good idea.

UNDERSTANDING PERSONALITY INCREASES COMPATIBILITY

School collegiality is strengthened when faculty understand each other and know how to effectively communicate with each other. A teacher who understands the nuances of different personalities understands how to meet the needs of other teachers and navigate through the complexity of problems that can arise because of individual personality differences. Problems attributed to personality differences affect how teachers feel about their jobs, colleagues, and even classrooms. Work relationships are also important because people develop many personal relationships through

Reprinted from Martinez, M. C. (2004). *Teachers working together for school success.* Thousand Oaks, CA: Corwin Press. Copyright © 2004 by Corwin Press, www.corwinpress.com. All rights reserved.

work. Buckingham and Coffman (1999) found that one important ingredient that contributes to a happy and effective employee is whether that employee has a best friend at work. Buckingham and Coffman's work points to the positive social interactions that every person desires, many of which are fulfilled in the workplace.

Compatibility between and among faculty is largely about effective interaction between different personality types. In this chapter, you will learn about four personality types. You will take an assessment to learn more about your own personality. Each personality type has certain preferences, needs, wants, strengths, and weaknesses. As you go through the assessment and identify the characteristics of your personality, you may discover that the two areas of improvement are linked to the strengths or weaknesses of your personality type.

The foundation of school collegiality lies in how teachers get along and work together. Those who learn about their own and their colleagues' personalities can work together more effectively. Teamwork and conflict resolution are also influenced by the personalities of the people who are working on a team or trying to resolve a conflict.

An equally important benefit for teachers who learn about personality and interaction is that the knowledge can be applied to multiple settings, with children or adults. Children, parents, teachers, and administrators all have different personality types. A teacher who has knowledge of personality types can respond and communicate more effectively with children in the classroom, parents in a conference, or administrators in a meeting.

Assessing Your Personality

The subject of personality has drawn considerable research interest. This interest gave birth to an entire field of study called *personality psychology* (Hunt, 1993). There are many instruments that have been used over the years to help people identify their personality types. Some instruments identify sixteen possible types, others as few as four. Most are conceptually similar even though the terms they use to describe different personalities may vary. Many of these instruments have withstood statistical testing and are deemed valid and reliable indicators of personality. These assessments owe their development to the work of early personality psychologists. Hunt identifies the work of early twentieth-century psychologists Hans J. Eysenck and Raymond Cattell, who independently tested for relationships among multiple traits that could describe distinct personality factors. The work of these psychologists was influenced by Carl Jung, who divided people into categories of extroversion and introversion, as well as thinking and feeling types.

From a practitioner's standpoint, the application and implication of personality types is evident. Accurate identification of different personality types can help teachers gain conscious insight into how different people think, act, and behave. A study of personality theory is also one of self-discovery, whereby you learn about your personality type and how it influences your relationships.

Salespeople have long used personality theory to aid them in their businesses. The classic and sometimes exaggerated claim is that salespeople apply this knowledge to gain insight into the prospects' personalities by an initial two-minute conversation. If salespeople perceive that prospects are direct, no-nonsense persons, they may get right to the point, briefly explain the most prominent features of their products, and inform the prospects of the price. They surmise that these particular prospects do not care about chatting and exchanging stories. Other prospects, who like to know who they are buying from, may want more interaction with the salesperson. These prospects may want to sit down and talk a bit longer to see if they can trust the salespeople and everything they are saying. The salespeople would obviously handle prospects differently, based on their personalities.

The application of personality theory is not limited to the business world. There have been great strides in applying the concepts behind personality theory to educational environments. Unfortunately, the majority of this information is disseminated to administrators in workshops or graduate students majoring in educational leadership. However, as the pace of change in education accelerates and teachers are increasingly called to work together, the need for teachers to learn about communication tools also increases.

It is more likely that people will focus on actual problems instead of personal differences when they appreciate personality differences. In a widely distributed book on negotiation, Fisher and Ury (1981) urge us to focus on the problem, not the people. These authors counsel us to separate the people from the problem. It is hard to solve problems when we can't get beyond individual differences with other people. If you know how personality influences behavior and communication, you will be less likely to personalize differences and disagreements.

Together, Table 5.1 and Tables 5.2a and 5.2b make up a personality assessment that I have developed as a tool to help educators learn about themselves and others. It integrates foundational concepts of early personality psychology and ideas adapted from several resources that speak to the subjects of personality and communication (LaHaye, 1984; National Seminars Group, 2001; Wilson Learning Corporation, 1989).

Table 5.1 and Table 5.2a contain the directions. Turn first to Table 5.1 and go through each of the four columns, placing a checkmark on any word or phrase that describes you. For the assessment to be accurate, you must follow one very important rule: Go with your *initial reaction*. For example, if you read the phrase "Emotional Extremes" in Column 2 and at first believe that this accurately describes you, place a checkmark next to this characteristic. Some assessment takers may perceive themselves as being emotional but on reflection associate such a characteristic as a weakness and therefore not check the space. Check every characteristic that describes you, be it a perceived strength or weakness. Every column has characteristics that may be perceived as strengths or weaknesses, so the important thing is to check those characteristics that accurately describe you. The effectiveness of any psychometric test requires this level of honesty. After you have checked every word or phrase that describes you, add up the total checkmarks in each column.

Turn to Table 5.2a and complete the subtraction as described in Steps 1 and 2, plotting the results along their respective axes on the table; you should end up with only two dots. Now draw a line to connect the two dots on your graph (Step 3). When you connect the two dots, there are two possible outcomes. The first possibility is that you formed a triangle. This will always be the case if the results from both Steps 1

Table 5.1   Personality Assessment Checklist

Check any attribute that describes you in Columns 1, 2, 3, and 4. Total the checkmarks in each column.	
Column 1	*Column 2*
_ Decisive	_ High energy
_ Factual	_ Motivator
_ Direct	_ Emotional extremes
_ Strict, legalistic	_ Impatient
_ Like information	_ Active
_ Orderly	_ Charismatic
_ Practical	_ Communicator
_ Cautious	_ Short attention span
_ Uncommunicative	_ People oriented
_ Responsible	_ Opinionated
_ Demanding	_ Talk before I think
_ Calculating	_ Risk taker
_ Formal	_ Loud
_ Goal oriented	_ Prefer quick pace
_ Industrious	_ Take charge
_ Economical	_ Enthusiastic
_ Reserved	_ High need to control
_ Traditional	_ Competitive
_ Total	_ Total
Column 3	*Column 4*
_ Happy-go-lucky	_ Prefer quiet environment
_ Noncommital	_ Calm
_ Diplomatic	_ Hard time saying no
_ Dependable when committed	_ Vulnerable, negative self-image
_ Carefree	_ Gentle
_ Untapped potential	_ Dependable
_ Impulsive	_ Exact
_ Open	_ Simple dress
_ Approachable	_ Work well under pressure
_ Informal	_ Supportive
_ Easily influenced	_ Deliberate actions
_ Undisciplined	_ Ask questions
_ Congenial	_ Good listener
_ Easy to get to know	_ Soft spoken
_ Friendly	_ Risk averse
_ Trusting	_ Team oriented
_ Good with people	_ Devoted
_ Sociable	_ Permissive
_ Total	_ Total

Table 5.2a   Sample Assessment Graph

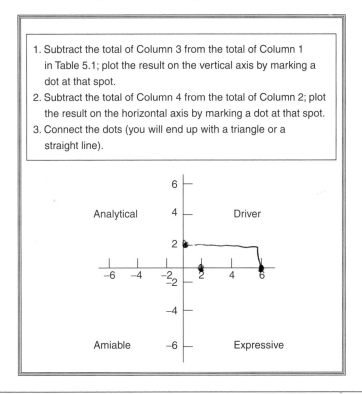

1. Subtract the total of Column 3 from the total of Column 1 in Table 5.1; plot the result on the vertical axis by marking a dot at that spot.
2. Subtract the total of Column 4 from the total of Column 2; plot the result on the horizontal axis by marking a dot at that spot.
3. Connect the dots (you will end up with a triangle or a straight line).

and 2 are different from zero. It is also possible that you simply formed a straight line. This will be the case if the result from either Step 1 or 2 was zero.

Table 5.2b is an example of a plot for a person who completed the personality assessment in Table 5.1 and Table 5.2a. This sample is included for illustration purposes only. The line that connects the two dots in Table 5.2b forms a triangle in the "Analytical" quadrant of the graph. It is likely that your triangle will be of a different size or location. If you ended up with a triangle of any size, then the quadrant in which your triangle resides contains the word that describes your personality type: Expressive, Driver, Amiable, or Analytical.

If your plot was a straight line rather than a triangle, look at the two personality quadrants that your line joins. The straight line means that the characteristics you exhibit, according to how you responded to the assessment, are evenly divided between these two personality types. The assessment is purposely designed to allow for the possibility that some people strongly exhibit characteristics of two personality types. Descriptions of the personality types are shown in Table 5.3.

The top of Table 5.3 lists commonly perceived strengths and weaknesses attributed to each personality type. These are described as "commonly perceived" because some of the listed weaknesses may actually be strengths, depending on the situation.

Table 5.2b   Completed Assessment Graph

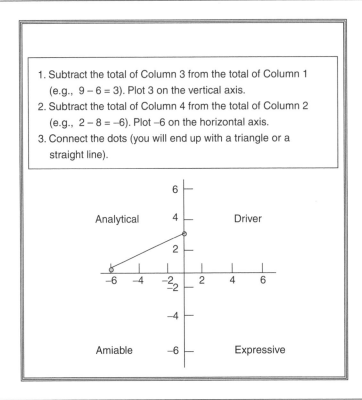

1. Subtract the total of Column 3 from the total of Column 1 (e.g., 9 – 6 = 3). Plot 3 on the vertical axis.
2. Subtract the total of Column 4 from the total of Column 2 (e.g., 2 – 8 = –6). Plot –6 on the horizontal axis.
3. Connect the dots (you will end up with a triangle or a straight line).

For example, a listed weakness for the Analytical personality is that this person is a perfectionist. Perfectionists are slow to get things done because they are constantly looking for more information and want to be exact in their decisions. This may be a strength if a team of faculty and staff is gathering information that is going to be used in a report to the state department of education. The more exact the report, the fewer questions later on.

As mentioned, the list of strengths and weaknesses in Table 5.3 provides a general sense of the common perceptions associated with each personality type. The strengths and weaknesses are more accurate for those teachers whose triangles in Table 5.2a are very large. If you ended up with a very small triangle or a straight line, the lists will be slightly less accurate. A small triangle indicates you more strongly exhibit characteristics of two or more personality types than a person who has a very large triangle. A large triangle indicates you strongly exhibit the characteristics described by your personality type. The fact is that everyone exhibits some characteristics of every personality type, but the strength of each characteristic associated with a given personality type varies for each individual.

There is a notable strength for those teachers who end up with a straight line or a very small triangle. Since these individuals more evenly exhibit characteristics from more than one personality type, they are usually able to effectively interact and communicate with a wide range of individuals. People with very large triangle plots are more likely to be viewed as extreme personalities and experience conflict with other people.

Table 5.3   Personality and Interaction

	Analytical	*Expressive*	*Amiable*	*Driver*
Strength	Thorough, calm, practical, high standards	Socially skilled, outgoing, persuasive	Team oriented, good listener, trusting, patient, helpful	Ambitious, goal oriented, dependable, organized
Weakness	Perfectionist, withdrawn, slow to get things done	Pushy, reactive, overbearing, manipulative	Hesitant, indecisive, vulnerable, too subjective	Stubborn, rigid, distant, critical
When Interacting				
Do	Be direct, provide evidence, be practical	Support brainstorms, discuss big picture, provide examples	Show sincere interest, be non-threatening, provide assurances	Show responsibility, control emotions, talk results, not personalities
Do not	Be disorganized, present half-baked ideas, be overassertive	Rush into business, debate, lack enthusiasm	Be cold or curt, be insensitive, be indecisive	Waste time visiting, try to build personal relationships

PERSONALITIES IN ACTION

Dan is a gentle man, quiet in manner but precise in action. He was a classroom elementary teacher for ten years before taking a position as a reading coordinator in his school. He is thorough in his work and ensures that teachers hold to the standards of the new reading program the school recently implemented. Most of the teachers work well with Dan, though some of them feel he could communicate a little more often and answer requests in a more timely manner. Dan gets along well with the school principal, but he sometimes feels the principal suggests ideas without having thought through their implications. This is disconcerting for Dan, because he likes to know that people offering suggestions aren't just "making things up" as they go. He has always liked to know the direct, practical implication of new ideas, and he wants people to walk the talk. Dan is an Analytical personality.

Sandra is an Expressive personality. She is an English teacher and works in a large, public high school. Sandra has been teaching for over twenty years, and her students see her as "cool" and fun. Sandra often organizes happy hour get-togethers with the other teachers and is not afraid to express her opinions. She recently worked on a committee to discuss the implications of inclusion in English and math courses. Inclusion, as defined by Sandra's school, meant that all students, including special education students, would be included in general education courses. Sandra found herself in the heat of many committee discussions, with some teachers perceiving her as trying to take over the conversation about how to effectively implement inclusion in the high school. Overall, Sandra is able to bring people together and lead a group, and she is now studying at the local university for her administrative license.

Eleanor works in a middle school that has recently transitioned from a junior high to a middle school. The middle school philosophy, as articulated by Eleanor's principal, embraces much of what Eleanor believes. Teachers are organized into interdisciplinary teams, and there is an emphasis on collaboration. Eleanor has always liked working in teams and in fact prefers it to working alone. She has never considered herself a spokesperson but takes pride in contributing to the team and helping others. Eleanor sees herself as able to put other people's needs above her own—this was actually the driving self-discovery that led her into teaching. Eleanor's friends say that people tend to take advantage of her because she does not know how to say "no." There is some truth to this assessment, as Eleanor has at times taken on too many assignments and duties because people recruited her or gave her additional tasks without really discussing it with her. Eleanor is best described as an Amiable personality.

Carlos is a high school history teacher and basketball coach. He is a stereotypical Driver personality. Carlos was a star player when he was in high school and graduated with honors from college. The principal in Carlos's high school regularly asks for his help with students who have been experiencing trouble in their studies and need structure. Carlos's businesslike approach in the classroom and on the basketball court has proven effective with problem students.

When Carlos first started coaching three years ago, the basketball teams were perennial losers, but under his guidance, the team now has a winning record and is probably a year away from state contention. Some parents have said that Carlos pushes students too hard and is critical of those who disagree with him. Carlos insists that his approach works. He spends little social time with other faculty and is not seen as the friendliest of teachers.

APPLYING THE CONCEPTS OF PERSONALITY TO YOUR SCHOOL

The major premise of personality theory is that people are different. Personality influences our actions, and our actions influence others. The framework that describes the four personality types offers a practical way to help teachers understand their own actions and those of their colleagues. Teachers can apply the tool of personality theory to their situations by answering questions specific to their schools. Answer the three application questions that follow. The depth of thought you give to each question determines the level of application you perceive in each question. If you are working through this book with other teachers, answer these questions as a group.

1. Reflect on your experience as a teacher. What personality type do you have most difficulty with? Why?

2. Reflect on your experience as a teacher. What personality type do you get along best with? Why?

3. Does your ability to get along with a specific personality type depend on whether you are in a work setting or a social setting?

The three questions are useful for discussion without specifically naming individuals. The focus is on the personality type. Your answer to the questions also depends on your personality type, but there are some generalizations that tend to surface when a large number of people answer these questions. Tannen (1994), who has written extensively on relationships between men and women in the workplace, states that individuals do not always fit the general patterns of behavior that we might use to categorize them. However, there is value in identifying patterns and outlining generalizations. Generalizations help us organize our thoughts and make sense of the world, as long as we use caution in applying these generalizations and understand that there are exceptions.

The first prominent generalization that emerges from the three questions is that people have an easier time answering Question 2 than Question 1. Most people, regardless of their personality, generally agree that it is easy to get along with an Amiable person. This makes sense since Amiable people are good listeners. They are also team oriented and helpful. Amiable people tend to be genuinely interested in others, so they make friends very easily.

People do not generally agree as strongly on an answer for Question 1, but most people tend to experience difficulty with those personality types that demonstrate strong emotions or evoke those emotions in others. Expressive and Driver personalities tend to do this. Expressive personalities are themselves emotional. Expressive people may be talkative and loud if excited; they may be negatively vocal when offended. Drivers may be perceived as stubborn and critical, and this may hurt and offend others. People may form negative perceptions of Expressives or Drivers simply because they illicit strong emotions in others. Amiable and Analytical people do not tend to be as vocal, so people are not as quick to produce a strong judgment about them.

Effective communication between the various personality types is also influenced by situation: work or social. Analytical or Driver personalities may be very bothered by Expressive or Amiable faculty members who like to "visit" during planning periods. They may view this visiting as unnecessary socializing that cuts into the planning period. In a social setting, two Analytical personalities standing by the punch bowl at the holiday party may welcome an Expressive personality. The dynamics of any relationship is therefore influenced by the characteristics of the personalities and the situations in which those personalities interact.

Conclusion

We all have people with whom we get along and those we would rather avoid. You can think about your interactions with different people using the lens of personality theory to improve your relationships. The three application questions below will help you build productive relationships in your school. It is best to answer these three questions on your own rather than in a group.

1. Identify one person in your school with whom you have experienced conflict. Identify this person's personality.

2. How can you use the information in this chapter to improve your interaction with this person?

3. What is your administrator's personality? How can you use the information in this chapter to improve your interaction with your administrator?

Personality theory is not an exact science, nor can it solve every relationship problem. It is, however, a much-used tool across different disciplines and has helped people resolve conflict, improve teamwork, and generate understanding among and between colleagues. This knowledge put into practice can improve school collegiality.

REFERENCES

Buckingham, M., & Coffman, C. (1999). *First break all the rules.* New York: Simon & Schuster.

Fisher, R., & Ury, W. (1981). *Getting to yes: Negotiating agreement without giving in.* New York: Penguin.

Hunt, M. (1993). *The story of psychology.* New York: Doubleday.

LaHaye, T. (1984). *Why you act the way you do.* Wheaton, IL: Living Books, Tyndale House.

National Seminars Group. (2001). *Management and leadership skills for first time managers and supervisor* [Training booklet]. Shawnee Mission, KS: Rockhurst University, Author.

Tannen, D. (1994). *Talking 9 to 5: Men and women in the workplace.* New York: Avon.

Wilson Learning Corporation. (1989). *Managing interpersonal relationships at Hewlett-Packard* [Training Booklet]. Eden Prairie, MN: Author.

6

Differentiated Coaching

Changing Your Approach to Meet Teacher Needs

Jane A. G. Kise

A teacher we'll call Sara volunteered to be coached by me on differentiated instruction, excited to learn about ways to reach more children. She and the others on her team were so enthusiastic to get started that they actually scheduled two afterschool meetings in one week with me—on their own time! So how quickly did Sara adopt the strategies she was eager to learn?

She corrected papers during those meetings. She failed to participate in brainstorming sessions. She ignored even the shortest of suggested readings. She said, "If I'm using the District curriculum, then I'm already differentiating." She irritated her teammates by asking detailed, seemingly irrelevant questions.

Was Sara resistant? Literature on the subject often places teachers on continuums from "innovators" to "laggards" (Tye, 2000) or "key members" to "deadwood" (Evans, 2001). Usually, blame for resistance is placed solidly with the teacher.

Sara, though, was unique. I use a framework called personality type to examine teacher strengths and beliefs. You may have encountered the theory through the Myers-Briggs Type Indicator®. It's a theory about normal differences in how people take in information and make decisions. Coaches can use other theories and frameworks for the same purpose, but data collected over decades by the Center for Applications of Psychological Type show that Sara's personality type is least frequent among teachers— less than 1% of all teachers share her personality type. Staff development is seldom designed with teachers like Sara in mind.

However, Sara was the first on her team to try the new differentiation techniques, *once I differentiated my coaching methods to meet her concerns, beliefs, and learning style.* Then I did the same for the other teachers on the team, and they changed, quickly.

I hadn't done so at first because, after all, they'd chosen to work with me. I'd assumed that a small group approach, with rich dialogue around lessons from their own curriculum and a proven planning process, would be enough. That coaching practice had worked for me at other schools. But the concerns and beliefs of these teachers made them hesitant to change their classrooms until I changed my coaching plan in ways that produced evidence that countered those beliefs.

RESISTANCE?

Often, information on coaching teachers suggests that we consider differentiating for content areas, grade levels, and years of teaching experience. However, what if the following is true, as I've found in working with countless teachers?

- Teachers form their practices around what they do best.
- Their strengths are related to their own personalities and learning styles.
- Their personalities and learning styles drive their core educational beliefs.
- Changing their teaching practices means changing those core beliefs.

That makes change very, very difficult. As Fullan and Hargreaves (1991) put it, changing teacher beliefs involves changing the person the teacher is.

It also makes the job of a coach more intricate, removing the concept of resistance and substituting the following: *How can I adjust my coaching style to meet the needs of this teacher?* Changing styles goes far beyond choosing from such coaching roles as modeling, coteaching, providing resources, and so on, which mainly focus on delivery methods, although this is part of it. Extensive research (Barger & Kirby, 1995; Clancy, 1997) found the following:

- There are clear differences in the kinds of information people with different personalities and learning styles need, how they process that information, and what makes change most stressful.
- Resistance to change increases when those needs aren't met.
- Leaders in general fail to recognize and deal effectively with those needs.

In differentiated coaching, then, the goal is to identify what information an individual teacher needs during change. That information will be affected by his or her personality type, which in turn influences the teacher's teaching style, beliefs about education, and main concerns during change.

The purpose of using a framework such as personality type isn't to label the teacher, but to *undo* the label of "resistor," to unearth needs that the coach, who most likely has a different personality type, doesn't naturally think of or meet. Let's look at a process for understanding a teacher's personality and beliefs, informational needs, and the coaching strategies that have the best chance of bringing about change.

STEP 1: DRAW A HYPOTHESIS ABOUT THE TEACHER'S NATURAL STYLE

While I use personality type, other learning styles models can also be used to foster strengths-based conversations about teaching and learning. If you use another model, consider whether you can adapt it for the same purposes I describe. Personality type is simply the model with which I am most familiar and can use to provide the richest examples.

Why Personality Type?

Coaches can use other learning styles frameworks for differentiating teacher needs. However, personality type is a strengths-based model that can turn the focus away from "right" and "wrong" to "Which students will this curriculum/teaching strategy/ assessment format reach?" This theory holds that people take in information and make decisions differently, two key processes in education. Further, these variations in behavior are quite orderly and consistent. Using a framework such as personality type makes coaching less threatening to a teacher, who after all is teaching from his or her core self.

Personality type is also well researched; search the bibliography at www.capt.org to see over 10,000 studies and articles, including reliability and validity studies, correlations with other learning styles models, connections between type theory and misdiagnosis of conditions such as Attention Deficit Disorder, the overrepresentation of

(Continued)

(Continued)

some types in Teacher of the Year awards, the use of type concepts to improve student achievement, and so on.

If you choose a different framework, make sure that it (Kise, 2006)

- Describes teaching and learning in nonjudgmental ways. No one should feel labeled.
- Is strengths-based, emphasizing each person's natural teaching and learning style rather than placing limits on what the person can do.
- Describes what learning styles a practice will reach.
- Works for both adults and students, and across cultures, to facilitate conversations about classrooms.

As you read through the information on the preferences, take notes. Which is your *preferred* style? Most people have elements of each, but one is easier and takes less energy. And, bring to mind a teacher whom you have struggled to coach. Which preferences might they have? Does this explain any of your coaching struggles?

Extraversion and Introversion

This preference pair describes our source of *energy*. In personality type theory, it is not about gregariousness or shyness; it's even spelled differently. Instead, people who prefer Extraversion are energized by interacting with others and through activities. People who prefer Introversion are energized by time alone for reflection.

Most Extraverted teachers run classrooms that have Extraverted characteristics—lots of activities, interactions, student work and learning aids on display, and so on. Introverted teachers run more Introverted classrooms, usually with less noise, fewer pieces of furniture or artwork, more individual time, and so on.

As you think about your "resistant" teacher, which style fits best? Then, consider whether his or her needs are being met (Kise, 2006) in the coaching process:

Extraversion	*Introversion*
Is there time for productive conversations regarding the changes?	Is information available for reflection before teachers are asked to respond or act?
Are there active roles for those who want them?	Are there one-to-one opportunities for communicating, both to share thoughts and to ask questions?
Is action as well as talk taking place?	Is there time to internalize the meaning of the change before having to act?

Sensing and Intuition

This preference pair describes the kinds of *information* people pay attention to first. Those who prefer Sensing pay attention to *what is*, first attending to facts verifiable by the five senses and to past experiences. Those who prefer Intuition pay attention to *what could be*, first attending to hunches, connections, analogies, and inspirations.

Sensing teachers tend to give structured assignments that can be objectively graded. They often search for what has worked for other teachers and may be content to use curriculum. Some even resist skipping over sections, concerned about missing something vital.

Intuitive teachers tend to prefer open-ended assignments that allow for student individuality and creativity. They love trying new ideas and often treat curriculum as a starting place, adding, subtracting, or innovating as ideas occur to them.

As you think about your "resistant" teacher, might that person be more Sensing or Intuitive? Consider whether his or her needs are being met (Kise, 2006) through the current change or coaching process.

Sensing	*Intuition*
Is real data available to demonstrate why the change needs to be made and why it is better than the present?	Have you provided the big picture—the underlying theories and the long-term vision?
Have specific details been provided regarding schedules, costs, and responsibilities?	Are there options for implementation to allow for creativity and individuality?
Have you made specific connections between the proposed changes, past practices, and other change efforts?	Do teachers have opportunities to influence the change effort design?

Thinking and Feeling

This preference pair describes how we make *decisions*. People who prefer Thinking make decisions through logic and universal principals, objectively considering precedents and consequences. People who prefer Feeling make decisions by stepping into the shoes of those involved to subjectively consider the impact on individuals and community values. Note that both are rational decision-making processes. In educational decisions, the Thinking preference considers data, standards, and benchmarks while the Feeling preference considers student engagement, motivation, and relationships. Both considerations are vital to student achievement, and the best decisions balance the two decision-making styles.

The classroom of a Thinking teacher might emphasize rigor over relationships. Yes, these teachers will build relationships with their students, but they're motivated first by ensuring that their students are working toward high standards and learning how to reason.

The classroom of a Feeling teacher might emphasize relationships over rigor. Yes, Feeling teachers will hold their students accountable to high standards, but they're motivated first by ensuring that their students are engaged in the learning process and the learning community.

As you think about your "resistant" teacher, consider whether his or her needs are being met (Kise, 2006) during the change or coaching process.

Thinking	*Feeling*
How clear is the logic of how the change measures were chosen? What about the internal logic of the proposed changes?	Is the change consistent with the values of the organization and people involved?
Has leadership demonstrated competency in implementing change?	Do plans take into account the needs of people?
Has leadership shown the fairness and equity of the proposed changes?	Do those most affected have a voice in the implementation plan?

Judging and Perceiving

This preference pair describes how we *approach life and work*. People who prefer Judging approach life by planning their work and working their plan. People who prefer Perceiving approach life by staying open to more information and leaving room for spontaneity.

Note that almost all schools in the United States—and around the world—have a Judging culture. Bells tell us when learning is to start and end, curriculum maps outline what is to be learned regardless of world or personal events, students are to be ready for the same test on the same day even as we give lip service to individual needs and differences, and so on.

The classrooms of Judging teachers often reflect time management skills and they may engage in lesson planning or curriculum mapping more willingly. Perceiving teachers may be able to change classroom direction more quickly when children's needs or circumstances change. They may dislike making lengthy plans because things always change and children are unpredictable, anyway.

As you think about your "resistant" teacher, consider whether his or her needs are being met (Kise, 2006) during the coaching or change process.

Judging	*Perceiving*
Are there clear goals and time frames for the change process?	Is the plan open-ended enough that goals and time frames can be adjusted as the process unfolds?
Are priorities clear? What will be left undone to implement this program?	How will the change effort stay open to new information?
Are surprises being minimized?	Is there flexibility for how each person implements these changes?

Have you identified your own natural preferences? If you are unsure of one or more, think through a change effort that frustrated you and consider the aforementioned needs during change. Which of your needs weren't met? Consider the information in Table 6.1, Type Preferences and Coaching Implications. Additional references on learning about personality type are listed at the end of the chapter.

Table 6.1   Type Preferences and Coaching Implications

Extraverted types *may*	Introverted types *may*
• Need to talk, not listen, to understand • Change their minds as they talk • Prefer act-reflect-act patterns of learning; for Extraverts, the doing gives them something to think about • Be stressed by too much lecture/inaction/quiet	• Prefer to reflect on materials or experiences in advance • Take on a "deer in the headlights" feeling if the meeting focus changes from what they expect • Prefer a reflect-act-reflect pattern of learning, anticipating or reading about what might happen in advance of trying it • Be stressed by noise, changes without reflective time, being asked to self-disclose too much information
Sensing types *may*	Intuitive types *may*
• Want immediate applications and relevant examples • Prefer step-by-step implementation strategies and details to take them from what they know to what you want them to do	• Be less interested in isolated skills than in how they fit into overall goals and strategies • View curriculum or instructional practices as a starting place for innovation *unless* given clear reasons not to deviate from them

(Continued)

Table 6.1 (Continued)

- View theory as beside the point; they want to know what will work in *their* classroom
- Be stressed by removal of what is working with no proof that the change will be better

- Respond more to metaphors or theories than to facts
- Be stressed by details, structure, no room for creativity

Thinking types *may*

- Want to know a coach is competent; tout your credentials and experience
- Need logic and the rationale for changes
- Distrust nonspecific praise
- Be stressed by displays of emotion, assumption of a personal relationship, lack of fairness or equity

Feeling types *may*

- Take problems or critiques personally. Start with concrete positive reinforcement.
- Be concerned about the impact of practices on the *whole* person— teachers and students—not just academic achievement
- Want students (and coaches) to like them
- Be stressed by disharmony, not being listened to, or awareness that the needs of some teachers or students are not being met

Judging types *may*

- Find good practices and stick with them.
- Have things planned out and resist coaching interventions that interfere
- Seem rigid without sufficient attention to their informational and timing needs
- Be stressed by changes—they had it all planned!

Perceiving types *may*

- Avoid planning very far ahead— things could change! A coach needs flexibility regarding the when's and what's of interactions.
- Resist deciding quickly about lessons or practices—or may easily change their minds with new information
- Be more likely to over or underestimate how long activities will take
- Be stressed by closure: something better or more appropriate may be revealed through waiting

SOURCE: Kise, J. A. G. (2006). *Differentiated coaching: A framework for helping teachers change.* Thousand Oaks, CA: Corwin Press.

Have you hypothesized about the personality type of a teacher who seems resistant? Let's turn to using that hypothesis to come up with a new coaching plan for that teacher.

Perhaps you're thinking, "This is too complicated—eight preferences make sixteen types!" Note that the process can easily be broken down:

- In coaching, Extraversion and Introversion mainly affect how you interact with a teacher. See Table 6.1 for suggestions on what

Extraverted and Introverted teachers may need, and take note of how you might need to adjust your style when working with teachers of the opposite preference.

- In coaching, Judging and Perceiving mainly affect a teacher's natural drive for planning and closure. Again, Table 6.1 contains suggestions for adjusting to meet the needs of teachers with the opposite preference.

- This means that the bulk of differentiated coaching involves the remaining four preferences. The essence of what teachers need during change can be described by how they take in information and make decisions—Sensing or Intuition and Thinking or Feeling—resulting in just four different coaching styles.

Think of these styles as shorthand for meeting the teacher's needs during change. Table 6.2 outlines the four styles, the kinds of information and evidence that will be most influential, and the coaching roles and methods teachers with each style are likely to respond to.

The information in Table 6.2 serves as a starting place for conferencing with teachers about how you might best approach them, especially if you're working from a hypothesis of their personality type or other learning style. A conversation about whether your approach will fit their needs usually increases buy-in. However, working through the next two steps will provide even more information to help you coach most effectively. Let's look at some ways to discern if teacher beliefs, often closely tied to their personality type, might be blocking their willingness to change.

STEP 2: IDENTIFYING TEACHER BELIEFS

When I began coaching Sara, I quickly discovered that as a Sensing type, she looked for tried-and-true methods. To her, a standardized curriculum, developed by experts, would certainly meet the needs of her students and she hesitated to add or subtract from it. Especially in their first years of teaching, Sensing types often rely on curriculum or pacing schedules or other "expert" resources.

In Sara's case, this belief that her curriculum must be meeting the needs of her students kept her from examining it closely. When we used the framework of personality type, she quickly learned to identify overstructured activities that demotivated Intuitive students as well as understructured activities that undermined the confidence of Sensing students. We were then able to move forward on making adjustments to the curriculum.

A variety of beliefs can block a teacher from change. Here are some examples:

- *Students don't receive enough home support, so it's inevitable that many won't complete major projects.* Through differentiated coaching, we helped teachers see that their low expectations had kept them from

(Text continues on page 90)

Table 6.2   The Four Coaching Styles

Sensing and Thinking (ST): Coach as Useful Resource

For this style, coaches need strategies and methods—almost a bag of tricks—that they can tailor to meet the specific content area or situation the teacher faces. Buy-in comes through seeing something work or seeing evidence that it worked in a very similar classroom with similar students.

- Provide hands-on, relevant exercises or tips that produce tangible results. These teachers want to test something out to see if it works. If it *does* work, they'll take the time to learn more.
- Provide evidence of effectiveness of these strategies as used by others. The ST does not want to experiment. Further, knowing exactly for whom and where it worked is important information to these teachers.
- Give examples that are easily customized to their jobs. These teachers may discount examples that do not deal with their specific responsibilities.
- Listen carefully to their concerns about new methods or theories. Often their informational needs have not been met.
- Show them it works. These teachers naturally prefer to see results rather than read about theories. Background information is almost irrelevant.

Information and Evidence They Want

- Immediate applications with specific, step-by-step directions.
- Implementation details—their responsibilities, time line, training, trouble-shooting contact.
- Proof that the new is better than their current practices. ST teachers have often modified practices over time and believe they work quite well. Evidence from student work or progress toward meeting objectives may convince them of the need to change what they are doing.

Effective Coaching Roles

- *Modeling.* STs often thrive when using the gradual release of responsibility model. They want to hear about a strategy, watch you use it with their students (or in a classroom like theirs), talk through questions and anticipated problems before they try it themselves, and finally try it while the coach watches so they can ask for help if they need it and receive suggestions afterward. *Keep your schedule open; they may request a second modeling or coteaching session—reflecting their hands-on learning style.*
- *Lesson Planning.* STs may not engage in revising or creating new lesson plans until they have enough evidence of the worthiness of the change. These teachers often like being handed a ready-to-go lesson. If it works, they'll be ready to sit down and plan another one with you.
- *Providing Resources.* These teachers are seldom insulted when coaches hand them relevant curriculum supplements, activities, or project directions. To deepen the coaching relationship, offer to locate what they need.
- *Providing Alternatives.* ST teachers want your ideas and are often demotivated by facilitative questioning designed to draw ideas out of them. They may bluntly say, "If I had an idea I'd be using it." Instead, start with concrete alternatives, answer all their questions, and then help them choose.

Sensing and Feeling (SF): Coach as Encouraging Sage

These teachers often thrive when a coach can adopt the traditional mentoring role, providing custom-designed pathways for growth.

- Meet the teacher's needs for encouragement, clear goals, and concrete tasks. They take personally the day-to-day events in their classrooms, assuming that deviations from perfect results or performance are their fault.
- Offer to join them on the job when applicable. Show them what is going right and make concrete suggestions to fix "molehills" that seem like "mountains" because of their desire to serve each student.
- Don't provide too many choices—they may be overwhelmed.
- Model one new strategy at a time and provide methods to document progress. Keep the focus on the overall objective; otherwise, the teacher may get sidetracked by perfectionism over details.

Information and Evidence They Want

- Stories and examples from peers who have used the strategy or technique. They also respond to stories of specific students who experienced growth.
- Specific, step-by-step instructions.
- A clear understanding of what is expected of them. Most SFs are very conscientious. Give them a list of alternatives and they may assume they're expected to try them all.

Effective Coaching Roles

- *Data Coach.* You'll often need data to convince an SF teacher that one of her favorite practices isn't effective, but a high percentage of people with math anxiety prefer Sensing and Feeling. A coach may need to compare test scores, disaggregate data, and engage in more of the data analysis, presenting conclusions for discussion with the teacher. The teacher may gradually take over more of the tasks after seeing how it's done and why the process was valuable.
- *Modeling.* SF teachers often gain confidence by watching and also respond to the gradual release of responsibility model. Often, once they've seen a coach model a practice, they easily come up with suggestions for improving it for their particular students.
- *Coteaching.* SF teachers like to work with people, so coteaching is a great coaching activity. They often need immediate feedback as to whether they've done something correctly. Also, being present allows a coach to point out what is working well. Things seldom go smoothly when students are introduced to something for the first time, and the SF teacher may need an objective voice before he or she is willing to try it again.
- *Coplanning.* SF teachers often enjoy brainstorming ideas with others. They may not see themselves as inherently creative, but a suggestion, or an example of what worked for another teacher, often jump-starts their ability to innovate. Also, coplanning provides a vehicle for answering the teacher's questions immediately.

(Continued)

Table 6.2 (Continued)

Intuition and Feeling (NF): Coach as Collegial Mentor

These teachers march to their own beat, and coaches need to keep this in mind. They love new ideas but then need to make them their own. Provide space for their creativity and they can become staunch supporters of any strategy.

- Engage in conversations to help these teachers use their creativity. Let them generate their own ideas for critique rather than work only from a coach's suggestions.
- Show them how to communicate with concrete examples of abstract concepts and techniques, providing demonstrations and directions for each technique.
- Demonstrate how to provide structure while still allowing for student creativity. Provide examples of rubrics or objectives that give clear direction yet avoid the overstructuring that NF's hate.
- Let them talk through several scenarios before deciding on strategies.

Information and Evidence They Want

- *The Big Picture.* These teachers are motivated by improving student motivation, opportunities in life, self-esteem, and altruism, not by improving test scores, even though they're well aware of the importance of measurable student achievement.
- *A Vision of How Each Student Will Be Affected.* They may filter new ideas through their potential impact on students at both extremes of the achievement spectrum, those from every culture, past key students they succeeded or failed to reach, and so on. Objective data leaves them cold unless it's accompanied by qualitative evidence that students will also grow personally.
- *Stories of Systemic Change.* They'll often pursue in-depth knowledge of a model or theory if it's presented with case studies of how a school changed or how a targeted group of students embraced academics.

Effective Coaching Roles

- *Study Groups.* NF teachers often like to read about and discuss new ideas. If they prefer Introversion, their best route to change is independent study. They enjoy trying things in their classrooms and then sharing results and student work.
- *Collegial Observations.* NF teachers may appreciate specific feedback when implementing classroom changes. Use a preobservation conference to identify the information they'd like to receive from you. They are less open to modeling and coteaching, unless a new strategy is out of their comfort zone. For example, one NF teacher only asked for modeling when she agreed to implement a strategy for helping students plan out how to complete projects. She knew she struggled with the same planning skills and welcomed the opportunity to learn with her students.
- *Consultant.* NF teachers often prefer to proceed independently with a new idea until they need additional input. Instead of working with them in the early stages of lesson planning or strategy implementation, ask if they'd like to outline their ideas and then run them by you.
- *Troubleshooter.* Advertise coaching as a way to receive help with the most reluctant learner, the class that's most difficult to settle down, the subject they least prefer to teach, and so on.

Intuition and Thinking (NT): Coach as Expert

When coaching these teachers, prepare to be challenged—not intentionally, but because NT teachers learn by comparing any new instructional strategy or change to the models and schemas they've developed about how students learn. That comparison can come across as confrontational if the coach isn't prepared. The coach can't take things personally.

- Provide credentials and references to establish trust in your expertise. They expect a coach to answer any question to satisfy their informational needs.
- Provide instructional methods for balancing theory and creativity with hands-on experimentation and structure. NTs can assume that everyone is as interested in models as they are.
- Allow them to probe suggestions, fit them into their own mental models, and then improve on them. A response of "That's plausible" to your most brilliant idea is *high praise* from these teachers. Often, people with this learning style are viewed as contrary, resistant, or abrasive rather than the deep thinkers they are.
- Meet their needs for evidence and data. If they embrace a change as valid and important, they often become enthusiastic.

Information and Evidence They Want

- *Depth of Knowledge.* If a coach can't answer an NT's questions, he or she might recommend Web sites, books, articles, and other resources to satisfy the teacher's need to know.
- *Data and Statistical Studies.* This is the one group of teachers who are very interested in objective research studies.
- *Logical Theories and Models.* NTs need to know how and why things work.

Effective Coaching Roles

- *Coleadership.* NT teachers thrive when they have a say in implementation planning. Carefully considering their critiques often increases buy-in. Ask about areas where they feel competent enough to coach other teachers or perhaps lead a study group.
- *Observation.* NT teachers are generally interested in making improvements and appreciate the preconference/observation/postconference model.
- *Study Groups.* Group discussions allow NT teachers to formulate ideas and receive feedback. They may prefer a more in-depth approach—research or theory-based books or more than one meeting on the same topic—than other teachers.
- *Collaborative Conversations.* Ask these teachers about the problems they want to solve in their classroom. Offer a hypothesis of the root source of the problem and a few alternatives. Then provide time for an extended conversation (perhaps via e-mail if the teacher also prefers Introversion). Expect to discuss alternative hypotheses, the pros and cons of each alternative, other alternatives, and the difficulties of implementation.

SOURCE: Kise, J. A. G. (2006). *Differentiated coaching: A framework for helping teachers change.* Thousand Oaks, CA: Corwin Press.

(Text continued from page 85)

believing that assignments can be structured for success. When they added those structures, the completion rate rose from 70%–75% to 95%–100% (Kise, 2005).

- *Basic skills need to come first.* Intuitive students balk at skills practice if they don't have the big picture of how those skills are worthwhile. Teachers saw student engagement skyrocket when they helped to provide that big picture.
- *All-class instruction lets me make sure all students are grasping concepts.* With modeling and support, this teacher learned that independent learning activities allowed her to target struggling students while those who understood what to do could keep moving forward.

The list is endless—assumptions that arise based on a teacher's own learning experiences, stereotypes about groups of students, inherent difficulties with a teaching strategy that's out of the teacher's style and therefore isn't implemented with fidelity, and so on. Often, the dissonance is so great that these beliefs block the individual from hearing a coach's advice or evidence of a strategy's research-based effectiveness.

How do you unearth these beliefs? First, assume that the teacher is resisting the change for a rational reason and not because of laziness or anger or other negative emotion.

Second, look for clues. For example, if a teacher has folders filled with tried-and-true lesson plans, is he or she going to be enthusiastic about jettisoning all of it for a new curriculum? Combine Sensing with Judging, and you'll have teachers who've found proven methods and may be suspicious of alternatives. One told me, "I will not experiment on my students!" Or, is the classroom uncluttered and class time filled with listening activities or seatwork? This teacher, who may prefer Introversion, may struggle to implement any kind of group work, perhaps even interpreting student difficulties in working together as a sign of their disinterest or immaturity rather than a lack of collaboration skills that can be taught.

Third, ask questions. Much is written about the power of establishing trust with teachers. In differentiated coaching, part of that trust comes from using the right coaching style (Table 6.2) so the teacher feels free to express his or her concerns and struggles. Questions that usually let them speak freely, and from their strengths, include the following:

- If you could wave a magic wand, what is one thing you would change about your school (or classroom)?
- Give me a specific example of a time when you felt successful helping a student (or colleague).
- If you could get all of your colleagues (teachers) to be consistent in one thing, what would it be?
- Describe your ideal classroom.
- What kind of situation causes you the most frustration?
- What do you think all students need to learn?

You'll develop new questions that work with your own style, but these are a good starting place. Record your beliefs about the teacher's beliefs in Table 6.3. You'll use them later to determine the kinds of *evidence* that you'll need to provide to change those change-blocking beliefs.

STEP 3: IDENTIFYING THE PROBLEMS THE TEACHER WANTS TO SOLVE

The third step in differentiated coaching recognizes the reality that even in schools with the best possible leadership, a classroom teacher may be preoccupied with different concerns than those addressed in the strategic plan or through the initiatives in which you are engaged as a coach.

With some of the urban teachers I've coached, maintaining classroom control is their biggest concern. If they believe that a new teaching strategy could result in losing that control—even temporarily—the coaching plan needs to ensure that this doesn't happen. Other examples include the following: "I've got to get students to turn in more homework," "These students don't trust me," "Parents don't like our new report cards," and "I spend too much time correcting papers and can't seem to get ahead on lesson planning."

The best way to find out the problems the teachers want to solve is to ask. At one high-poverty school, even though the teachers gave lip service to the initial goal of increasing student engagement, the teachers finally admitted, "We're so stressed by all the things our students need that we're losing sleep!" We worked on stress management before any other initiative.

This doesn't mean that you focus on whatever the teachers feel like focusing on. Instead, work to solve their most pressing problem in a way that builds buy-in for the change you do want them to make. Show them how the proposed change is relevant to their biggest needs. For example, our work on stress management included prioritizing all of the things they hoped to accomplish. That allowed me to reinforce the school's priorities as they admitted it couldn't all happen at once.

Once you've identified the presenting problem, ask yourself the following:

- Is the problem defined correctly or are there other possibilities? Often we leap to problem solving before completing this step, which is dangerous since different problems bring to mind different solutions.
- What evidence can be produced in solving the problem that will influence the teacher's beliefs and therefore motivate them to change?

For example, a math teacher told me that students didn't care about math. No matter what he did, they refused to engage in learning activities. He told me, "At the last test, only 7 of the 25 students even tried. The rest put their names on the top and just sat there." What was his solution?

Table 6.3   Information-Gathering Sheet

Communication				
Your coaching style is:	ST	SF	NF	NT
Teacher's Preferred Style is:	ST	SF	NF	NT

Style adjustments to keep in mind, including **Extraversion and Introversion, Judging and Perceiving (Tables 6.1 and 6.2):**

Teacher Beliefs	Evidence of Success
Which of the teacher's habits or beliefs work against success? (Examples: All students like ___; All teachers should ___; Learning can only happen if ___; Our students can't ____.)	**What evidence would persuade the teacher of the value of a new approach?** (See Table 6.2, The Four Coaching Styles.)
Which strengths can you build on?	
Goals	**Roles**
Teacher's Main Concern or Presenting Problem: (Examples: Need to have authority acknowledged; Student engagement, etc.)	**Coach's Role: What kind of support would the teacher like?** (See Table 6.2, The Four Coaching Styles.)
School's Requirements or Initiative Needs:	**Teacher's Role: What first step might the teacher be comfortable taking?** (Examples: Trying a specific, ready-to-go strategy; reading about a theory; looking at data.)
What teacher interests could be "hooks" for change?	

Keep marching through the curriculum to reach the seven engaged students. He felt he'd tried everything humanly possible.

I watched the classroom and formulated a different problem: The students didn't know *how* to learn math. If they didn't care I thought I'd see more misbehavior. My solution set involved explicitly teaching how to be mathematicians and active learners. However, the math teacher needed evidence that his students didn't know how to learn math, evidence to change his initial definition of the problem and motivate him to change. In this case, I suggested, and he agreed, to have students write down what came to mind when they thought of math and what they need to do to learn math.

The students described math as hard, boring, difficult to understand, and confusing. One student wrote, "Huh? Why? What? Too many numbers." As for what they needed to do, all but one student listed *passive* roles such as listening to the teacher, having a teacher who explained more, bringing a pencil. One student wrote, "I don't know how to do math. I don't learn. I watch." Only a handful of students—perhaps the seven who took the test?—listed active strategies such as practicing math facts, asking for homework help, or asking for more examples. Once the teacher saw this evidence, he was ready to try strategies designed to help students learn to ask questions, engage in problem solving rather than waiting for solutions, and take responsibility for their own learning.

Should the teacher be involved in defining the problems and looking for alternatives, as the cognitive coaching model advocates? Yes, but with "resistant" teachers, I've found that the alternatives are often so far removed from their natural teaching style that they don't seem like viable alternatives. The coach's role becomes more directive while keeping in mind the teacher's concerns, beliefs, and learning style.

STEP 4: DEVELOPING A COACHING PLAN

At this point, the coach is ready to take all the information about the teacher's natural strengths, beliefs, and major concerns and wrap it together into a coaching plan. Another way to describe the process is as follows:

- Choose the coaching style and strategies that best meet the learning style and informational needs of the teacher, whether you use personality type or another framework.
- Identify teacher beliefs that might block change.
- Talk with the teacher about the biggest problem he or she would like to solve.
- Reframe or redefine that problem if necessary. Involve the teacher in this process unless he or she believes the problem is hopeless or the teacher seems resistant, perhaps because proposed solutions are so foreign to his or her natural style.

- Develop alternatives, evaluate them, and choose one that will produce evidence that can influence the beliefs that are blocking this teacher from change.

Table 6.3 can help you organize your thoughts. Filling it out is seldom a linear process. Instead, one insight may provide new information for other elements of your draft plan. You might first discover a "hook"—the teacher reveals a vibrant interest in teaching a new novel or in developing a lesson that effectively uses an interactive whiteboard—that you know you can use to help the teacher implement the new strategy the principal wants adopted.

If this sounds complicated, remember that some teachers have the same style as yours. You can coach them as you would like to be coached. Many, many others share part of your style. In personality type terms, you might share Feeling, but then be opposite on Sensing and Intuition. Much of your natural style will work for these teachers. Those with the opposite style require the most work, but without that extra effort they're the ones least likely to accept what you have to offer as a coach. They may be your "resistors." It's worth the effort.

Sara, for example, was my total opposite. The coaching style she responded to—having me hand her a complete lesson plan to try, for example—would have been *insulting* to me. Yet once she'd experienced that complete plan with her students, she quickly developed others on her own.

Thus, what seems to be a complicated coaching process often becomes the most direct route to change. Guskey (2002) wrote as follows:

> The crucial point is that it is not the professional development *per se*, but the experience of successful implementation that changes teachers' attitudes and beliefs. They believe it works because they have seen it work, and that experience shapes their attitudes and beliefs ... the key element in significant change in teachers' attitudes and beliefs is clear evidence of improvement in the learning outcomes of their students. (p. 384)

Differentiated coaching acknowledges that teachers need different experiences and evidence to change those beliefs and thus makes it possible for more teachers to embrace change. Does it work? Here's what one teacher leader had to say about his first attempt:

> Teacher Y was having difficulty in her class. By the end of the first term she was considering ... quitting teaching in general. I knew she was working hard and I knew she knew her math. Initially, when I was trying to help her with her classroom issues, I was very

direct with her. I would give her a detailed list of teaching practices she should implement to better instruct her class. Then, when I would observe her class again, I would see the same issues. She was not being an effective teacher, I was not being an effective coach and worst of all, the students were not learning. Things were bad and getting worse.

Then we, the teacher and I, discussed her type. It turns out she prefers Feeling and I was coaching her as if she preferred Thinking. After this conversation, I dramatically changed my coaching approach. I stopped handing her lists of practices to implement. I started listening instead of talking. I would ask her how she felt about the class and what she thought could be done to improve the class. I listened to her ideas, empathized and validated her feelings and made suggestions on how to implement them in the class. She had many great ideas and her class started improving almost immediately. By utilizing the notion of type I was able to help Teacher Y help herself. Now Teacher Y is one of the strongest teachers in the department and I look forward to her return in the fall.

Differentiated coaching provides teachers with the best kind of freedom— not freedom to do as they please, but the freedom to recognize, embrace, and move toward their full potential as educators.

RESOURCES FOR USING DIFFERENTIATED COACHING

Practice case studies are available for downloading at www.edcoaching .com. These can be used by individuals or for group discussion and contain descriptions of the teachers' styles, information from interviews, and a sample coaching plan.

Fairchild, A. M., & Fairchild, L. L. (1995). *Effective teaching, effective learning: Making the personality connection in your classroom.* Mountain View, CA: Davies-Black.

Kise, J. A. G. (2006a). *Differentiated coaching: A framework for helping teachers change.* Thousand Oaks, CA: Corwin Press.

Kise, J. A. G. (2006b). *Differentiation through personality types: A framework for instruction, assessment, and classroom management.* Thousand Oaks, CA: Corwin Press.

Lawrence, G. (1993). *People types and tiger stripes* (3rd ed.). Gainesville, FL: Center for Applications of Psychological Type.

Murphy, E. (1992). *The developing child: Using Jungian type to understand children.* Palo Alto, CA: Consulting Psychologists Press.

Pajak, E. (2003). *Honoring diverse teaching styles: A guide for supervisors.* Alexandria, VA: Association for Supervision and Curriculum Development.

REFERENCES

Barger, N. J., & Kirby, L. K. (1995). *The challenge of change in organizations: Helping employees thrive in the new frontier.* Palo Alto, CA: Consulting Psychologists Press.

Clancy, S. G. (1997). STJs and change: Resistance, reaction, or misunderstanding? In C. Fitzgerald & L. K. Kirby (Eds.), *Developing leaders: Research and applications in psychological type and leadership development* (pp. 415–438). Palo Alto, CA: Consulting Psychologists Press.

Evans, R. (2001). *The human side of school change: Reform, resistance and the real-life problems of innovation.* San Francisco: Jossey-Bass.

Fullan, M., & Hargreaves, A. (1991) *What's worth fighting for in your school.* Toronto: Ontario Public School Teachers' Federation.

Guskey, T. R. (2002). Professional development and teacher change. *Teachers and teaching: Theory and practice, 8,* 380–391.

Kise, J. A. G. (2005). Coaching teachers for change: Using the concepts of psychological type to reframe teacher resistance. *Journal of Psychological Type, 65*(6), 47–58.

Kise, J. A. G. (2006). *Differentiated coaching: A framework for helping teachers change.* Thousand Oaks, CA: Corwin Press.

Tye, B. B. (2000). *Hard truths: Uncovering the deep structure of schooling.* New York: Teachers College Press.

7

Stages in Teacher Development

Kathleen Feeney Jonson

I was elated to get the job but terrified about going from the simulated experience of student teaching to being the person completely in charge.

—A teacher in the stage of anticipation

I thought I'd be busy, something like student teaching, but this is crazy. I'm feeling like I'm constantly running. It's hard to focus on other aspects of my life.

—A teacher in the stage of survival

I thought I'd be focusing more on curriculum and less on classroom management and discipline. I'm stressed because I have some very problematic students who are low academically, and I think about them every second my eyes are open.

—A teacher in the stage of disillusionment

I'm really excited about my writing center, although the organization of it has at times been haphazard. Story writing has definitely revived my journals.

—A teacher in the stage of rejuvenation

I think that for next year I'd like to start the letter puppets earlier in the year to introduce the kids to more letters.

—A teacher in the stage of reflection

Teachers can generally be counted on to talk about developmental needs and stages when they discuss children. It may be meaningful to think of teachers themselves as having developmental sequences in their professional growth patterns as well. At the Santa Cruz New Teacher Center, researchers found that beginning teachers move through several developmental stages within their first year of teaching—from anticipation, to survival, to disillusionment, to rejuvenation, to reflection, and back to anticipation. In another model, Lilian Katz describes the developmental stages of teachers over the course of their career. Katz's model begins with the stage of survival and moves through consolidation to renewal and then to maturity. It is often helpful for the mentor to learn to recognize the particular stages new teachers go through and to adapt to the new teacher's needs. This understanding gives mentors a framework to design support that can make the mentee's first year of teaching a more positive experience.

THE FIRST YEAR:
THE NEW TEACHER CENTER MODEL

After supporting some 1,500 new teachers, leaders of the Santa Cruz New Teacher Project noted several developmental phases common to beginning teachers (see Figure 7.1). Although not all teachers go through the phases in exactly the same sequence or timeframe, most follow the pattern to some degree (Moir, *Phases of First-Year Teaching*). Those working with new teachers may benefit from understanding these phases.

Anticipation

This first phase of teacher development precedes the teacher's first assignment, occurring at the end of student teaching during preservice training. Beginning teachers become excited and anxious about their pending assignments and may romanticize the role they will fill. They enter their own classroom for the first time with a sense of idealism and excitement that may carry them through the first few weeks of school.

Figure 7.1 Phases of first-year teachers' attitudes toward teaching

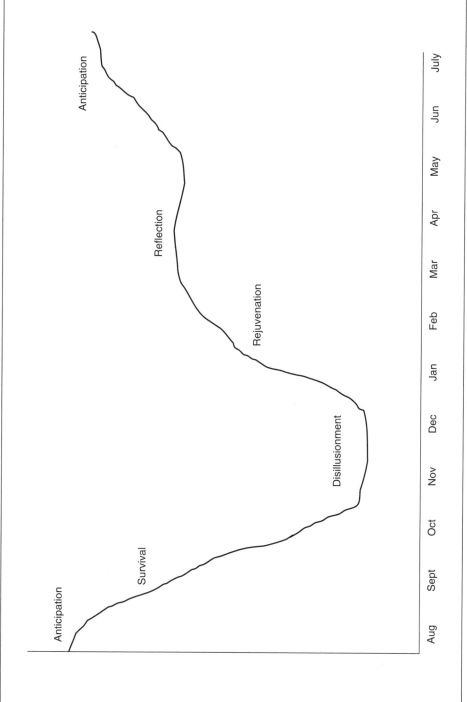

SOURCE: From Moir, E. *Attitudinal phases of new teacher development*. Retrieved from www.btsa.ca.gov/ba/profdev/princ_orient/docs/2-04.doc. Copyright by Ellen Moir. Reprinted with permission.

Survival

Within the first month, the amount of material to be learned may quickly overwhelm new teachers. Despite their preparation and the anticipation they felt in the beginning, the reality of the job may catch them off-guard. Day-to-day routines take all of their time, leaving little room for reflection. Beginning teachers may spend 70 hours a week just trying to keep up. Even in their exhaustion, though, they may remain energetic and committed, hoping that things will get easier.

Disillusionment

After six to eight weeks of hard work and nonstop stress, new teachers begin to lose energy and to question their commitment to the profession. Extensive demands on their time and discouragement may lead teachers to question their competence as they enter the phase of disillusionment. Back-to-school night, teacher conferences, and initial teacher evaluations all add to the stress, compounded sometimes by complaints from family members and friends about the excessive amount of time spent in teaching. Teachers experience self-doubt, have low self-esteem, and question their own professional commitment. Classroom management becomes a primary area of focus. Often teachers become ill during this time. "Getting through this phase may be the toughest challenge [new teachers] face," according to Moir (*Phases of First-Year Teaching*).

Rejuvenation

Usually around January, after winter break, new teachers' attitudes begin to improve. They have been able to spend some time with family and friends during the holiday and to get proper rest, food, and exercise, possibly for the first time since beginning the school year. They have had a chance to organize their materials and plan lessons and are beginning to understand and accept the realities of teaching. Many new teachers have learned coping strategies and skills during the first half of the year and are better able to manage. Now they can focus on the business of curriculum development, long-term planning, and teaching strategies.

The phase of rejuvenation often lasts into the spring, with ups and downs throughout. Toward the end of the phase, new teachers may begin to wonder whether they will be able to accomplish everything necessary by the end of the school year and whether their students will be able to perform on tests. Just how effective has their teaching been?

Reflection

Beginning in about May, first-year teachers enter an invigorating phase of reflection. Looking back over the year, they think about their successes and about the things they did that were not so successful. They begin to plan things they will do differently next year: different methods of management, ways of presenting curriculum, and teaching strategies. From here, they circle back to anticipation as they look forward to the next year.

An understanding of these phases is critical in designing support systems for new teachers and offering mentoring services. While the teacher going through the survival mode may need support and help mostly with management, one in rejuvenation may be more interested in curriculum development. With an understanding of this common sequence, the mentor can tailor guidance to be most meaningful.

THROUGH THE YEARS: THE KATZ MODEL

In another model, Katz (1972) describes the developmental stages that teachers go through over time, which are generally linked to experience. Katz describes these stages as survival, consolidation, renewal, and maturity. Individual teachers vary greatly in the length of time spent in each of the stages outlined here, Katz says, but most progress through all four. This section outlines the four stages as described by Katz, with comments regarding developmental tasks and training needs for each stage.

Because mentoring and training needs change as mentors gain experience, a basic understanding of these stages may shape the assistance a mentor provides. See Figure 7.2 for teacher training needs at various developmental stages.

Survival

The first stage of teacher development according to Katz is the same as one of the early stages in the Santa Cruz model: survival. In Katz's model, this stage often lasts throughout the first full year of teaching.

Developmental Tasks. During the stage of survival, teachers' main concern is whether or not they can endure. They may ask such questions as, "Can I get through the day in one piece? Without losing my patience, my temper, my ideals? Can I make it until the end of the week—the next vacation? Can I really do this kind of work day after day? Will my colleagues accept me?"

The first full impact of responsibility for a group of immature but energetic students provokes teacher anxieties; approaching encounters with parents add to the stress. Discrepancies between anticipated success and classroom reality intensify feelings of inadequacy and unpreparedness.

Mentoring Needs. During the period of survival, teachers need support, understanding, encouragement, reassurance, comfort, and guidance. They need instruction in specific skills and insight into the complex causes of behavior—all at the classroom site. On-site mentoring must be constantly and readily available from someone who knows well both the trainee and the teaching situation. The mentor should have enough time and

Figure 7.2   Training needs of teachers at different developmental stages

Developmental Stages	Training Needs
Stage IV	Seminars, institutes, courses, degree programs, books, journals, conferences
Stage III	Conferences, professional associations, journals, magazines, films, visits to demonstration projects
Stage II	On-site assistance, access to specialists, colleague advice, consultants
Stage I	On-site support and technical assistance
	0 1YR. 2YR. 3YR. 4YR. 5YR.

SOURCE: Katz, L. G. (2005). *The developmental stages of teachers*. Champaign, IL: Clearinghouse on Early Education and Parenting, University of Illinois at Urbana-Champaign. Retrieved July 25, 2007, from http://ceep.crc.uiuc.edu/pubs/katz-dev-stages.html.

flexibility to be on call as needed by the trainee. Schedules of periodic visits that are arranged in advance cannot be counted on to coincide with the mentee's crises.

Consolidation

The second stage in Katz's model may begin late in the first year or early in the second year of teaching and often lasts into the beginning of the third year.

Developmental Tasks. By the end of their first year, teachers have usually decided that they are capable of surviving. They are ready to consolidate the overall gains made during the first stage and to differentiate specific tasks and skills to be mastered next. During the consolidation stage, teachers often begin to focus on individual problem students and problem situations. They look for answers to such questions as, "How can I help an inattentive child? How can I help a particular student who does not seem to be learning?"

During the stage of consolidation, the new teacher acquires a baseline of information about what students are like and what to expect of them. The teacher begins to identify individual students whose behavior departs from the pattern of most of the children.

Mentoring Needs. During the consolidation stage, on-site mentoring continues to be valuable. A mentor can help the teacher through mutual exploration of a problem. Take, for example, the case of a young elementary school teacher who was eager to get help and expressed her problem in the question, "How should I deal with a clinging child?" An on-site mentor could observe the teacher and child in the situation and suggest possible solutions fairly quickly. Without firsthand knowledge of the child and context, however, the mentor might best help the teacher interpret the experience and move toward a solution to the problem through an extended give-and-take conversation. The mentor might ask the teacher such questions as, "What have you done so far? Give an example of some experiences with this particular child during this week. When you did such and such, how did the child respond?"

Also in this stage, a wider range of resources might be necessary to help the new teacher gain information about specific students. Psychologists, social and health workers, and other specialists can strengthen the teacher's skills and knowledge during this stage. Exchanges of information and ideas with more experienced colleagues may help teachers master the developmental tasks of the period. Opportunities to share feelings with other teachers in the same stage of development may help reduce some of the teacher's sense of personal inadequacy and frustration.

Renewal

Katz's third stage of development often occurs during the third and fourth years of teaching.

Developmental Tasks. During the renewal stage, teachers begin to tire of doing the same old things. They start to ask more questions about new developments in the field: "Who is doing what? Where? What are some of the new materials, techniques, approaches, and ideas?" Although what they have been doing for each annual group of students may have been adequate, they find the recurrent Valentine cards, Easter bunnies, and pumpkin cutouts insufficiently interesting. If it is true that the interest and commitment of teachers to their projects and activities contribute to their educational value, then their need for renewal and refreshment should be taken seriously.

Training Needs. During the renewal stage, teachers find it especially rewarding to meet colleagues from different programs both formally and informally. Teachers in this stage are receptive to experiences in regional and national conferences and workshops, and they profit from membership in professional associations and participation in their meetings. They widen the scope of their reading, scan numerous magazines and journals, and view films. They may be ready to take a close look at their own classroom teaching through videotaping. This is also a time when teachers welcome opportunities to visit other classes, programs, and demonstration projects. The teacher center, designed to help teachers increase skills, may have the greatest potential value during this stage. Here teachers gather to help each other learn or relearn skills, techniques, and methods; to exchange ideas; and to organize special workshops. From time to time, specialists are invited to the center to meet with teachers and discuss curriculum, child growth, or other areas of concern for teachers.

Maturity

The fourth and final stage of teacher development in Katz's model might begin as early as the third year but often starts after five or more years.

Developmental Tasks. Teachers who have reached the stage of maturity have come to terms with themselves as teachers. They have enough perspective to begin to ask deeper and more abstract questions, such as "What are my historical and philosophical roots? What is the nature of growth and learning? How are educational decisions made? Can schools change societies? Is teaching a profession?" Perhaps they have asked these questions before, but with their greater experience, the questions now represent a more meaningful search for insight, perspective, and realism.

Training Needs. Throughout the maturity stage, teachers need opportunities to participate in conferences and seminars and perhaps to pursue other educational goals. Mature teachers welcome the chance to read widely and to interact with educators working on problem areas at many different levels. Training sessions and conference events enjoyable to teachers in the consolidation stage may be tiresome to the mature teacher. Teachers in this last stage, on the other hand, might enjoy introspective and searching discussion seminars that would lead to restlessness and irritability among teachers early in the survival stage.

CONCLUSION

It is often said that experience is the best teacher. Even so, we cannot assume that experience teaches what the new teacher should learn. One major goal of the teacher-mentor should be to direct learning, to try to make sure that the beginning teacher has informed and interpreted experience. Understanding the different phases of growth for teachers—through the first year and beyond—can help the mentor support and guide the beginner in meaningful ways. This chapter has looked at these various phases.

Chapter 8, Practical Strategies for Assisting New Teachers, looks at specific ways for mentors to help their new teachers develop professionally.

REFERENCES

Katz, L. (2005). *The developmental stages of teachers.* Champaign, IL: Clearinghouse on Early Education and Parenting, University of Illinois at Urbana-Champaign. Retrieved July 25, 2007, from http://ceep.crc.uiuc.edu/pubs/katz-dev-stages .html.

Katz, L. (1972). Developmental stages of preschool teachers. *Elementary School Journal, 23*(1), 50–51.

Moir, E. *The phases of first-year teaching.* Santa Cruz New Teacher Center. Retrieved February 3, 2007, from www.newteachercenter.org/article2.php

8

Practical Strategies for Assisting New Teachers

Kathleen Feeney Jonson

Karen Kawasaki, a new teacher at Mt. Carmel High School, "had great lesson plans, great ideas and projects, and an interactive style of teaching," according to Charlotte Kutzner, a veteran teacher in the Poway School District where Kawasaki teaches north of San Diego. But Kawasaki had a problem. As a new teacher, she also had trouble with classroom management, and after the school principal visited her classroom a couple of times, he told her that she needed to improve. She worried that she might lose her job.

In the Poway School District, teachers with two years or less of experience are assigned to teacher consultants. Unfortunately, Kawasaki's consultant had been out on sick leave. In November, a new consultant—Kutzner—was assigned.

"I was in her classroom once or twice a week," says Kutzner. "We talked a lot. We observed veteran teachers to see how they dealt with the problem. We even role-played ideas for how to handle students at the beginning of the class."

"Charlotte helped me a lot," Kawasaki says. "She made suggestions.... My confidence level went up."

At the end of the year, Kawasaki's job was assured, and she is now considered an excellent teacher.

—*California Teacher* (Bacon, 1997, pp. 1, 6)

Karen Kawasaki's situation was similar to that of many beginning teachers across the country: She was doing a lot right, but just couldn't figure out *everything* by herself. Unlike many beginning teachers, however, Kawasaki was fortunate enough to connect with an effective mentor who could guide her, who was available to her, and who was able to provide her with the quality time necessary for her to work through her problems at an appropriate pace (Fraser, 1998, p. 26). Charlotte Kutzner was able to be the kind of mentor Portner (1998, pp. 7–8) describes as ideal: one who can relate to new teachers' experiences, assess their abilities, coach them as they develop new skills, and guide them to reflect on their experiences.

"As consultants, we applaud what's going well, but also help teachers with their next best step," Kutzner says. "It's important to tailor assistance to the needs of the individual teacher" (Bacon, 1997, p. 7).

To get the most from their relationship, a mentor and a mentee need to plan together to determine goals that they will work toward. They should be realistic about the time they have and explicit about the things they want to work on (Stanulis & Weaver, 1998, p. 138). To help the beginning teacher reach these goals, the mentor must perform a variety of functions, ranging from observing in the classroom and providing feedback to helping the beginning teacher develop specific skills through serving as a role model in the full scope of daily professional activities (see Box 8.1).

BOX 8.1

Strategies a Good Mentor Can Use to Help the Beginning Teacher

- Share school protocol and traditions with the new teacher.
- Guide the mentee through the daily operation of the school.
- Explain school procedures as appropriate.
- Brainstorm with the mentee to help develop lesson plans.
- Provide occasional lesson plans.
- Suggest classroom management techniques.
- Role-play a parent conference.
- Examine student work together.
- Demonstrate lessons for the mentee.
- Demonstrate record keeping.
- Arrange for the mentee to visit a different teacher's classroom, and discuss the observation afterward; if time, join the new teacher during observation for later discussion.
- Observe the mentee's teaching and provide feedback.
- Meet regularly with the mentee, both formally and informally.

- Support and counsel the mentee, providing perspective when needed.
- Ask questions to help the beginning teacher prioritize issues and concerns.
- Assist the beginning teacher in developing an action plan for professional growth.
- Share resources, including materials for a curriculum unit, professional readings, children's literature, and so on.
- Attend a workshop together with the mentee.
- Role-model all aspects of professionalism.
- Encourage reflection.

Many of the strategies that experienced mentors find most helpful in aiding their mentees can be grouped into the following categories:

- Direct assistance
- Demonstration teaching
- Observation and feedback
- Informal contact
- Assistance with an action plan for professional growth
- Role modeling
- Assessing student work

Figure 8.1   Mentor functions

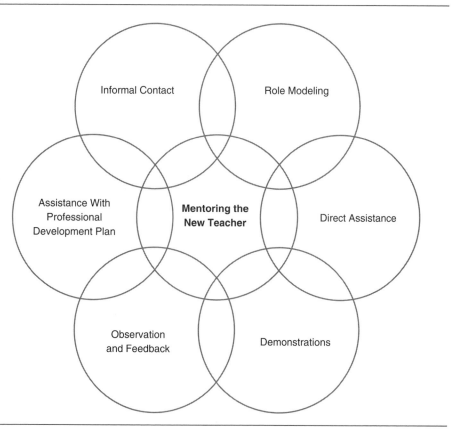

Table 8.1   The Importance of Mentoring Strategies

	Very Useful	Somewhat Useful	Not Useful	Not Practiced
Direct assistance	25	3	0	0
Demonstration teaching	18[a]	8	0	2
Observation and conferences	21[b,c]	5	0	2
Informal contact	24[d]	4	0	0
Assistance with professional growth plan	13	10	2	3
Role modeling	24[e,f]	3	1	0

SOURCE: Jonson (1999b).

NOTE: The following notes are quotes from the mentors surveyed.

a. When used to make a point.
b. If there is a trusting relationship.
c. If conferences are informal to minimize stress.
d. Informal contact may be several times/day . . . builds relationship and provides many quick "fixes" easily.
e. Useful if done before mentee takes over class. Less useful afterward because it dissipates mentee's position of authority in the eyes of the students.
f. The aspect of role modeling is not one I consciously set about doing. But, more than other areas, mentees tell me, in conversations several years later, that they wanted to "be like you." To me, it is a hidden part of mentoring. But, if the mentee doesn't feel that respect and admiration for the mentor, why would they pay attention to the mentor's ideas? I also think the respect other colleagues show for the mentor gives the mentee more reason to want to learn from the mentor.

A full description of each function follows. See Figure 8.1 for the range of mentor functions and Table 8.1 for the relative importance given to the first six functions by mentors surveyed in the San Francisco School District. No matter what the strategy, however, mentors should remember that the mentor-mentee relationship becomes more personally caring and professional when their mentees perceive them as being genuinely interested— "helpful, caring, willing to take time, dedicated, friendly, outgoing, patient, influential" (Jonson, 1999b)—and as being professional role models.

DIRECT ASSISTANCE

The new teacher looked distressed after school, so I engaged her in small talk for a few minutes. She then explained that a parent was giving her a hard time, and she asked me what to do about it. First, I had to let her know that it was the mother with the problem. I told her how I had handled similar problems and we came up with things she could do that are comfortable for her. She hasn't had any problems with that parent since then, but I believe she has a more positive self (teacher) image, and she feels more comfortable in dealing with unhappy parents.

—A mentor (Jonson, 1999b)

Mentor-teachers carry out many specific tasks while helping beginning teachers. Various titles apply to these tasks: behaviors, functions, roles. Though some may fall under other categories of strategies as well, all involve the mentor giving assistance in some direct way.

Because beginning teachers want to achieve professional autonomy and status equality with their colleagues, a large percentage of them do not seek help from colleagues except indirectly by swapping stories about personal experiences. This behavior hides the weaknesses of beginners, but does not enable them to obtain help with those factors—inexperience, unavailability of expertise, and ambiguity about goal attainment—that produce teacher stress related to performing professional tasks.

Beginning teachers need practical suggestions for preventing problems, solving them when they occur, and resolving conflicts and other minor emergencies. Mentors who directly assist their mentees tend to be the most helpful. In fact, mentors in the San Francisco survey ranked direct assistance as being *very useful* more often than any other function (Jonson, 1999b).

In a classic study of first-year teachers in New York City, Sacks and Brady (1985) identified the following areas of need in which a mentor might directly assist a mentee:

- Moral support, guidance, and feedback
- School routines and scheduling
- Discipline and management
- Curriculum and lesson planning
- Individualized instruction
- Motivational techniques

In addition, mentors often offer direct assistance to help the new teacher with career development.

Some mentors offer this help only when the mentee requests it; others step in whenever they see it as appropriate. Each mentor must personally decide when and how to offer direct assistance. Some mentees might see direct assistance as meddling or bossy—either because of the mentor's manner or because the mentee is not ready to receive help. But many are happy for the help. As one mentee in the Santa Cruz New Teacher Project advised new mentors, "Don't worry about being too direct. It's okay to give us specific suggestions. We don't always see what might not be working" (UCSC, 2003, p. 15).

"It helps if you can anticipate and help us prepare for events that are coming up, like reports," says another new teacher in the Oakland New Teacher Project. "Offer assistance in multiple forms—assessing for us or releasing us to assess. Meet for a useful period of time. Ten minutes is not enough" (UCSC, 2003, p. 15).

Recommended Procedures

Mentors need to offer to share the wealth of knowledge and experience they have gained but at the same time take care not to intimidate or overwhelm. It is important that the mentor make time available on a regular basis to address the mentee's concerns and progress and to ensure interaction. Sharing the same planning period helps a great deal. Box 8.2 lists a number of ways a mentor can directly assist a mentee.

BOX 8.2

Ways for a Mentor to Provide Direct Assistance

For moral support, guidance, and feedback:

- Respond to specific requests by mentees
- Encourage mentees in their efforts to develop their own ideas, teaching styles, and classroom management plans
- Encourage and support self-direction and autonomy
- Assist with room arrangement
- Model or suggest techniques for conferencing with parents
- Role-play a parent conference
- Act as a confidant for the mentee to express personal and professional concerns

With school routines and scheduling:

- Discuss written and unwritten rules, norms, and traditions in the school and community
- Assist in socializing within the school environment
- Give a tour of the district office and facilities
- Assist in filling out school forms
- Help the mentee develop and maintain a record-keeping system
- Identify resource people, such as the principal and staff development specialists in the district or in district and regional support agencies
- Explain school procedures regarding field trips

With discipline and management:

- Help the mentee develop a classroom management system
- Suggest options for classroom discipline
- Help the mentee develop a discipline plan

With curriculum and lesson planning:

- Help the mentee organize and manage materials
- Bring new methods, materials, and resources to the attention of the mentee and provide assistance in their implementation
- Provide examples of unit plans and course syllabi
- Co-plan an instructional unit or co-create a one-day lesson plan
- Co-develop a thematic unit
- Provide materials for a curriculum unit
- Brainstorm ways to introduce the curriculum unit
- Create materials together
- Suggest a strategy for reviewing literature
- Ask the new teacher how a strategy might affect student learning
- Point out gaps in lesson procedures
- Identify strengths in a lesson plan

With individualized instruction:

- Model skillful teaching strategies
- Confer with the mentee regarding effective ways to meet student learning objectives and district instructional goals
- Help the mentee diagnose students' learning styles and modify teaching strategies to meet all students' needs
- Arrange for the new teacher to observe another teacher
- Co-observe another teacher and discuss it afterward

With motivational techniques:

- Encourage the new teacher to try a new strategy
- Ask questions to help the new teacher prioritize issues related to instruction

With career development:

- Inform the mentee of workshops and other activities and opportunities for professional involvement
- Ask the new teacher to identify areas of strength and an area for professional growth
- Help the mentee assess current skills
- Ask questions to help the mentee self-assess
- Help the mentee identify specific competencies that need improvement
- Accompany the mentee for an evaluation conference with an administrator
- At the request of the mentee, assist in building competencies in areas of concern identified by the mentee's evaluator
- Assist the new teacher in developing a professional growth plan
- Help the new teacher select items to include in a portfolio
- Give feedback on the mentee's progress in meeting instructional goals

DEMONSTRATION TEACHING

A wealthy woman asked a famous millinery designer to design a hat for her. He placed a canvas form on her head, and in eight minutes with a single piece of ribbon, he created a beautiful hat right before her eyes. The matron was delighted. "How much will that be?" she asked. "Fifty dollars," he replied. "Why, that's outrageous," she said. "It's only a piece of ribbon!" The milliner quickly unraveled the ribbon and, handing it to her, said, "Madame, the ribbon is free!"[1]

A demonstration occurs when an experienced teacher shows a beginning teacher the proper use of a strategy, technique, or skill by incorporating it into an actual classroom lesson. One of the more important functions of a mentor-teacher is to prepare and teach demonstration lessons so that a mentee can observe specific techniques or materials being used. Often the beginning teacher can learn from watching how the mentor manages the class, presents curriculum, and deals with problems. At other times, the mentor might suggest that another teacher demonstrate a particular technique.

Videotapes, whether prepared locally or commercially, also can be used to demonstrate effective teaching. Videotapes offer some specific advantages, including convenience and consistency, but they cannot replace the effect of a live demonstration and subsequent conferences with the demonstrating teacher.

"Be willing to model lessons with the (new) teacher's class," a new teacher in the Santa Cruz New Teacher Project advises mentees. "It's neat to see what the advisor will do with my kids as things come up in a lesson" (UCSC, 2003, p. 15).

When to Use Demonstrations

Following are examples of appropriate times for demonstrations by a mentor-teacher:

- On request of the mentee
- After a mentor's observation of the mentee and identification of a technique that could be useful to the mentee
- By mutual agreement
- When the mentor has a specific technique to share
- On a regularly scheduled basis
- As part of the mentee's professional development plan

---

1. As seen in DEAR ABBY written by Abigail Van Buren a.k.a. Jeanne Phillips and founded by her mother, Pauline Phillips. © Universal Press Syndicate. Reprinted with permission. All rights reserved.

Recommended Procedures

A number of mentor/mentee teams have used the following procedure successfully when providing demonstration lessons (Jonson, 1999b).

- *Predemonstration conference.* The mentor and mentee determine the goal of the demonstration/observation and what the mentee should observe and record.
- *Demonstration.* The mentor demonstrates the preestablished lesson at the scheduled time while the mentee observes.
- *Postdemonstration conference.* The mentor and mentee review and analyze what was accomplished by the demonstration. In so doing, the mentor must remember that the idea is to help, not to threaten. The two then make plans for the mentee to practice the observed skill(s), for additional observations in the mentor-teacher's classroom, or both.

This procedure uses the pre- and postconference format advocated in the cognitive coaching model of Costa and Garmston (1994).

OBSERVATION AND FEEDBACK

When she observed my teaching, my cooperating teacher would always offer feedback in a very positive way, even when it was critical. I never felt that what she said was threatening to me, or that sense of "Oh, no, she really hated what I did" or anything like that.

—New teacher (Developmental Studies Center, 1998, p. 31)

The demanding pace of the classroom gives beginning teachers little time to monitor or reflect on their behavior. As a result, they tend to use automatic rather than deliberate responses to handle recurring classroom situations. A variety of studies in teacher expectations and attitudes, teacher-student relationships, student attitudes, and student learning progress have demonstrated that more effective teachers tend to be "proactive," that is, to assume and maintain the initiative in structuring classroom events. Less effective teachers tend to be more "reactive," lacking clarity of objectives and methods of reaching them and less "in charge" in their classrooms.

Observing the beginning teacher and providing feedback through a postobservation conference are important mentoring activities that can help beginning teachers. Research findings indicate that formal observation and feedback are especially effective for improving instruction (Costa & Garmston, 1994; Hunter, 1994; Showers, 1985). Feedback provided through written critiques, descriptions of classroom interaction analysis, behavior analysis, self-critiqued videotape, and other methods can also be helpful— but the use of a conference is preferred.

Feedback based on classroom observations makes beginning teachers aware of problems and helps bring about change. Sometimes the changes are obvious and simple to make, such as altering a physical arrangement in the classroom. Other changes are less obvious, and systematic feedback is needed to clarify the problem and explore ways to make appropriate changes. The mentor may find that several observation-feedback cycles are necessary to focus on the beginning teacher's patterns of calling on students and involving them in classroom discussions, for example. Additionally, the beginning teacher may need to be encouraged to attend specific professional development programs to make changes because the teaching skills are complex. In general, the value of the mentor's feedback depends on its quality and presentation. All feedback should

- address specific, concrete behaviors or characteristics;
- be focused, nonjudgmental, and evidence based;
- be credible and presented with caring intentions and in understand-able terms;
- include specific guidelines for growth; and
- lead to a commitment to initiate new or expanded strategies.

When mentors observe a mentee, they must note specifically what the beginning teacher is doing, what is working well, and where guidance is needed. The idea is for mentors to record exactly what is seen and then share observations in a way that is productive and supportive. If possible, mentors should help the beginning teacher see which existing behaviors are successful and raise the possibility of extending those behaviors rather than switching to entirely new ones. Mentors must describe the problem(s), but allow for lots of input from the beginning teacher. Feedback conferences tend to be especially productive if the beginning teacher has jotted down questions for discussion before the conference (Developmental Studies Center, 1998, p. 31).

Observation and feedback can initially be uncomfortable for both parties. With a good, trusting, supporting relationship, however, the mentor and the mentee will be able to achieve their goals through this process. A beginning teacher in California who participated in an extensive observation process found the experience worthwhile—despite the fact that the process was rigorous, with the mentor collecting information before and during the observation, comparing the results with the state standards for the teaching profession, and sharing the results in great detail with new teachers:

> The greatest benefit for me [in the mentoring program] was to be observed by an objective party who was able to tell me the good things that I was doing and the areas where I could improve.

My observer affirmed my strengths but also helped me let myself "off the hook" of perfection. I allow myself to be in a learning process—like the children in my class.

—Laura Wong, new teacher (Schultz, 1999, p. 103)

When to Use Observation and Feedback

What are beginning teachers interested in having observed? When mentors ask their mentees what concerns them and what they would like the mentor to observe, record, and provide feedback about, teachers request information about two distinct categories of behaviors: their own and that of their students. Behaviors can further be classified as verbal or nonverbal. Tables 8.2 through 8.5 give examples of verbal and nonverbal behaviors that teachers often want mentors to observe in the classroom (Costa & Garmston, 1994, pp. 29–31).

Recommended Procedure: The Formal Conference

A formal observation-and-conference cycle follows steps similar to those described for demonstrations. In this case, though, the mentee is the focus of the observations discussed.

The formal mentor observation and conference has three parts:

1. Preobservation conference

2. Observation

3. Postobservation conference

Ideally, the mentor and the mentee engage in the formal observation-conferencing process at least once a month. They should remember that this is a collaborative decision-making process, with the mentor and the mentee discussing and agreeing on each point.

Preobservation Conference

The reliability and usefulness of a classroom observation relate directly to the amount and kind of information the observer has obtained beforehand (McGreal, 1983, p. 98). During the preconference, the mentor should gather information, and both mentor and mentee should determine a focus for the observation.

"I appreciate when my advisor is receptive to hearing my needs instead of having their own agenda," a new teacher in the Santa Cruz New Teacher Project says (UCSC, 2003, p. 15). "Help me with what I need rather than what we're supposed to do. . . . It's important for me to have a say in scheduling the time and focus of our meetings."

Table 8.2   Nonverbal Feedback Most Often Requested by Teachers About Themselves

Description	Example
A. Mannerisms	Pencil tapping, hair twisting, handling coins in pocket
B. Use of time	Interruptions; transitions from one activity to another; time spent with each group; time spent getting class started, dealing with routines (such as attendance), etc.; punctuality in starting/ending times
C. Movement throughout the classroom	Favoring one side of the classroom over another; monitoring student progress and seatwork
D. Modality preference	Using balanced visual, kinesthetic, and auditory modes of instruction
E. Use of handouts	Clarity, meaningfulness, adequacy, and/or complexity of seatwork
F. Use of AV equipment	Placement, appropriateness, operation
G. Pacing	Too fast, too slow, "beating a dead horse" (tempo/rhythm)
H. Meeting diverse student needs	Considering/making allowances for: gifted/challenged; cognitive styles; emotional needs; modality strengths; languages, cultures, etc.
I. Nonverbal feedback	Body language, gestures, proximity, eye contact; moving or leaning toward students when addressing them
J. Classroom arrangements	Furniture placement, bulletin board space, environment for learning, provision for multiple uses of space/activities

SOURCE: Costa, A. L., & Garmston, R. J. (1994). *Cognitive coaching: A foundation for renaissance schools* (p. 29). Norwood, MA: Christopher-Gordon Publishers.

Table 8.3   Verbal Feedback Most Often Requested by Teachers About Themselves

Description	Example
A. Mannerisms	Saying "okay," "you know," or other phrases excessively
B. Sarcasm/negative feedback	Gender references; criticism; put-downs; intonations
C. Positive/negative feedback	Use of praise, criticism, ignoring distracting student responses
D. Response behaviors	Silence, accepting, paraphrasing, clarifying, empathizing; responding to students who give "wrong" answers
E. Questioning strategies	Posing taxonomical levels of questions; asking questions in sequences
F. Clarity of presentation	Giving clear directions, making assignments clear, checking for understanding, modeling
G. Interactive patterns	Teacher—>Student—> Teacher—>Student Teacher—>Student—> Student—>Student
H. Equitable distribution of responses	Favoring gender, language proficiency, culture, perception of abilities, placement in room, etc.
I. Specific activities/teaching strategies	Lectures, group activities, lab exercises, discussion videos

SOURCE: Costa, A. L., & Garmston, R. J. (1994). *Cognitive coaching: A foundation for renaissance schools* (p. 29). Norwood, MA: Christopher-Gordon Publishers.

Table 8.4   Nonverbal Feedback Most Often Requested by Teachers About Their Students

Description	Example
A. Attentiveness	On task/off task, note taking, volunteering for tasks
B. Preparedness	Participation, sharing, homework, materials, volunteering knowledge
C. Movement	Negative: out of seat, squirming, fidgeting, discomfort, interfering with others
	Positive: following directions, transitioning, self-direction, taking initiative, consulting references/atlases/dictionaries, etc.
D. Managing materials	AV equipment, textual materials, art supplies, musical instruments, lab equipment, care of library books, returning supplies, etc.

SOURCE: Costa, A. L., & Garmston, R. J. (1994). *Cognitive coaching: A foundation for renaissance schools* (p. 29). Norwood, MA: Christopher-Gordon Publishers.

Acheson and Gall (1980, p. 98) suggest the following agenda for determining goals during a preconference. They also recommend following these steps in order. By doing so, they say, mentor and mentee together identify the teacher's concerns about instruction.

1. Translate the teacher's concerns into observable behaviors

2. Identify procedures for improving the teacher's instruction

3. Assist the teacher in setting self-improvement goals

4. Arrange a time for classroom observation

5. Select an observation instrument and behaviors to be recorded

6. Clarify the instructional context in which data will be recorded

The emphasis for the observation is on collecting data regarding matters of interest to the beginning teacher. Use the preconference log in Figure 8.2 to help organize the procedure and focus for observation of the new teacher.

Table 8.5   Verbal Feedback Most Often Requested by Teachers About Their Students

Description	Example
A. Participating	Positive: volunteering verbal responses, speaking out—on task, student-to-student interaction—on task, requesting assistance
	Negative: speaking out—off task, student-to-student interaction—off task
B. Social interaction	Positive: listening, allowing for differences, sharing, establishing ground rules, assuming and carrying out roles, following rules of games, etc.
	Negative: interrupting, interfering, hitting, name calling, put-downs, culturally insensitive language, swearing, hoarding, stealing
C. Performing lesson objectives	Using correct terminology; applying knowledge learned before or elsewhere; performing task correctly; conducting experiments; applying rules, algorithms, procedures, formulas, etc.; recalling information; supplying supportive details, rationale, elaboration
D. Language patterns	Using correct grammar, spelling, punctuation, counting; using correct syntax; supplying examples
E. Insights into student behaviors/difficulties	Learning styles: verbal, auditory, kinesthetic, etc.; cognitive styles: field sensitive, field independent, etc.; friendships/animosities; tolerance for ambiguity/disorder; distractibility

SOURCE: Costa, A. L., & Garmston, R. J. (1994). *Cognitive coaching: A foundation for renaissance schools* (p. 29). Norwood, MA: Christopher-Gordon Publishers.

First Observation

Observation in this case does not mean simply watching; rather, it means intentionally and methodically observing interaction between the teacher and students. It should be planned, careful, focused, and active. Once the focus has been determined at the preconference, the mentor needs to keep

Figure 8.2   Preconference log

Preconference Log (to be filled out by member)

Date of preconference: _____

Teacher: _____

Mentor: _____

Lesson background:

- What subject will the teacher be teaching when observed?
- What is the purpose of the lesson that will be observed?

Observation:

- What is the reason and purpose for the observation?
- What is the specific focus of the observations?
- How will the observation be recorded?

Date of observation: _____

Location of observation: _____

Time of observation: _____

Date of postconference: _____

Location of postconference: _____

Time of postconference: _____

SOURCE: Glickman, C. D. (2002). *Leadership for learning: How to help teachers succeed* (Appendix A, p. 110). Alexandria, VA: ASCD. Used with permission. The Association of Supervision and Curriculum Development is a worldwide community of educators advocating sound policies and sharing best practices to achieve the success of each learner. To learn more, visit ASCD at www.ascd.org.

that focus during the observation. The more narrowly the mentor is able to focus, the more accurate will be the classroom observation (McGreal, 1983, p. 102). The mentor also needs to record data during the observation to be recalled later in a postconference. Several techniques for recording data are discussed under the heading "Tools for Observation," later in this chapter.

Postobservation Conference

During this last phase of the observation-and-conference cycle, the mentor provides feedback to help the mentee improve. The idea is for the mentor to describe what has been observed, not to pass judgment. Any feedback should be in strict confidence; in most districts, the mentor is not part of the system of teacher evaluation and avoids discussing the performance of the beginning teacher with other staff. Inexperienced mentors, being quite proud of their data-gathering ability and having worked hard during the observation to take notes, may be eager to tell the beginning teacher everything they have seen. Doing so, however, will make it impossible for the beginning teacher to process all of the information. Costa and Garmston (1994) offer the following tips on data reporting to help avoid this common problem:

- Sit side by side with the mentee so that the mentee can see the mentor's notes.
- Begin by having the *mentee* recollect the lesson. This gives the mentor something to build on and also helps the mentee develop self-reflecting and self-coaching skills.
- If the mentee introduces important but tangential problems or concerns during the postconference, deal with them briefly—but don't abandon the originally planned discussion. Keeping focus enables the mentor to manage time.
- Give the mentee notes to have. In some cases, it might even help to give the mentee notes *before* the postobservation meeting.

Offering feedback in positive terms will enhance trust and support and will reduce anxiety. But it is also important for feedback to be honest. "If mentors are unwilling to criticize," writes Glenn, "perhaps out of fear of negatively affecting the relationship . . . progress will be slow in coming. Unless . . . teachers know where their areas for improvement lie, they are likely to flounder with no direction" (2006, p. 91).

The following guidelines will help the mentor provide positive but constructive feedback:

- Focus feedback on the behavior, rather than on the person
- Provide objective feedback, and cite specific examples
- Describe rather than judge
- Point out specific causes and effects
- Share ideas rather than give advice
- Explore alternatives, rather than give solutions
- Give only the amount of feedback the receiver can use
- Provide feedback valuable for the receiver, rather than for the giver

It is important to keep the focus on the topic determined in the preobservation conference. Without such a focus, the discussion is likely to move to issues outside the classroom, away from the goal of improving learning for students (Glickman, 2002, p. 35).

Second and Subsequent Observations and Conferences

Mentors and mentees will require more than one observation-and-conference sequence to establish a strong, trusting relationship. Once this level of trust has been achieved, the mentor and the beginning teacher are ready to proceed to other observations and conferences focused on specific instructional growth for the beginning teacher. This process of preconference, observation, and postconference should continue throughout the year, changing focus as the needs of the beginning teacher change. See Box 8.3 for helpful guidelines.

BOX 8.3

Guidelines to Help a Mentee in Subsequent Observations and Conferences

Preobservation Conference (5–10 minutes)

- Set dates and times for the observation and postconference
- Determine what the mentee would like to have observed
- Determine where the observer is to sit in the class
- Discuss the lesson plan and material to be taught
- Specify the observation tools to be used (see next section)

Observation (20–50 minutes)

- Observe one or two teaching behaviors or strategies
- Use the observation form agreed on in the preconference

Postobservation Conference (10–30 minutes)

- Set a relaxed tone
- Discuss objective data, not viewpoints or judgments
- Explore strategies, alternatives, causes, and effects
- Discuss areas of focus for future observations and other activities

---

Tools for Observation

Using observation tools is like taking snapshots of classroom events.

The purpose is to record, in an objective and usable manner, the verbal and nonverbal behaviors of students and teachers. Many types of observation tools exist; following are some examples. Mentors and their mentees are encouraged to use whatever observation tools and techniques they agree will be helpful or to develop their own.

Seating Charts

Several techniques for observing student and teacher behaviors make use of the seating chart format. These techniques have several advantages:

- They are easy to use and interpret.
- A large body of information can be recorded on a single chart.

- They deal with relatively important aspects of classroom behavior.
- They enable the observer to record one student's behavior while at the same time observing the teacher and the class as a whole.

1. *Student/Teacher Question Patterns.* A seating chart can be used to record the frequency of each student's interaction with the teacher during a question-and-answer session.

Directions. When the teacher asks an individual student a question, place an arrow in that student's box on the seating chart. The arrow should be pointing away from the teacher. Each subsequent question directed to that student should be marked with a slash through the same arrow. In Figure 8.3, one student was asked two questions, and the other student was asked four questions.

Figure 8.3   Question patterns: Teacher to individual student

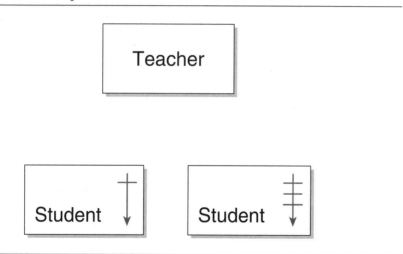

When the teacher directs questions to the entire class, place an arrow in or near the teacher's box on the classroom map/seating chart (see Figure 8.4). The arrow should point in the direction of the class. Subsequent questions directed to the entire class should be recorded as slash marks through the same arrow.

When a student asks a question or responds to the teacher's question, place an arrow in or near that student's box on the seating chart (see Figure 8.5). In this instance, the arrow should point toward the teacher. Subsequent questions and responses by the student should be marked by slashes through the same arrow.

2. *On-Task Behavior.* A seating chart or classroom map is useful for providing data on whether students are engaged in appropriate, "on-task" behavior at specified times during a lesson or activity.

Figure 8.4   Question patterns: Teacher to entire class

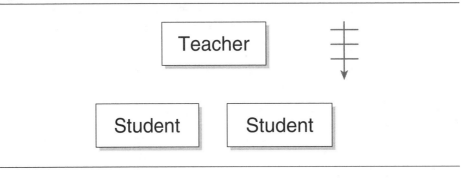

Figure 8.5   Question patterns: Student to teacher

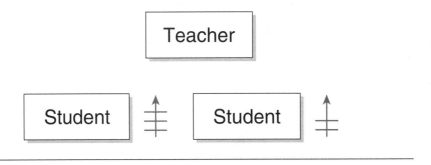

Directions. Observe the class at three- or five-minute intervals. Using the agreed-on behavior categories, note what each student is doing at the specified times, and mark the appropriate symbols in the student's box. In Figure 8.6, two students were chatting with others (i.e., were off task) at 9:00, but all students were on task at 9:03.

3. *Reinforcement and Feedback.* A seating chart may also be used to record teacher responses to individual student behavior. An observer/ mentor (with the beginning teacher's agreement) may wish to learn whether the beginning teacher's communications with the class (or with an individual student) are predominantly positive, for example.

Directions. Each time the teacher provides feedback to an individual student, decide whether the feedback is a reprimand, a positive response (such as a compliment or affirmation), a correction, or a neutral response. Then place the symbol for that feedback in the student's box (see Figure 8.7).

4. *Classroom Movement Patterns.* The observer/mentor and the beginning teacher may be interested in recording teacher and/or student movement around the classroom during a period of time. Data on a seating

Figure 8.6   On-task behavior

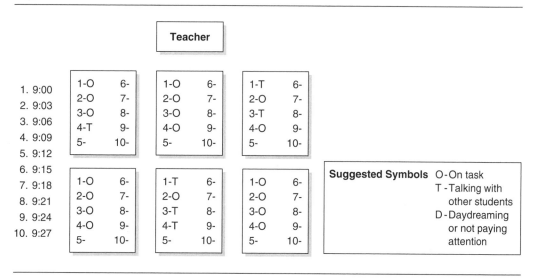

Figure 8.7   Reinforcement and feedback

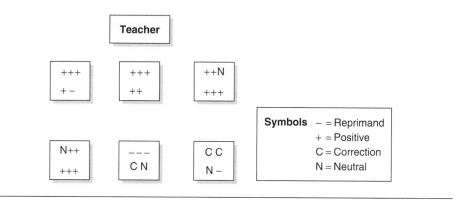

chart or classroom map may provide information concerning teacher bias, classroom management procedures, student engagement, or some other aspect of classroom behavior.

Directions. Use lines with arrows to show which students move about the room during the observation period (see Figure 8.8).

Draw lines with arrows to record *teacher* movement during the observation (see Figure 8.9).

Figure 8.8   Student movement patterns

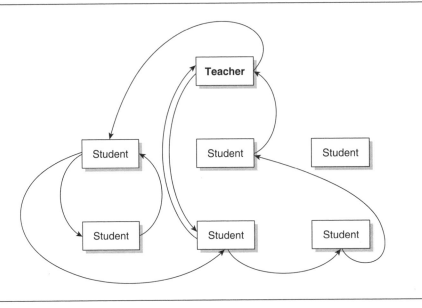

Figure 8.9   Teacher movement patterns

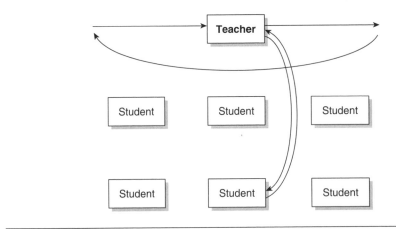

5. *Cause-and-Effect Records.* This observation tool is designed to give the observer/mentor and the beginning teacher information concerning the influence of the teacher's actions on student response in the classroom. It can be useful for observing a teacher's classroom management, questioning strategies, direction giving, and other behaviors that call for a student response.

Directions. Divide a blank sheet of paper into two columns. Record teacher actions in the left-hand column and student response to these actions in the right-hand column (see Figure 8.10).

Figure 8.10   Cause-and-effect record

Teacher	Student (response)
Bell	Students moving to their seats
Roll taken	Students talking quietly to each other
Surveys class	Room quiets down
Teacher turns on overhead and says, "Take out a piece of paper and answer the following questions about yesterday's reading assignment."	Students look at overhead and some students begin to take out paper

6. *Verbatim Transcripts.* Many mentors and supervisors have been trained to use an exact written record of teacher-and-student verbal inter-actions during an observation period. Whether it is selective (i.e., whether the kinds of verbal events to be recorded have been decided on before-hand) or a complete account of teacher-and-student verbal behavior, the verbatim transcript allows for a rather thorough analysis of what has transpired in the classroom during the observation. Many experts advocate the use of the verbatim transcript because of its specificity in providing the beginning teacher with feedback.

7. *Videotapes.* Videotaping a lesson for the mentor and the beginning teacher to review together later can also provide valuable information. This is especially helpful if the camera is set up to catch student body language and facial expressions. In this way, both participants can "observe" the lesson together during the feedback cycle.

INFORMAL CONTACT

"I didn't even think of this until we started talking about it today," a first-year teacher in middle school language arts professed to her mentor one day as the two conversed. "Oh, now that makes sense when I hear myself saying it," she said another time. Yet a third time, she exclaimed, "I feel like the sun's come out! I know this is the way we need to go."

—"Kelly," first-year middle school teacher
(Stanulis & Weaver, 1998, p. 136)

In their report of the study involving this inexperienced teacher, Stanulis and Weaver (1998) write, "In setting aside the time to talk, we were honoring one of the primary ways in which teachers do business and make meaning: talking about issues and problems with a colleague" (p. 136).

In fact, informal contact, the easiest form of assistance to provide, may also be the most helpful overall. Beginning teachers and mentors frequently state that informal discussions with experienced teachers are the most valuable type of assistance. The beginning teacher needs to know about so many "nuts and bolts"—but doesn't. Even the policies and procedures that *are* explained in preservice orientation often are forgotten in the excitement of the new school year. A bit of information, some timely suggestions, or a few words of understanding and encouragement can be a big help.

Effective mentors make a point of visiting their mentees and generally being around, especially during the first few days of school. In fact, when asked to list qualities in a good mentor, one respondent to the survey of San Francisco mentors noted simply, "being *available* to the mentee for discussions, exploration, etc." (Jonson, 1999b). Close physical proximity between the mentor's and the mentee's classrooms is highly desirable to facilitate informal contact. This allows the mentor to meet informally but frequently with the beginning teacher to discuss such day-to-day concerns as

- taking attendance,
- understanding school discipline policies,
- acquiring supplies and materials,
- planning classroom instruction,
- coping with daily problems, and
- understanding contracts and benefits.

Any concerns of beginning teachers are valid subjects for frequent informal conferences. Consequently, the mentor should make an effort to be both available and easily accessible to the beginning teacher, especially during the first few weeks of the school year.

ASSISTANCE WITH AN ACTION PLAN FOR PROFESSIONAL GROWTH

An important premise of coaching shared by other promising practices is the view of professional growth as ongoing learning. Conditions necessary for the professional growth of teachers parallel essential ingredients of adult development. Educators, like all adult learners, need the autonomy to direct and take responsibility for their own learning.

—Sarah L. Levine (1989, p. 243)

One important key to successful mentoring is moving the mentee from some level of dependence on the mentor-teacher to a high level of self-direction. As a logical step in this process, the mentee can begin to plan, formally or informally, a professional development process. In several states, in fact, new teachers must come up with a Professional Development Plan during their first year to be implemented over the next three to five years to qualify for a renewable license. This process is separate from any evaluation of the mentee and can follow the processes of observation, demonstration, coaching, and reflection.

Mentors must be conscious of how their own professional development serves as a model for their mentees. Lifelong learning is as much an attitude as an activity. It is a way of life for professionals.

Many kinds of professional planning assistance are possible. The mentor-teacher can assist in planning professional development by doing the following:

- Sharing views concerning possible career paths and goals
- Providing direct assistance: answering questions, suggesting strategies, supplying resources
- Creating opportunities for mentees to become involved in professional activities—such as faculty activities, professional associations, special projects—and to "prove" themselves as professionals
- Providing information on the mentor's own professional development plan as a model
- Assisting the mentee in setting short- and long-term professional goals
- Acting as a resource to help the mentee obtain information such as certification and continuing education requirements
- Suggesting or providing books, articles, professional videos, and so on

A good plan should do the following:

1. Clarify the *roles and responsibilities* of the mentor and mentee

2. Provide a *focus and framework* for mentor-mentee teamwork

3. Become an *informative resource* when shared with others

Goals should be short-term, achievable within a few months. Plans should be revisited and revised or rewritten two or three times per year so that the beginning teacher can gain a sense of accomplishment and growth.

In addition, the mentor should be sensitive to the beginning teacher's own agenda for professional development. Many beginning teachers are as busy as they can be just filling the requirements of maintaining their credentials. Some work to complete a master's degree in the first year or two while on the job. Any other plans for development should be coordinated with these activities.

ROLE MODELING

The aspect of role modeling is not one I consciously set about doing. But, more than in other areas, mentees tell me in conversations several years later that they wanted to "be like [me]." To me, that is a hidden part of mentoring. But if the mentee doesn't feel that respect and admiration for the mentor, why would he pay attention to the mentor's ideas? I also think the respect other colleagues show for the mentor gives the mentee more reason to want to learn from the mentor.

—A mentor (Jonson, 1999b)

Literature on mentoring emphasizes the importance of providing beginning teachers with role models for personal and professional behavior. What seems to confirm and enhance the mentoring relationship is the mentee's respect for the mentor as a professional and as a human being who is living a life worthy of that respect. In addition to helping the beginning teacher acquire skills and knowledge, the mentor-teacher must model a commitment to professional growth (see Box 8.4). Important to the mentoring relationship is not just what mentors *know*, but who they *are*.

BOX 8.4

The Mentor-Teacher as a Model

The mentor-teacher becomes a model

- In relations with colleagues, students, parents, and others
- By demonstrating a commitment to student growth and development
- By demonstrating exemplary skills in the classroom
- In collaborative endeavors with other professionals (collegial interaction and support)
- In work habits
- By modeling a professional growth commitment and having a personal and professional development plan
- By active involvement in professional activities and professional organizations
- By seeking knowledge of trends in education, including new teaching materials, methodology, and research
- By expressing a positive set of values and beliefs concerning teaching as a career
- By being a facilitator of change and improvement

Role modeling means much more than the mentor doing demonstration teaching. It means exhibiting professionalism; it means showing the mentee how to get things done within the political climate of the school; it means demonstrating realistic ways of solving problems; it means exhibiting energy, self-confidence, security, and competency.

With the aid of an effective role model, the mentee develops a sense of professional identity and competence. The mentor, in turn, profits in the areas of technical and psychological support, internal satisfaction, and increased respect from colleagues (Kram, 1985).

ASSESSING STUDENT WORK

Is the work good? What is good?

In a survey of first-year teachers, Mandel asked what novices most want help with. High on the list was grading fairly (2006, p. 68). "They want the grades to be accurate, but not to hurt a student's self-esteem," Mandel writes. "Efficient and fair grading, one of the most fundamental teacher tasks, is not a skill normally taught in education classes or new teacher workshops. Somehow, our education system seems to assume that new teachers already know effective grading techniques or can easily learn them on their own. But fair grading is complicated."

Writing, exams, projects, and portfolios all can be used to measure student achievement. Examining student work is a large part of every teacher's job, for two reasons: (1) Grades let students know how they are progressing and (2) they let teachers know how effective their instruction is. A good assessment of student work can help the teacher develop classroom instruction. In isolation, though, a new teacher may not have a clear context for assessment. Discussion with a colleague can help the new teacher focus and analyze the work on a broader scale.

Together, a mentor and mentee might assess several samples of work from one student, one assignment as completed by several students, or successful and less successful samples of a given assignment. Blythe, Allen, and Powell (1999, p. 10) suggest several questions to guide an assessment of student work. They relate to the work itself, teaching practice, student understanding, student growth, and student intent. For a list of these questions, see Box 8.5.

Recommended Procedures

Before meeting, mentees decide what they would like to learn from the assessment, select samples of student work for discussion, and prepare context information: a description of the assignment, the rubric, and so on. If appropriate, mentees make an extra copy of work so that they and their mentors can each have one.

BOX 8.5

Kinds of Questions to Guide the Examination of Student Work

About the quality of student work:

- Is the work good enough?
- What is good enough?
- In what ways does this work meet or fail to meet a particular set of standards?

About teaching practice:

- What do the students' responses indicate about the effectiveness of the prompt or assignment?
- How might the assignment be improved?
- What kinds of instruction support high-quality student performances?

About the student's understanding:

- What does this work tell us about how well the student understands the topic of the assignment?
- What initial understanding do we see beginning to emerge in this work?

About the student's growth:

- How does this range of work from a single student demonstrate growth over time?
- How can I support student growth more effectively?

About the student's intent:

- What issues or questions is this student focused on?
- What aspects of the assignment intrigued this student?
- Which parts of the assignment called forth the most effort from the student?
- To what extent is the student challenging herself? In what ways?

Following a meeting on "Examining Student Work and School Change" in Chicago in October 1998 (hosted by the Chicago Learning Collaborative and the Annenberg Institute for School Reform), an association of individuals and educational organizations developed a Web site (www.lasw.org) focused on looking at student work to strengthen connections between student learning and instruction, curriculum, and other aspects of school life. The Web site gives suggestions for teachers looking together at student work and reflecting on important questions about teaching and learning. Although the focus is not on mentors working with mentees, many of the ideas are important and transferable. According to advice given on the Web site, the teacher bringing work for discussion (perhaps the mentee) should choose a particular focus for discussion. The question might be broad: *How can I support higher-quality presentations? What are the strengths and weaknesses in the student presentations?* Or the focus might be narrow: *How can I use a prompt to bring out more creativity in students' work? What evidence of mathematical problem solving is in the students' work?*

CONCLUSION

This chapter has reviewed many strategies and tools that mentors use to work with beginning or other new teachers, including information about when to use the strategies and recommended procedures.

REFERENCES

Acheson, J., & Gall, M. (1980). *Techniques in the clinical supervision of teachers.* New York: Longman.

Bacon, D. (1997, October 6). Veteran teachers lend a hand: Peer Assistance and Review Program celebrates ten years. *California Teacher, 1,* 6–7.

Blythe, T., Allen, D., & Powell, B. S. (1999). *Looking together at student work: A companion guide to assessing student learning.* New York Teachers College Press.

Costa, A. L., & Garmston, R. J. (1994). *Cognitive coaching: A foundation for renaissance schools.* Norwood, MA: Christopher-Gordon.

Developmental Studies Center. (1998). *The master teacher handbook.* Unpublished manuscript.

Fraser, J. (1998). *Teacher to teacher: A guidebook for effective mentoring.* Portsmouth, NH: Heinemann.

Glenn, W. J. (2006). Model versus mentor: Defining the necessary qualities of the effective cooperating teacher. *Teacher Education Quarterly, 33*(1), 85–95.

Glickman, C. D. (2002). *Leadership for learning: How to help teachers succeed.* Alexandria, VA: Association for Supervision and Curriculum Development.

Hunter, M. (1994). *Enhancing teaching.* New York: Macmillan.

Jonson, K. (1999a). Parents as partners: Building positive home-school relationships. *The Educational Forum, 63,* 121–126.

Jonson, K. (1999b). [Survey of 28 mentor-teachers in the San Francisco Unified School District]. Unpublished raw data.

Kram, K. E. (1985). *Mentoring at work.* Glenview, IL: Scott Foresman.

Levine, S. L. (1989). *Promoting adult growth in schools.* Needham Heights, MA: Allyn & Bacon.

Mandel, S. (2006, March). What new teachers really need. *Educational leadership.* Alexandria, VA: Association for supervision and curriculum development.

McGreal, T. L. (1983). *Successful teacher evaluation.* Alexandria, VA: Association for Supervision and Curriculum Development.

Portner, H. (1998). *Mentoring new teachers.* Thousand Oaks, CA: Corwin Press.

Sacks, S. R., & Brady, P. (1985, March–April). *Who teaches the city's children? A study of New York City first year teachers.* Paper presented at the annual meeting of the American Educational Research Association, Chicago.

Schultz, B. (1999). Combining mentoring and assessment in California. In M. Scherer (Ed.), *A better beginning: Supporting and mentoring new teachers.* Alexandria, VA: Association for Supervision and Curriculum Development.

Showers, B. (1985, April). Teachers coaching teachers. *Educational Leadership, 42*(7), 43–48.

Stanulis, R. N., & Weaver, D. (1998). Teacher as mentor, teacher as learner: Lessons from a middle-school language arts teacher. *The Teacher Educator, 34*(2), 134–143.

University of California Santa Cruz, Department of Education (UCSC). (2003). Tips for new mentors. *Reflections, 6*(1), 15.

9

Instructional Coaching

Jim Knight

Instructional coaching, more completely described in *Instructional Coaching: A Partnership Approach to Improving Instruction* (Knight, 2007), provides intensive, differentiated support to teachers so that they are able to implement proven practices. Like other coaches using other models described in this book, instructional coaches (ICs) have excellent communication skills and a deep respect for teachers' professionalism. Additionally, ICs have a thorough knowledge of the teaching practices they share with teachers. Unlike some other approaches, instructional coaches also frequently provide model lessons, observe teachers, and simplify explanations of the teaching practices they share with teachers.

This chapter provides an overview of the specific components of Instructional Coaching that grew out of our ongoing study of onsite professional development. The chapter also describes the framework we use to identify where to start with teachers—The Big Four—and several factors that we have found to be important when it comes to the success of coaching programs.

WHAT IS INSTRUCTIONAL COACHING?

ICs partner with teachers to help them incorporate research-based instructional practices into their teaching. They are skilled communicators, or relationship builders, with a repertoire of excellent communication skills that enable them to empathize, listen, and build trusting relationships. ICs also encourage and support teachers' reflection about their classroom practices. Thus, they must be skilled at unpacking their collaborating teachers' professional goals so that they can help them create a plan for realizing those goals, all with a focus on improving instruction.

Instructional coaches deeply understand many scientifically proven instructional practices. ICs focus on a broader range of instructional issues, which might include classroom management, content enhancement, specific teaching practices, formative assessment, or other teaching practices, such as the Strategic Instruction Model, Reading in the Content Areas, Marzano's strategies, or other proven ways to improve instruction. ICs help teachers choose appropriate approaches to teaching for the different kinds of learning students are experiencing. They frequently model practices in the classroom, observe teachers, and engage in supportive, dialogical conversations with them about what they observed. An instructional coach, in other words, partners with teachers so they can choose and implement research-based interventions to help students learn more effectively.

WHAT IS THE PARTNERSHIP PHILOSOPHY?

One of the most important aspects of Instructional Coaching, as I define it, is the theory behind the approach. Theory provides a foundation for all aspects of our professional and personal life. When we undertake any task, we operate from a set of taken-for-granted rules or principles of how to be effective, and these tacit rules represent the *theory* for that particular task. Theory is the gravity that holds together any systematic approach, including Instructional Coaching.

I describe the theoretical framework for Instructional Coaching as a partnership approach, seeing coaching as a partnership between coaches and teachers. This approach is articulated in seven principles, which are derived from research and theoretical writing in a variety of fields, including adult education (Friere, Knowles) cultural anthropology (Eisler,) Leadership (Block, Greenleaf), organizational theory (Senge), and epistemology (Kuhn, Bernstein, Feyerabend). The principles were also validated in a study of two approaches to professional development (a partnership approach and a traditional approach) (Knight, 1999).

The Partnership Principles

ICs use the partnership principles as touchstones for reflecting on the work they have done in the past and for planning the work they will do in the future. More information on the partnership approach is available in *Partnership Learning: Scientifically Proven Strategies for Fostering Dialogue During Workshops and Presentations* (Knight, 2009b). The seven partnership principles are as follows:

1. Equality: Instructional Coaches and Teachers Are Equal Partners

Partnership involves relationships between equals. Thus, instructional coaches recognize collaborating teachers as equal partners, and they truly believe that each teacher's thoughts and beliefs are valuable. ICs listen to teachers with the intent to learn, to really understand, and then respond, rather than with the intent to persuade.

2. Choice: Teachers Should Have Choice Regarding What and How They Learn

In a partnership, one individual does not make decisions for another. Because partners are equal, they make their own individual choices and make decisions collaboratively. For ICs this means that teacher choice is implicit in every communication of content and, to the greatest extent possible, the process used to learn the content. ICs don't see it as their job to make teachers think like them; they see their goal as meeting people where they are and offering choices.

3. Voice: Professional Learning Should Empower and Respect the Voices of Teachers

All individuals in a partnership have opportunities to express their point of view. Indeed, a primary benefit of a partnership is that each individual has access to many perspectives rather than the one perspective of a leader. ICs who act on this principle encourage teachers to express their opinions about content being learned. ICs see coaching as a process that helps teachers find their voice, not a process determined to make teachers think a certain way.

4. Dialogue: Professional Learning Should Enable Authentic Dialogue

To arrive at mutually acceptable decisions, partners engage in dialogue. In a partnership, one individual does not impose, dominate, or control.

Partners engage in conversation, learning together as they explore ideas. For ICs this means that they listen more than they talk. ICs avoid manipulation, engage participants in conversation about content, and think and learn with participants.

5. Reflection: Reflection Is an Integral Part of Professional Learning

If we are creating a learning partnership, if our partners are equal with us, if they are free to speak their own minds and free to make real, meaningful choices, it follows that one of the most important choices our collaborating partners will make is how to make sense of whatever we are proposing they learn. Partners don't dictate to each other what to believe; they respect their partners' professionalism and provide them with enough information, so that they can make their own decisions. Thus, ICs encourage collaborating teachers to consider ideas before adopting them. Indeed, ICs recognize that reflective thinkers, by definition, have to be free to choose or reject ideas, or else they simply are not thinkers at all.

6. Praxis: Teachers Should Apply Their Learning to Their Real-Life Practice as They Are Learning

Partnership should enable individuals to have more meaningful experiences. In partnership relationships, meaning arises when people reflect on ideas and then put those actions into practice. A requirement for partnership is that each individual is free to reconstruct and use content the way he or she considers it most useful. For ICs this means that in partnership with collaborating teachers, they focus their attention on how to use ideas in the classroom as those ideas are being learned.

7. Reciprocity: Instructional Coaches Should Expect to Get as Much as They Give

In a partnership, all partners benefit from the success, learning, or experience of others—everyone is rewarded by what each individual contributes. For that reason, one of an IC's goals should be to learn along with collaborating teachers, such as learning about each teacher's classroom, the strengths and weaknesses of the teaching practices being learned when used in each teacher's classroom, various perspectives of the teaching strategy when seen through the eyes of teachers and students, and so on.

WHAT TEACHING PRACTICES DO INSTRUCTIONAL COACHES SHARE WITH TEACHERS? THE BIG FOUR

If instructional coaches are going to share proven teaching practices with teachers, they likely need a framework to help them identify where to start. ICs working with the University of Kansas Center for Research on Learning employ a framework we refer to as "The Big Four," which includes (1) classroom management, (2) content, (3) instruction, and (4) assessment for learning. More information on The Big Four is available in *The Big Four: A Framework for Instructional Excellence* (Knight, 2009a), *Instructional Coaching: A Partnership Approach to Improving Instruction* (Knight, 2007), and *Coaching Classroom Management: A Toolkit for Coaches and Administrators* (Sprick, Knight, Reinke, & McKale, 2006).

> **The Big Four**
>
> 1. Classroom Management
> 2. Content
> 3. Instruction
> 4. Assessment for Learning

1. Classroom Management

If a teacher's students are on task and learning, an IC and collaborating teachers can turn to a variety of other issues related to student learning. However, if student behavior is out of control, in our experience, the coach and collaborating teacher will struggle to make other practices work if they do not first address classroom management issues. More information about classroom management is available in the book *Coaching Classroom Management: A Toolkit for Coaches and Administrators* (Sprick et al., 2006). ICs can explore starting points for coaching by considering several questions that might help identify whether behavior is an issue that needs to be addressed immediately:

- Are students on task in class?
- Does the teacher make significantly more positive comments than negative comments (at least a three to one ratio)?
- Has the teacher developed clear expectations for all activities and transitions during the class?
- Has the teacher clearly communicated those expectations, and do the students understand them?
- Do students have frequent opportunities to respond during the class?

More difficult to identify, but no less important to ask, are the following questions:

- Does the teacher care about his or her students' welfare?
- Does the teacher respect his or her students?

- Does the teacher communicate high expectations?
- Does the teacher believe his or her students can achieve those expectations?

2. Content

Does the teacher understand the content, have a plan, and understand which information is most important? If a teacher's class is well managed, a second question is whether the teacher has a deep knowledge of the content. Teachers need to know which content is most important, and they also need to know how to explain that content clearly. Several questions might help a coach determine whether a teacher has mastery of his or her content. They include the following:

- Does the teacher have a complete, detailed plan for teaching the course?
- Has the teacher developed essential questions for all units?
- Do those questions align with the state standards?
- Can the teacher identify the 10 to 15 core questions that are answered by the course?
- Can the teacher identify the top 10 concepts in the course?
- Can the teacher clearly and simply explain the meaning of each of the top 10 concepts?

3. Instruction

Is the teacher using teaching practices that ensure all students master content? If teachers hold a deep understanding of their content, and if they can manage their classroom, the next big question is whether they can teach their knowledge to their students. Effective instruction involves numerous teaching practices, the need for which may be surfaced by the following questions:

- Does the teacher properly prepare students at the start of the class?
- Does the teacher effectively model thinking and other processes for students?
- Does the teacher ask questions at an appropriate variety of levels?
- Does the teacher use cooperative learning and other activities to keep students engaged?
- Does the teacher provide constructive feedback that enables students to improve?
- Does the teacher use language, analogies, examples, and stories that make it easier for students to learn and remember content?
- Does the teacher effectively sum up lessons at the end of the class?

4. Formative Assessment

Do the teacher and students know if students are mastering content? If a teacher's students are on task, if the teacher has a deep knowledge of the content, knows what's most important and can communicate that knowledge using effective instructional practices, then the final question is whether the teacher and student know how well the students are learning. Several questions will help ICs explore a teacher's understanding of formative assessment:

- Does the teacher know the target or targets the students are aiming for in the class?
- Do the students know the target they are aiming for in the class?
- Does the teacher use formative assessments or checks for understanding to gauge how well students are learning?
- Are students involved in the development and use of formative assessments?
- Can a teacher look out into the classroom and know with some degree of accuracy how well each student is doing?

WHAT DO INSTRUCTIONAL COACHES DO? THE COMPONENTS OF INSTRUCTIONAL COACHING

Instructional coaching, as we define it, has very clear components that enable ICs to respond to the unique challenges of personal change. The eight components of this process (Enroll, Identify, Explain, Model, Observe, Explore, Refine, Reflect) are described as follows.

Enroll

How does an IC get people on board? We propose five methods: (1) one-to-one interviews, (2) small-group presentations, (3) large-group presentations, (4) informal conversations, and (5) administrator referral.

1. One-to-One Interviews

Perhaps the most effective way for coaches to enroll teachers is through the use of one-to-one interviews. One-to-one interviews help ICs achieve at least three goals. First, they are a way to gather specific information about teacher and administrative challenges, student needs, and cultural norms specific to a school. Coaches can use this information to tailor coaching sessions and other professional learning to the unique needs of teachers and students. Second, interviews enable ICs to educate participants about the partnership philosophy, methods, and opportunities offered by Instructional Coaching. During interviews, ICs can explain their partnership approach to coaching, listen to teachers' concerns, and explain that as coaches they are there to help, not to evaluate.

Finally, interviews provide an opportunity for ICs to develop one-to-one relationships with teachers.

How Should One-to-One Interviews Be Conducted? Interviews are most effective when they last at least 30 minutes, and more effective when they are 45 minutes to one hour long (generally, one planning period per interview). While a longer interview allows more time to learn about each person's particular burning issues, and provides more time to build a relationship, a great deal of information can be gathered from 15-minute interviews.

Whenever possible, interviews should be conducted one-to-one. In a group, people tend to comment in ways that are consistent with the cultural norms of their organization (Schein, 1992). One-to-one, on the other hand, allows people to speak much more candidly. Since effective Instructional Coaching may involve overcoming negative or even toxic cultural norms, creating a setting where teachers feel safe stepping outside their culture and speaking frankly is important.

During the Interviews. In most cases, your goals during an interview will be the same regardless of the amount of time available. We have found that it is most valuable to seek answers to at least four general questions:

1. What are the rewards you experience as a teacher?

2. What obstacles interfere with you achieving your professional goals?

3. What are your students' strengths and weaknesses?

4. What kinds of professional learning are most or least effective for you?

When you have more time to conduct interviews, you can broaden or focus the scope of your questions depending on the nature of the professional development session you are planning to lead. (A fairly extensive list of interview questions from which you might draw in structuring your interview can be found in Knight, 2007.)

How to Build Relationships During Interviews. Using interviews as a way to build an emotional connection with collaborating teachers can make it easier for coaches to communicate their message. By positioning themselves as listeners during the interviews, ICs have a chance to make many bids for emotional connection with participants (Gottman, 2001).

During an interview, ICs can share stories, laugh and empathize, offer positive comments, discuss personal issues, and listen with great care. If done well, enrolling interviews provide ICs with many opportunities to listen with empathy, offer encouragement, and reveal themselves as real, caring people.

Asking Teachers to Commit: Contracting. As important as the interview process is for providing you with information about teachers, students, and your school, the most important outcome of the interview process is to obtain commitment from teachers to the coaching process. Many coaches in business and education refer to this as contracting. ICs must find time during the interview to tactfully explain how Instructional Coaching works and what benefits it might offer for the teacher being interviewed. An IC should search for appropriate times in the middle of the interview to explain aspects of Instructional Coaching in response to the teacher's comments.

The goal is to ensure that the teacher knows enough about coaching so that he or she can make an intelligent choice about whether to work with the coach. For that reason, ICs should see the interview as their first chance to demonstrate the respectful, partnering relationship that is at the heart of Instructional Coaching. At the end of the one-to-one interview, ICs should know whether a teacher is ready to collaborate with them, and in most cases the interview is an IC's best strategy for enrolling teachers. As Lucy West (whose chapter appears later in this book) has said, a coach's goal is to meet teachers where they are and offer them resources that uniquely respond to their particular needs.

2. Small-Group Presentations

In some cases, one-to-one interviews are not practical or necessary. One alternative to one-to-one interviews is small group meetings. Usually an IC meets with the teachers during a team meeting, a grade-level meeting, or whatever small group meeting is available.

During the get-together, an IC's goals are quite simple: (a) to explain the opportunities that exist for teachers' professional growth, (b) to clarify the partnership perspective that underlies the coaching relationship, (c) to explain other "nuts and bolts" issues related to instructional coaching, and, most important, (d) to sign up teachers who want to work with a coach.

The presentation during small-group meetings should be short, clear, and respectful. In many cases, this initial conversation is the IC's first opportunity to communicate an authentic respect and admiration for the important activity of teaching. If ICs honestly communicate their genuine respect for teachers, that may go a long way toward opening doors. On the other hand, if an IC appears to communicate a lack of respect for teachers, that may put the IC into a hole that will be very difficult to climb out of.

We suggest that ICs plan for about 20 minutes during small-group meetings. Following the informal presentation, ICs should answer any questions teachers raise. ICs can also provide a one-page summary of the teaching practices teachers can learn as a result of Instructional Coaching, such as classroom management, curriculum planning, teaching to mastery, or formative assessment.

At the close of the small-group presentation, after teachers have heard about the IC's partnership philosophy, the way the IC works, and the teaching practices that the IC can share, ICs should hand out a short form asking teachers to note whether they are interested in collaborating with their IC at this time. The form provides an opportunity for teachers to communicate their interest privately.

3. Large-Group Presentations

In some cases, ICs enroll teachers through a single presentation to a large group, possibly the entire staff. Such a presentation is usually held at the start of the school year, ideally before classes begin, or at the end of the year, to enroll teachers for the following year. A large-group presentation is a good idea when an IC wants to ensure that all teachers hear the same message. Large-group presentations are also effective when an IC is confident that teachers are interested in collaborating with them. As a general rule, the greater the resistance an IC expects to experience with teachers, the smaller the group should be, and when there is any concern that teachers will resist collaborating with ICs, one-to-one interviews are recommended.

ICs can enhance large-group presentations by employing partnership learning structures (Knight, 2009b), learning activities that foster dialogue in the middle of the presentation. For example, ICs might ask teachers to work in groups to identify the top needs of students and then match possible interventions to the identified needs.

At the end of the session, the IC asks participants to complete a form to indicate whether they are interested in collaborating with them. The form might be the same as the one proposed for the small-group session, or the IC might have participants complete a form throughout the presentation. When they employ this presentation tactic, ICs provide a brief explanation of a few teaching practices or interventions, and then they pause to provide time for the audience to write down their thoughts or comments about the practices or interventions that are described. In this way, the teachers have an opportunity to express their thoughts about what they are hearing, and ICs get a lot of helpful feedback. What is essential is that at the end of the session, teachers have a chance to write down whether they are ready to work with the coach, and the IC will have a list of people with whom to start coaching.

4. One-to-One Informal Conversations

Frequently, ICs enroll teachers through casual conversations around the school. ICs who are skilled at getting teachers to commit to collaboration usually are highly skilled relationship builders. An IC shouldn't feel compelled to get every teacher on board immediately; a better tactic is to win over a few teachers with high-quality professional learning on an intervention that really makes a difference for students. In most cases, the IC should seek out a highly effective solution for a troubling problem a teacher is facing. If you respond to a real challenge a teacher is facing with a real solution, word will travel through the school, and teachers will commit to working with their coach.

5. Administrator Referral

When an IC and a principal work together in a school, inevitably there will be occasions when the principal or other administrators identify teachers who need to work with the IC. Principal referral can be a powerful way to accelerate the impact of coaching in a school, but it must be handled with care. If the partnership principles are ignored and struggling teachers are told they must work with a coach (or else!), the IC can be seen as a punishment, not a support, and teachers may come to resent the coach's help.

We suggest a different approach for principal referral, one consistent with the partnership principles. Rather than telling teachers they must work with coaches, we suggest principals focus on the teaching practice that must change, and offer the coach as one way the teacher can bring about the needed change. Thus, a principal might say, "John, when I observed your class I noticed that 10 of your 24 students were off task during your lesson. You need to implement ways to keep those kids on task. Our Instructional Coach Tamika is great at time on task. You might want to talk with her about this, but if you can find another way, that's fine, too. What matters is that more kids are learning. I'll check back in a few weeks, and I expect to see a difference."

In this way, the principal can apply pressure on the teacher while at the same time leaving the IC as one option. Thus, the coach isn't a punishment forced on the teacher, but a lifeline, someone who provides a meaningful support for teachers doing this important and complex work in the classroom. When led to the coach in this way, many teachers are grateful for their coach's support and assistance. If other teachers are able to address the problem in the class in other ways, that is fine too, and it provides ICs with more time to work with teachers who want to work with their coach.

Identify

After enrolling teachers (either through interviews, one-to-one meetings, in small groups, in large groups, or through administrator referral), the IC will have a list of potential collaborating teachers. It is important that ICs reply promptly to every teacher expressing an interest in working with them. If the coach waits too long, the teachers may run out of time to collaborate, become focused on other priorities, or lose their desire to collaborate with the coach.

ICs shouldn't worry too much if their starting list of potential collaborating teachers is short. The list could include most of the school's teachers, but frequently it consists of fewer than 25% of the staff. The length of the list is not that important initially. What really matters is that the experiences of the first few teachers the IC collaborates with are successful because the first teachers will start the word-of-mouth process that should eventually lead to widespread implementation of the teaching practices provided by the coach.

The First Meeting

A lot can be accomplished during the first conversation after a teacher has enrolled in the coaching process. Both parties share the goal of identifying which of the teaching practices the coach has to offer might be most helpful to the teacher. On many occasions, the first conversation is all that is needed for the teacher and coach to identify the teaching practices to be implemented in the teacher's classroom. On other occasions, the first conversation, what some call a preconference, does not always provide enough data to identify where the coach and teacher start. In some cases, the collaborating teacher might not know where to start. Many ICs prefer to observe teachers before identifying a teaching practice. What counts is that the IC and teacher *together* identify a particular best practice that has the greatest chance of making a difference for students and naturally teachers' lives.

Explain

Once the IC and teacher have identified a proven practice to be implemented, the IC has to explain the teaching practice. This is not as easy as it seems. Many teachers' instructional manuals are more than 100 pages long, filled with fairly abstract language and concepts. Add to this, the reality that the amount of time a coach and teacher might spend together can be quite short, and no doubt, will occur in a context of competing priorities. Clearly coaches have their work cut out for them. Nonetheless, to be effective, an IC must translate research into practice. We suggest five tactics that enhance an IC's ability to do this.

1. Clarify

One of the most important and most frequently overlooked practices that ICs can employ is the simple task of reading, writing, and synthesizing what they plan to tell teachers. ICs need to read, reread, take notes, and reread the manuals and research articles that describe the instructional practices they are sharing. A simple overview of a manual is not sufficient. Coaches need to mark up their books, highlight key passages, write in the margins, and cover their manuals with sticky notes. They should have read these materials so frequently that they know the page numbers for key sections and recognize most pages in a manual the way one recognizes an old friend. During and after reading, ICs should write out their understanding of the materials they have read.

Five Tactics for Translating Research Into Practice

1. Clarify: Read, write, talk
2. Synthesize
3. Break it down
4. See it through teachers' (and students') eyes
5. Simplify

This activity might take the form of writing outlines of documents, creating semantic maps or webs, or paraphrasing what has been read into simple language.

Once they have read and written about the materials they've been studying, ICs should seek out opportunities to explain, clarify, modify, and expand their understandings by communicating with others who are knowledgeable about the same interventions. Some ICs use e-mail or the telephone to share ideas with other ICs who are sharing the same practices. Others even contact the authors of the research articles and manuals to ask for their insights. In the best-case scenario, ICs set up informal or formal professional learning communities so they can meet with other ICs to discuss and deepen their knowledge of teaching practices.

2. Synthesize

After clarifying the meaning of research articles and manuals, ICs need to synthesize what they have learned and describe the essential features of the teaching practices they've studied. For some this is accomplished by writing one-to-two sentence statements that capture the essence of the interventions they are sharing with teachers. What matters is that coaches are able to identify and summarize what is most important about the teaching practices they are sharing.

ICs can develop short checklists that summarize the vital teaching behaviors that are essential components of the teaching practices they're sharing. Checklists can provide focus to conversations with teachers and shape the modeling and observing practices used to enable teachers to master successful teaching new practices.

3. Break It Down

As a translator of teaching practices, ICs break down teaching practices into manageable components related to the specific teaching practices to be implemented. There is much coaches can do to make teacher manuals more accessible. Some literally tear apart manuals and divide them into easy-to-understand sections that they put into binders. ICs can also highlight important passages or put sticky notes beside especially important sections of a manual. When breaking down materials, ICs should ensure that teachers know exactly what needs to be done next. As personal productivity guru David Allen (2001) has observed, "It never fails to greatly improve both the productivity and the peace of mind of the user to determine what the next physical action is that will move something forward" (p. 237).

4. See It Through Teachers' (and Students') Eyes

ICs must plan their explanations by thinking carefully about what the new practice will look like in the classroom. In this way, ICs can address the practical concerns that teachers might have. For example, they might think through a number of classroom management issues, such as handing out papers, organizing grading assignments, or handling movement in the classroom. ICs might also discuss how to incorporate formative assessments into a lesson or explain what expectations should be taught when a certain teaching practice is introduced. Throughout the explanation, the IC should be intent on removing teachers' anxiety and making it easier for them to understand and eventually use a new teaching practice.

5. Simplify

ICs should not dumb down complex ideas and make them simplistic. As Bill Jensen said in his book *Simplicity: The New Competitive Advantage in a World of More, Better, Faster* (2000), we should not confuse "simplistic" with simplicity. Simplicity, Jensen explains, is "the art of making the complex clear" (p. 2). And "making the complex clear always helps people work smarter. Because it is a lot easier to figure out what's important and ignore what isn't" (Jensen, 2000, p. i).

There are many things coaches can do to attain simpler explanations. Jensen (2000) proposes storytelling as a communication strategy that "easily creates common meaning and purpose for everyone" (p. 88). ICs can use stories to help teachers see what a teaching practice might look like in the classroom. Additionally, ICs should look for analogies, anecdotes, or simple explanations and comparisons that bring the materials to life.

Model: You Watch Me

ICs, as we define them, spend a great deal of their time in classrooms modeling lessons, watching teachers teach, and having conversations about what teachers saw when they watched the IC, or what the IC saw when he or she watched the teachers. Since some teachers find the business of observation somewhat intimidating, ICs try to keep the experience as informal as possible: "You watch me; I watch you."

The Observation Form

Before conducting a model lesson, an IC must ensure that the collaborating teachers are prepared to get the most out of it—that they know what to watch for and, in fact, are actually watching the model lesson. ICs can develop a shared understanding of the purpose of the model lesson by coconstructing with the teacher an observation form to help focus the attention of both the teacher and the IC. The observation form is a simple chart on which the IC, in partnership with the collaborating teacher, lists the critical teaching behaviors that a teacher should be watching for when watching a model lesson.

The observation form includes a column for listing these behaviors, one where teachers can put a check mark every time they observe a critical teaching behavior, and a column where they can include comments, questions, or thoughts about what they observe during a model lesson. By coconstructing the form with teachers prior to the model lesson, ICs can check for teachers' understanding of critical teaching behaviors. Later, by having teachers fill out the form during a model lesson, they can focus the teachers' attention on what matters most in the model. Of course, a coach and IC don't need a preconstructed form; they can simply create one on a sheet of paper.

Checklists of critical teaching behaviors can help coaches clarify and synthesize their understanding of teaching practices. However, we have found that giving a ready-made checklist to teachers is not as effective as coconstructing an observation form. Although the IC ensures that the coconstructed form includes most of the critical teaching behaviors on the original checklist, by involving the teacher in creating the form, a coach gets better buy-in to the form and can be more certain that the collaborating teacher understands all of the items listed on it. Also, teachers frequently suggest teaching behaviors for the form that the coach might not have considered but that are important. Thus, by involving teachers in the process as partners, we actually get a better product.

Giving a Model Lesson

Before providing model lessons, ICs must ensure that they have a deep understanding of the lesson they are modeling. Prior to the lesson, the IC and collaborating teacher also need to clarify their roles with respect to behavior management in the classroom. In some cases, teachers want to retain their role as manager of classroom behavior. In other situations, teachers are very comfortable with the IC taking primary responsibility for managing behavior during the model lesson. Both the teacher and IC must know how behavior will be managed. As every experienced teacher knows, students seem to have a sixth sense that makes them very sensitive to any vacuum in leadership with respect to classroom management, and if no one is in control, students can be off task in minutes, possibly seconds.

We have found that it is most effective for coaches to model only the specific practice that is described on an observation form, rather than model an entire lesson. During the model, the teacher observes the coach, using the observation form to focus his or her attention, checking off behaviors when the teacher sees them modeled by the coach. ICs need to be careful to include the teacher in the lesson and ensure that students know that they, the ICs, are just visitors in the teacher's classroom. Additionally, the coach should defer to the experience of the teacher throughout the lesson.

Observe: I Watch You

After the collaborating teacher has watched the coach provide a model lesson and then discussed his or her thoughts and questions about it with the IC, it is time for the IC to observe the teacher. While watching the teacher, the IC does the same as the teacher did while watching the model lesson: the IC watches for the critical teaching behaviors they identified using a copy of the coconstructed observation form that the teacher used to observe the coach when he or she did the model lesson. And, as the teacher did earlier, the IC watches the teacher carefully and checks off the form every time he or she sees the teacher perform one of the identified critical teaching behaviors.

Since teachers have already used the form to watch the IC's model lesson, they are usually quite comfortable with their IC using the form in the classroom. However, ICs need to be careful to stress the informality of the observation, which is why we emphasize the idea of simply saying, "You watch me, and I watch you." For some teachers, the very notion of "observation" is intimidating, and some ICs avoid using that term, choosing to say instead that they'll "visit" the classroom. If an IC is careful to watch for and record the many good aspects of the lesson that is observed, however, teachers will become much less reticent about inviting the IC to watch lessons.

As an observer, the IC should try to remove personal judgments from the activity of observing. Rather than seeing themselves as evaluating teachers, coaches should see themselves as a second set of eyes in the room, using the observation form or other data-gathering methods as tools for recording relevant data about how the lesson proceeds. While observing, the IC should especially attend to the collaborating teacher's efforts to use the critical teaching practices. Whenever the teacher uses one of the critical behaviors, the IC should check the appropriate column of the observation form, and write down specific data about how the teacher used the behavior. For example, if a critical teaching behavior is to explain expectations to students, the IC might jot down a quick summary of exactly what the teacher said when he or she clarified expectations.

What data the coach records during the observation vary, depending on what intervention teachers are learning to use. In many cases, the IC will only need to use the observation form to gather the necessary data. Other interventions require other kinds of data gathering. For example, ICs who are coaching teachers to increase the number of high-level questions used might simply write down each question posed by the teacher so that the coach and teacher can review them later. ICs who are coaching teachers with respect to "opportunities to respond" (the number of times students are invited to speak or interact during a lesson) might simply keep a tally of the number of opportunities to respond provided during a lesson. Thus, ICs may use the observation forms or other data-gathering methods depending on the teaching practice being learned.

While observing the lesson and gathering data, an IC has to be especially careful to note positive actions taking place in the class, such as effective interventional practices or positive student responses. While intuitively an IC might think that the most important part of observing a lesson is to find areas of weakness that need to be improved, in reality, the most important part of the observation may be to look for things the teacher does well. Seeing what needs to be improved is often quite easy; seeing, recording, and communicating what went well sometimes requires extra effort.

ICs who are highly sensitive to the positive things that take place in the classroom can provide a great service to the teachers and the school. Too often the challenges of being an educator, and the emotional exhaustion that comes with trying to reach every child every day, makes it difficult for teachers to fully comprehend the good they are doing. Furthermore, conversations in schools sometimes have a tendency to turn negative, perhaps as a defense mechanism for teachers who are frustrated that they cannot reach more students. Thus, ICs should consider it one of their goals to change the kind of conversations that take place in schools, one conversation at a time.

Explore: The Collaborative Exploration of Data

As soon as possible after observing a lesson, an IC should schedule a follow-up meeting with the collaborating teacher to discuss the data that was collected. This meeting, like other aspects of the Instructional Coaching process, is based on the mutual respect between professionals inherent in the partnership principles. The collaborative exploration of data taking place during this meeting is *not* an opportunity for the IC to share his or her "expert" opinion on what the teacher did right or wrong.

More than anything else it is a learning conversation where both parties use data as a point of departure for dialogue.

This meeting is not an opportunity for top-down feedback. Top-down feedback, as Figure 9.1 suggests, occurs when one person, an expert, watches a novice and provides feedback until the novice masters a skill. This might be a great way to teach some skills, but it is problematic as a model for interaction between professionals who are peers.

Figure 9.1   Top-Down Feedback

The problem with top-down feedback is that it is based on the assumption that there is only one right way to see things, and that right way is the view held by the feedback giver. Kegan and Lahey (2001) explain the assumptions of this approach:

> The first [assumption] is that the perspective of the feedback giver (let's call him the supervisor)—what he sees and thinks, his feedback—is right, is correct. An accompanying assumption is that there is only one correct answer. When you put these two assumptions together, they amount to this: the supervisor has the one and only correct view of the situation. (We call this "the super vision assumption"; that is, the supervisor has *super* vision). (p. 128)

During top-down feedback, the feedback giver is prepared to "(1) say exactly what the person is doing wrong, (2) give the sense the criticism is meant to help, (3) suggest a solution, and (4) give a timely message" (Kegan & Lahey, 2001, p. 128). The person giving top-down feedback, in other words, working from the assumption that he or she is right, does all of the thinking for the person receiving the feedback. That is hardly the partnership approach, and the reason why Kegan and Lahey (2001) say, "many a relationship has been damaged and a work setting poisoned by *perfectly delivered* constructive feedback!" (p. 128).

An alternative to top-down feedback is the partnership approach or the collaborative exploration of data. As depicted in the Figure 9.2, during the partnership approach, the IC and teacher sit side by side as partners and review the data that the IC has gathered. The IC does not withhold his

Figure 9.2   Collaborative Exploration of Data

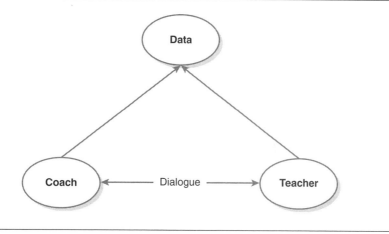

or her opinion, but offers it in a provisional way, communicating that he or she is open to other points of view.

A Language of Ongoing Regard

One important goal ICs should hold during the collaborative exploration of data is to communicate clearly the genuinely positive aspects of the lesson that was observed. I do not mean that they should be promoting thoughtless, vague, or empty happy words or phrases. A "language of ongoing regard" has specific characteristics. Kegan and Lahey (2001) stress that authentic, appreciative, or admiring feedback needs to be (a) direct, (b) specific, and (c) nonattributive. Most ICs recognize the importance of direct, specific feedback. Direct comments are spoken to a person in the first person, not about a person in the third person. Thus, it is preferable to tell someone directly, "I appreciate your help," rather than saying publicly, "I appreciate Jean's help." Specific comments clearly explain the details of what we are praising, rather than offering general statements. Thus, it is preferable to say, "You asked 42 questions today during your class," in contrast to "you asked a lot of questions today in your class."

The importance of making nonattributive comments may be less obvious. Kegan and Lahey (2001) explain that our positive comments about others are more effective when we describe our experience of others rather than the attributes of others. For example, it is less effective to say to someone, "You're very patient" (describing an attribute that we judge them to have), than it is to say, "You waited 10 seconds for Alison to give her answer, and when she got it right, she lit up like a Christmas tree." Kegan and Lahey explain why nonattribute feedback is more effective:

> It may seem odd to you that we're urging you not to make statements of this sort: "Carlos, I just want you to know how much I appreciate how generous you are" (or: "what a good sense of humor you have" or "that you always know the right thing to say"), or "Alice, you are so patient" (or, "so prompt," "so never-say-die," "always there when you are needed,"), and so on. . . . These seem like such nice things to say to someone. . . . The problem we see is this: the person, inevitably and quite properly, relates what you say to how she knows herself to be. You can tell Carlos he is generous, but he knows how generous he actually is. You can tell Alice she is very patient, but she knows her side of how patient she is being with you. (p. 99)

Learning how to give direct, specific, nonattributive feedback is a skill that every IC should develop and one that can be practiced and developed daily until it becomes a habit of thought. ICs can practice developing this "language of ongoing regard" at their workplace, but they can also practice it with their children, parents, spouse, or other people in their life. There is great benefit in practicing such feedback until it becomes a habitual way of communicating. Indeed, it seems strange that we often feel uncomfortable telling people directly and specifically why we appreciate them. Perhaps we're afraid our comments will seem insincere or self-serving flattery. Nothing could be further from the truth. As Kegan and Lahey (2001) state, "Ongoing regard is not about praising, stroking, or positively defining a person to herself or to others. We say again: it is about enhancing the quality of a precious kind of information. It is about informing the person about *our* experience of him or her" (p. 101).

Dialogue

Frequently, during the collaborative exploration of data, the IC and teacher swiftly move toward identifying next steps that they both agree will have the most positive impact on teaching. On other occasions, however, the IC and teacher hold different opinions about the significance of the data or what the teachers' next steps should be. The best route for ICs to take here is not to withhold their perspective or push for their perspective.

Partnership involves two equals sharing ideas, and this doesn't require one person to suppress or promote his or her ideas for another's. Rather, when the IC and the collaborating teacher see the data differently, the coach, acting on one of the partnership principles, can employ the tools of dialogue to foster an authentic learning conversation. When skillfully handled, a dialogue about differing perceptions of data can help both the IC and the teacher learn a great deal.

Refine

The components of coaching discussed in this chapter are the primary activities carried out by ICs. Usually, ICs use most or all of these components, but the sequence in which the components have been described is not always followed. Sometimes the IC opens the door to a teacher's classroom by offering to model a lesson. Sometimes coaching begins with the IC observing. Sometimes the IC provides several model lessons. Each coaching sequence must be tailored to the unique needs of each individual teacher.

During coaching, the IC provides as much support as necessary, but no more. In most cases, after a teacher has mastered a new teaching practice, the coach and teacher choose to move on to some other intervention. What matters is that the teacher and the IC keep learning together, working as partners to ensure that students receive excellent instruction.

Reflect

When an IC moves through the components of coaching with a teacher, both the teacher and the coach should be learning. The teacher is learning a new teaching practice. At the same time, the coach could be learning any number of new skills or insights related to working with students, providing model lessons, enrolling teachers in the Instructional Coaching process, building relationships, addressing teachers' core concerns, or any other aspect of Instructional Coaching. Every day provides numerous learning experiences for even the most experienced coaches.

To ensure that they do not forget what they learn along the way, many coaches keep journals, either on their computers or in hand-written notebooks, to record the important things they learn. ICs can also use a reflective practice developed by the U.S. Army—After-Action Review (AAR). According to *The U.S. Army Leadership Field Manual* (U.S. Army, 2004), "An AAR is a professional discussion of an event, focused on performance standards, that allow participants to discover for themselves what happened, why it happened, and how to sustain strengths and improve on weaknesses" (p. 6). Put another way, the AAR structures reflection on (a) what was supposed to happen, (b) what really happened, (c) why there's a difference between (a) and (b), and (c) what should be done differently next time.

WHAT FACTORS INCREASE THE SUCCESS OF COACHING PROGRAMS?

If ICs are going to be successful, they must work in a context that supports their focus on instruction. A few simple factors can make all the difference in the effectiveness of any coaching program.

Time

The simplest way to improve the effectiveness of a coaching program is to increase the amount of time coaches are actually coaching. This seems obvious, but the most frequent concern raised by the more than 2,000 instructional coaches we have worked with in the past four years was that they are asked to complete so many noninstructional tasks they have little time left to work with teachers. Because instructional coaches' job descriptions are often vague or nonexistent and because their schedules are more flexible than the schedules of others, they often are asked to do many clerical or noninstructional tasks. Paying ICs to copy and bind standards documents or shop for math lab furniture or serve as substitute teachers is a poor way to spend money and perhaps an even poorer way to improve teaching practices in schools.

In Cecil County, Maryland, ICs and administrators address this issue by drawing up a pie chart that depicts exactly how much time they agree coaches should spend on various tasks. Then, each week the coaches report to their principals how their time was spent. If necessary, this allows the coach and principal to adjust the time allocations so they can focus their efforts on improving instruction.

Proven Research-Based Interventions

If ICs are going to make a difference in the way teachers teach, they need to have scientifically proven practices to share. Hiring coaches but not ensuring they have proven practices is a bit like trying to paint a beautiful painting without any art supplies. ICs need to have a repertoire of tools to help them assist teachers in addressing their most pressing concerns.

ICs working with the Center for Research on Learning discover interventions that address The Big Four areas of behavior, content knowledge, instruction, and formative assessment. The coaches develop a deep understanding of scientifically proven practices they can share with teachers to help them improve in any or all of the four areas.

One way to address this concern is for the coach, principal, and other school leaders to come to a shared understanding of excellent instruction. Then, the team should identify what tools are necessary for all teachers to become excellent. Finally, the coach and team should identify how the coach can develop proficiency in those practices so that they can be shared with others in the school. Tools such as *The Big Four: A Framework for*

Instructional Excellence (Knight, 2009a) or Charlotte Danielson's (1996) *Enhancing Professional Practice: A Framework for Teaching* can be very helpful when doing this task.

Professional Development for Instructional Coaches

Coaches need to understand the interventions they are sharing, and they need to understand how to productively employ the coaching process. Without their own professional development, ICs run the risk of being ineffective, wasting time and money, or even misinforming teachers. Therefore, the coaches need to participate in their own professional development to ensure that they know how to coach and what to share when they coach teachers.

Professional development for coaches should address at least two subjects. First, coaches should engage in various professional learning activities designed to improve their coaching practices. Specifically, ICs affiliated with our center learn how to employ powerful, proven practices to (a) enroll teachers in coaching, (b) identify appropriate interventions for teachers to learn, (c) model and gather data in the classroom, and (d) engage in dialogue about classroom and other data. Additionally, they improve their professional skills in areas such as communication, relationship building, change management, and leadership.

Second, professional development for coaches should deepen ICs knowledge about the teaching practices they are sharing with teachers. Obviously, if coaches have a superficial knowledge of the information they share with teachers, they will not know what to emphasize when they discuss, model, or observe during professional learning with teachers. Indeed, coaches who do not deeply understand what they are sharing with teachers could misinform teachers and actually make things worse, not better, for students.

Protecting the Coaching Relationship

Many, perhaps most, teachers see their profession as an integral part of their self-identity. Consequently, if coaches or others are careless with their comments or suggestions about teachers' practices in the classroom, they run the risk of offending teachers, damaging relationships, or at the very least not being heard. Because teaching is such a personal activity, coaches need to win teachers' trust. Trust is an essential component of an open coaching relationship.

To make it easier for coaches to maintain trusting partnerships with teachers, educational leaders must protect the coaching relationship. If leaders ask coaches to hold the dual role of administrator and coach, they put their coaches in a difficult situation. Administrators, by definition, are not peers. Usually people are more guarded when they talk with their bosses than when they talk with their peers. Coaches will find it easier to have open conversations about teaching practices if their collaborating teachers do not view them as bosses and, therefore, do not have to worry about how their comments might affect the way they will be evaluated.

Ensuring That Principals and Coaches Work Together

The IC can be and should be the right-hand person of the principal when it comes to instructional leadership in schools, but the principal must remain the instructional leader. No matter how much a coach knows, and no matter how effective a coach is, the principal's voice is ultimately the voice most important to teachers. For that reason, coaches must understand fully what their principal's vision is for school improvement, and principals need to understand fully the interventions that their coach has to offer teachers.

One way to ensure that principals get the most out of their ICs is to provide them with sufficient training. Principals who do not understand the importance of protecting the coaching relationship may act in ways that make it difficult for a coach to be successful. Also, a principal who is unaware of the tools that an IC can offer will be unable to suggest them to teachers who might benefit from learning them. District administrators around the country are addressing these issues by providing coaching professional development for principals. Another way to ensure that principals are on the same page as their coaches is for coaches and principals to meet frequently.

Hiring the Right Instructional Coaches

All the factors described here will not yield success if the wrong people are hired to be coaches. Indeed, the most critical factor related to the success or failure of a coaching program may be the skills and attributes of the IC.

Over the past 10 years, we have found that ICs must be excellent teachers, particularly because they will likely provide model lessons in other teachers' classrooms. They also need to be flexible since their job requires them to change their plans almost daily to meet the changing needs of teachers.

Coaches should be highly skilled at building relationships. In our experience, whether a teacher adopts a new teaching practice has as much to do with the IC's communication skills as with whatever intervention the coach has to share. Simply put, if teachers like a coach, they usually will try out what the coach suggests. If they don't like the coach, they'll resist even good teaching practices.

Jim Collins' study of great organizations offers additional insight into the desirable attributes of effective coaches. Great leaders, Collins (2005) writes, "are ambitious first and foremost for the cause, the movement, the mission, the work—not themselves—and they have the will to do whatever it takes to . . . make good on that ambition" (p. 11).

The attributes Collins identifies in great leaders are also found in the best ICs. They need to be ambitious for change in their schools and willing to do, as Collins emphasizes, "whatever it takes" to improve teaching practices. If a coach is too passive about change, chances are that little will happen in the school. At the same time, if a coach is too self-centered or aggressive, there is a good chance the coach will push teachers away.

Effective coaches embody what Collins (2001) describes as a "compelling combination of personal humility and professional will" (p. 13). They are affirmative, humble, and deeply respectful of teachers, but they are unwilling to rest unless they achieve significant improvements in teaching and learning in their schools.

Evaluating Coaches

Evaluation is a major mechanism for continuous improvement of any coaching program. Evaluating ICs can offer unique challenges because no one in a district, including the principal, may ever have been a coach before, and there may be no guidelines for evaluating coaches.

One way to address this challenge is to involve coaches in the process of creating guidelines, standards, and tools to be used for their evaluation. Involving coaches in the process of writing their evaluation guidelines accomplishes at least three goals. First, it enables school districts to develop a rubric for evaluating coaches that is especially designed for coaches. Second, it increases coaches' buy-in to the guidelines and the process of being evaluated since they created them. Third, the dialogue coaches have while creating the guidelines is an excellent form of professional learning.

CONCLUSION

ICs make a very important contribution to school improvement by partnering with teachers to help them find better ways to reach more students. ICs who work from the partnership perspective can employ the components of coaching as a methodology for sharing proven practices with teachers. In some cases, they might focus on The Big Four practices of (1) classroom management, (2) content enhancement, (3) instruction, and (4) assessment for learning. When coaches understand effective tools to address The Big Four, when they know how to work with teachers, and when they work in schools that embody the success factors listed earlier, there is every reason to assume that they will have an unmistakable positive impact on how teachers teach and how students learn in schools.

REFERENCES

Allen, D. (2001). *Getting things done: The art of stress-free productivity.* New York: Penguin.

Bernstein, R . J. (1983). *Beyond objectivism and relativism: Science, hermeneutics, and praxis.* Philadelphia: University of Pennsylvania.

Billmeyer, R., & Barton, M. (1998). *Teaching reading in the content areas: If not me, then who?* (2nd ed). Denver, CO: Mid-continent Research for Education and Research.

Block, P. (1993). *Stewardship: Choosing service over self-interest.* San Francisco: Berrett-Koehler.

Block, P. (2001). *The answer to how is yes: Acting on what matters.* San Francisco: Berrett-Koehler.

Collins, J. (2001). *Good to great: Why some companies make the leap . . . and others don't.* New York: HarperCollins.

Collins, J. (2005). *Good to great and the social sectors: A monograph to accompany* Good to Great. Boulder, CO: Collins.

Danielson, C. (1996). *Enhancing professional practice: A framework for teaching.* Alexandria, VA: Association for Supervision and Curriculum Development.

Eisler, R. (1998). *Chalice and the blade: Our history, our future.* New York: HarperCollins.

Eisler, R. (2000). *Tomorrow's children: A blueprint for partnership education for the 21st century.* Boulder, CO: Westview.

Feyerabend, P. (1988). *Against method* (Rev. ed.). London: Verso.

Friere, P. (1970). *Pedagogy of the oppressed.* New York: Continuum.

Gottman, J. M. (2001). *The relationship cure: A five-step guide for building better connections with family, friends, and lovers.* New York: Crown.

Greenleaf, R. K. (2001). *Servant leadership: A journey into the legitimate nature of power and greatness* (L. C. Spears, Ed.). Mahwah, NJ: Paulist.

Jensen, B. (2000). *Simplicity: The new competitive advantage in a world of more, better, faster.* New York: HarperCollins.

Kegan, R., & Lahey, L. (2001). *How the way we talk can change the way we work: Seven languages for transformation.* San Francisco: Jossey-Bass.

Knight, J. (1992). Strategies go to college. *Preventing School Failure, 38*(1), 36–42.

Knight, J. (1999). *Partnership learning: A dialogical method for planning and delivering staff development sessions.* Paper presented at the meeting of the American Educational Research Association, Montreal, Canada.

Knight, J. (2007.) *Instructional coaching: A partnership approach to improving instruction.* Thousand Oaks, CA: Corwin Press.

Knight, J. (2009a). *The big four: A framework for instructional excellence.* Manuscript in preparation.

Knight, J. (2009b) *Partnership learning: Scientifically proven strategies for fostering dialogue during workshops and presentations.* Manuscript in preparation.

Knowles, M. S. (1988). *The modern practice of adult education: From pedagogy to andragogy* (Rev. ed.). Englewood, CO: Prentice Hall Regents.

Kuhn, T. S. (1970). *The structure of scientific revolutions* (2nd ed.). Chicago: University of Chicago.

Marzano, R. J., Pickering, D., & Pollock, J. E. (2001). *Classroom instruction that works: Research based strategies for increasing student achievement.* Alexandria, VA: Association for Supervision and Curriculum Development.

Schein, E. H. (1992). *Organizational culture and leadership* (2nd ed.). San Francisco: Jossey-Bass.

Senge, P. M. (1990). *The fifth discipline: The art and practice of the learning organization.* London: Random House.

Sprick, R., Knight, J., Reinke, W., & McKale, T. (2006). *Coaching classroom management: A toolkit for coaches and administrators.* Eugene, OR: Pacific Northwest Publishing.

U.S. Army. (2004). *The U.S. Army leadership field manual.* New York: McGraw-Hill.

10

Content Coaching

Transforming the Teaching Profession

Lucy West

Content coaching is a practical and powerful method for improving instruction and student learning. The *essence* of content coaching is simple: to improve learning teachers must focus on relevant, important, rich content. Robust lessons center around big ideas in a given domain and give students opportunities to grapple with significant problems or issues using reasoning and discourse particular to that domain. For example, mathematicians may seek to prove a conjecture logically whereas literary critics might attempt to make inferences about characters based on excerpts from a text. The premise of content coaching rests on the hypothesis that improved instruction significantly improves learning.

The *practice* of content coaching is sophisticated and nuanced. Content coaching is an iterative process centering on thoughtful lesson design, skilled enactment of lessons, reflective analysis of student learning, and use of that analysis to construct ensuing lessons. Content coaches possess knowledge and understanding of the content of their discipline, awareness of which concepts within that discipline are appropriate for students at various stages, knowledge of current learning theories, a varied repertoire of instructional strategies aligned with those theories, and an understanding of organizations as living, dynamic systems. The goal of content coaching is to cultivate teachers' academic habits of reasoning and discourse associated with their particular discipline and to help them develop a specific skill set that will enable them to cultivate those same habits in their students, habits which will promote student appreciation and understanding of the subject at hand. Unlike some models of coaching, which focus almost exclusively on building collaborative professional learning cultures, content coaching views attending to content as a critical aspect of the coaching process.

THE BIG PICTURE

Content coaching is *evolving* in tandem with the standards movement, the trend toward the professionalization of teaching (Saphier, 2005), growing research findings on the nature of learning (Dweck, 2002; National Research Council, 2005; Resnick, 1995), and complexity or systems theories of change (Elmore, 2004; Fullan, 2004; Senge, 1990; Wheatley, 2001). Content coaching is grounded in a set of principles of learning articulated by Lauren Resnick and initially practiced in Community School District 2, New York City (1995–2003), during the time the model was under development (see Figure 10.1). The principles of learning underpinning the model are gleaned from the research and based on an emerging theory of intelligence called the incremental theory of intelligence. The theory of incremental intelligence, in turn, is emerging from the fields of biology, brain research, and cognitive psychology. The theory posits that we can indeed become smarter by becoming cognizant of who we are as learners and by applying the right kinds of effort and metacognitive strategies to whatever it is we want to learn or accomplish. In practice, this theory of intelligence implies that educational models should be more effort based and less ability based. Resnick and Hall (2000) speak to the shift in emphasis from ability to effort when they say the following:

> There is a third logical possibility about the relationship between ability and effort, one that holds the potential to resolve the tension between aptitude- and effort-oriented belief systems. The third possibility, the newest vision, is that an effort-based system actually can *create* intelligence. Ability is created through certain kinds of effort on the part of learners and reciprocally on the part of educators who are working with those learners. Jeff Howard expresses this notion in a way that particularly captures young people's imagination: Smart isn't something you are, it's something you get. (p. 3)

The policies of most American schools (e.g., tracking systems, gifted programs, excessive use of special education) stem from an ability-based view of intelligence, which contributes in part to the kind of achievement gaps we see across the nation. Such a view sees children through a lens that may prove debilitating to many, a view that leads educators—thinking they are protecting the self image of students and preventing their failure—to deny them access to rigorous curriculum and to challenging experiences. The denial of such a curriculum is a reflection of a lack of belief in students' capabilities. These ingrained, insidious, ubiquitous, and unexamined beliefs proliferate in our schools, in spite of avowals that "every child can learn." The result is a large number of students drowning in a sea of low expectations, denied an optimal opportunity to learn. Unfortunately, supervisors and coaches too frequently hold similar views about teachers, such as "some people are born to teach; others just haven't got the knack," which leads to a failure to invest in the coaching that could help teachers develop their knowledge and skills.

Figure 10.1   Effort-Based Principles of Learning

• Socializing intelligence	• Self-management of learning
• Academic rigor in a thinking curriculum	• Learning as apprenticeship
• Accountable talk	• Fair and credible evaluations
• Clear expectations	• Recognition of accomplishment

SOURCE: Resnick and Hall (2000).

It turns out that Asian societies are more prone to effort-based beliefs (Stiegler & Hiebert, 1999) that result in effort-based professional learning opportunities like Lesson Study. Lesson Study is a Japanese model of improving teaching practice in part through collaborative attention to the details of a lesson, by a group of teachers ranging from novice to veteran, generally in primary school with assistance from university faculty. It is an example of implementing an incremental theory of intelligence in professional practice. Teaching is a complex and learnable craft (Saphier, 2005). People can learn to become very competent teachers. One is not necessarily "born" a great teacher. In other words, we can take the effort-based theory of intelligence and apply it to adult learning as well as to student learning. Content coaching aims to do just that.

PRINCIPLES OF LEARNING AND COACHING

These principles of learning are foundational in the work between coach and teacher just as they are in the classroom. The principles incorporate a learning stance that posits that all substantive learning requires effort. Intelligent effort results in the development of capacities we may not "naturally" possess. To put it simply, "effort creates intelligence" (Resnick,

1995). Content coaching is an effort-based process through which professionals learn to be more effective teachers.

Accountable Talk

Content coaching employs the same set of principles with adults that most of us want to see employed in classrooms, for example, dialog. It is well documented that people learn through conversation (Allington, 2000; Resnick, 1995). In content coaching we engage in substantive discourse around core instructional issues. The discourse (accountable talk) is accountable to the professional community, the academic domain, and to rigorous reasoning based on evidence (Resnick, 1995).

In our coaching sessions, we wonder aloud about the important dilemmas and complexities of meeting standards, getting high test scores, and, most important of all, ensuring that all our students are really learning important content. As we discuss such issues, we reflect on our talk to become aware of our professional habits of discourse. If we are committed to respectful, honest, focused dialog, we will more likely be able to facilitate robust, rigorous dialog in our classes.

In many coaching sessions we reflect on the discourse of students and how the teacher might facilitate student talk and learn from that talk. In class we invent techniques or try on research-based strategies designed to get our students talking about their thinking, and we then contemplate what student comments reveal about their understanding.

Self-Management of Learning

Each of the principles of learning can be used to influence how a lesson will be enacted and to shape the work among adults. *Self-management of learning* (Dweck, 2002; Resnick, 1995), also referred to as *habits of mind* (Costa & Kallick, 2000), is another principle that could be considered on both the adult and student levels. What habits of mind or learning strategies do each of us employ as we work to refine our craft? Can we articulate what we do as we try to learn a new instructional strategy or deepen our content knowledge? Do we know when to ask for assistance, where to go for information, when to persevere, and when to let go and give ourselves time and space for things to percolate? Such habits of self-reflection and self-awareness are crucial life skills and are all namable, learnable strategies that successful people employ. When we become conscious of such strategies personally and professionally, we can name them. Once we can name them, we can incorporate the cultivation of these life skills in our lesson designs so that our students can adopt them and learn to take charge of their own learning. This holistic approach to teaching and learning is foreign to many teachers, especially to secondary teachers who often view their job as teaching "math" or "science" rather than as also teaching *students* how to learn math or science.

Socializing Intelligence

The idea of working together to shape the learning among us might be called "socializing intelligence" (Resnick & Nelson-Le Gall, 1997). It is a principle that builds on Vygotsky's finding that we learn through social interactions. In fact, as professionals, we "enculture" one another just as we enculture our students. One of the prevailing cultural aspects of too many schools is the culture of isolation—teachers working independently from one another as if what they do or don't do in their classrooms has no impact on the school as a whole. Each teacher works in a vacuum, designing lessons and struggling to meet student needs, with neither input from others nor the opportunity to provide input to others, as if they were isolated heroes with the weight of the world on their shoulders. In many schools teachers are aware that a colleague's class is not one they would want their own child to be assigned to, and yet no one takes any productive steps toward upgrading the instruction in that room. Teachers who need help don't receive it, and teachers who have great success are often loath to share their secrets because the school culture is a competitive or "star" environment rather than a collaborative learning environment. Many veteran teachers become exhausted and cynical in such cultures.

Sometimes, as a survival strategy and to keep passion alive, teachers may tap informal networks for advice or companionship in the work. These informal networks, however, often lack focus, structure, or administrative support and ebb and flow under the dictates of time pressures and conflicting demands. In some schools today, there is a movement toward common meeting periods. While this is a step toward collaboration, unless the purpose of "common periods" is clearly centered on improving instruction and learning, we often perpetuate the very culture we are trying to change. Teachers may use the time to discuss administrative issues or to complain about administrators, other teachers, parents, and students, and myriad other things. As to what's working in the school or classroom, they may take a stand of "I know" rather than "I wonder" or "what if," and on issues of disagreement, they may just end up agreeing to disagree. Agreeing to disagree essentially leaves everyone comfortably right where they started.

Content coaching is one means of beginning to "reculture" schools into collaborative *learning* environments in which adults work together to help each other and to assist *all* the students in their community to succeed. Educators see the school as "the village" in which each student is everyone's student. Adults "publicly and explicitly" engage in learning as "learners," thereby giving their students a living model of what "lifelong learning" looks like. In a content coaching environment, common periods are used to design and analyze lessons, study student work, and collaboratively invent ways to assist students who aren't succeeding when we employ the prevailing instructional practices. Teachers often coteach and talk with each other in front of their students about the choices they're making or the questions they have. They walk the talk of taking risks and learning together publicly.

Learning as Apprenticeship

Another principle of learning is that of making the learning as experiential as possible. The coteaching example provided earlier is an "experiential" approach to improving practice. The people who are coteaching might be coach and teacher or two teachers who are peer coaching one another. Coaching can be thought of as an "apprenticeship model" of teaching. The important distinction about the content coaching apprenticeship model is that it is not idiosyncratic in nature. It employs the accumulated knowledge we have as a profession about teaching and learning and provides tools to develop coherence across practitioners. Content coaching is a principled practice which assumes that "best practice" is always evolving as new research informs the field. Content coaching takes a "scholarly" approach to the study of teaching and learning and focuses specifically on the pedagogical content knowledge needed for a particular domain.

THE WORK

Content coaching defines "the work" as lesson design, enactment, diagnosis, and enhancement of student learning—the instructional core. Content-focused coaching does not advocate for a specific program, set of materials, or one particular instructional strategy. Content coaches keep an eye on the bigger picture—effective instruction as *evidenced by student learning*. We engage in respectful, meaningful, ongoing dialog centering on the core issues of teaching and learning. We consider all resources, including curriculum materials, as *tools*. The job of the educator is to select and utilize the appropriate tools in the service of learning. No tool can do all things. Using a carpenter's tool kit as an analogy, you don't want to use a screwdriver when you need to hammer a nail. A worksheet would not be the appropriate tool for grappling with complex ideas. Group work is a good choice when the problem is rich enough to engage more than one person. Individual interviews or writing samples would be useful tools for discovering what individual students are thinking.

Too often coaches are hired to be "salespeople." The district wants the coach to convince the teacher to "buy in" to the use of particular materials or strategies instead of engaging with teachers to solve authentic dilemmas related to teaching and learning identified by the district and teachers. (I am not meaning to imply that teachers have carte blanche to ignore an adopted curriculum. I discuss this further later.) Whatever strategies or materials that are being used must make sense to the practitioner using them. It is possible to build coherence and also provide for individual freedom when everyone keeps an eye on student learning as the bottom line. This stance is critical to developing powerful and satisfying solutions to complex problems.

TOOLS OF THE PROFESSION

Curriculum materials, programs, pacing guides, standards, and assessments are tools. The use of a specific tool implies agreement with the beliefs informing the tool. Think of a compass. If you use a compass to find your way through the woods, you believe that the earth has a magnetic force, that the needle on the compass always points north, that there are four cardinal directions, and so forth, and that use of this tool can take you in the direction you want to go. If you lack belief in the tool or feel it's faulty, you won't choose to use it If we learn by examining our beliefs and by trying out and reflecting on new ones, then a *well-designed* and *well-understood* tool can, in fact, assist the process of change and improvement (hence the investment by the National Science Foundation into "standards-based" curriculum materials). I emphasize *well-understood* because too many times new programs, curriculum materials, or other *tools* are foisted on educators without the provision of enough time and support for people to grapple with and understand the underlying theory or beliefs embedded in the tool. People who question the implementation of a new text are often seen as "resistant" rather than as voices representing the need for more deliberate and in-depth inquiry into the use of the new tools. Inadequate, up-front inquiry often results in people attempting to use the new tools through the filter of their old beliefs or to resist using the tools at all. When this happens, superficial implementation is the result. The conflict and frustration this causes leads to endless debates—the math wars, for example, or whole language verses phonics. Content coaching takes a radical stance away from this policy-driven approach to implementation of curriculum materials and proposes a *mindful engagement* with programs and materials. Fidelity then becomes something to explore and investigate rather than a dictum to follow a script.

> Teaching is a very complex activity (Bromme, 1992; Stiegler & Hiebert, 1999; Leinhardt, 1993). It can be looked at from many perspectives and discussed at different levels of abstraction, depending on one's knowledge, theories, and beliefs. The conceptual frame presented here reflects a profound change in the definition of teaching—from teaching as *mechanically implementing* curriculum to *mindfully making use of curriculum*. Teaching requires sophisticated reasoning in choosing and prioritizing lesson goals and designing lessons that enable a given group of students to reach given standards. (West & Staub, 2003, p. 5)

What this means in practice is that although a lesson under discussion may be "the next lesson in the book," it is incumbent on the coach and the teacher to consider the lesson as described in the book to be the starting point for discussion, not the recipe for the lesson. This is an important distinction to understand. In many forms of coaching, coaches are expected to assist teachers in implementing a particular set of curriculum materials as written. Often the mantra is as follows: "teach the materials as they are written at the pace recommended in the pacing calendar" (a pace sometimes provided by the publisher or authors and sometimes by the district). This is what we refer to as "mechanistic teaching." It implies that every student, in every class, needs the same thing on any given day. In addition, the lessons described in many programs and curriculum materials are designed in bite-sized pieces, meaning they focus on one small idea or skill at a time in the belief that over time the student will put all the pieces together and thereby understand the whole picture. These notions fly in the face of everything we know about how people learn. Yet, policies requiring this type of practice abound.

At the same time that teachers are being told to "follow the curriculum as written" to ensure "fidelity" to its enactment at a prescribed pace, they are also being told to differentiate the lesson to meet the range of needs of every one of their students. The first directive is a push to "cover the curriculum," and the second comes from an acknowledgement of student differences. To follow the first is often to run roughshod over the needs of many students. These opposing directives cause a dissonance and are a source of great frustration for teachers.

The standards movement is one effort to try to move the field away from naïve and mechanistic approaches to teaching, but unfortunately, with the advent of "No Child Left Behind" legislation, it has had an unintended impact of emphasizing the importance of high-stakes test scores over substantive learning.

THE STANDARDS MOVEMENT

In fact, the standards movement has two premises: all students can learn to high standards *and* individual students will need differing amounts of time and types of interventions to meet the standards. Curiously, the standards movement has spawned a great deal of debate about what is to be learned as well as an array of sanctions for those who do not meet standards within a specified time frame based on one or two test scores. Less emphasis has been placed on flexible time and individualized interventions than on the idea of meeting the standards. Our schools are designed like factories of the early 20th century (Resnick, 1995; Senge, 1990), whose aim was the efficient mass production of a product. Materials came to the factory, were run along an assembly line, and ended up integrated into something of value in the marketplace. Working with this model, we devised schools where all six-year-olds were expected to enter a classroom in the fall, study the same things for the same amount of time (whether or not some of them already knew some of these things), and leave the classroom in June as finished first-graders, ready to advance en masse to the next grade with its set of skills. Not originally designed to address the needs of individual learners, our schools have not made the transition to flexible, vibrant learning organizations capable of dealing effectively with individual differences. Furthermore, we are not as sophisticated as we need to be about exactly what interventions will result in helping a range of students meet high standards. Thus educators who become mindful of a need for change have to learn to move in a new way in an old system while we all work to transform the system to one that supports the very goals it purports to support—high standards and respect for individual learning differences.

Content coaching takes a different, more complex, view of teaching and learning than the mechanistic view of the factory. Based on what we already know and emerging information about learning and teaching, it is not only possible to think deeply about lessons, about the mindful use of materials, and about evidence of student understanding or lack thereof, but it is essential that we do so. We can think about lessons in relation to a unit of study, a set of standards, essential questions, learning styles, prior knowledge, and a host of other things. By thinking in this way, we can better meet the standards and the demands of testing than we can by mechanically implementing lessons. We are not saying that every teacher should "do his own thing" or ignore the materials that may be "mandated for use" by the district. We are saying that there is a *mindful* way of using materials and a mechanistic way of using materials and that how one uses materials is as important as which materials are selected. There is a continuum of teacher stances when it comes to curriculum. At one end of the spectrum is the stance of following the book page by page, and at the opposite end is the stance of creating everything from scratch. Neither extreme is useful in today's world.

Mindful use of materials, of course, implies that teachers and coaches are deeply familiar with the design of the materials and the underlying theory (if any) in their design. It requires that they have a solid grasp of the content they want to teach and a large and flexible repertoire of effective teaching strategies to engage the specific learners who are sitting in front of them. This mindful use of materials is the focus of the content coach, to assist teachers in becoming skillful practitioners through thoughtful dialog around the what, how, why, and who questions described later.

THE USE OF TOOLS IN COACHING SESSIONS

In a content coaching session, for example, it would not be enough for the coach to say, "The pacing calendar dictates we do this lesson today, therefore, we are doing it." In addition to the pacing calendar, the coach would take into account what the students already know and can do based on their prior work and knowledge and would consider whether the lesson proposed actually meets their needs. The coach would also keep in mind that the "what" to be taught can be addressed in myriad ways, and that sometimes by connecting the focus of the proposed lesson to ideas with which the students are already familiar, the coach can create a lesson that will both honor the intended content of the pacing calendar and the needs of his or her students. In other words, we engage with the tools in our toolkit in a thoughtful manner that encourages teachers to be both accountable to the community and to be creative and resourceful enough to meet the true needs of their students. This is a *both/and* approach. We can both teach for understanding and be accountable to the assessment and standards demands of our context.

In addition to the tools described earlier, content coaches are guided by a set of tools that are drawn from both theory and practice. These tools situate the work into the big picture (see Figure 10.2) and provide a scaffold (see Figure 10.5) for diving into the details of crafting a powerful lesson. We discuss these tools in greater detail later in the chapter.

THE COACHING DIALOG

Content coaching is a dialogical practice that is designed to cultivate high quality instruction. The premise behind engaging in dialog to improve instruction is that improved instruction comes from an internal change in thinking, not just from an external mandate. Dialog changes thinking. In dialog, we each "stimulate the other to think." It is both "creative and recreative"

Figure 10.2   A Framework for Lesson Design

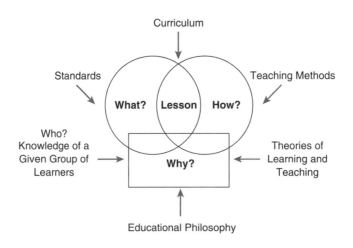

SOURCE: Adapted from Staub (1999, 2001).

(Shor & Freire, 1987, p. 2). In true dialog we reexamine our ideas and invent new, more informed perspectives. "We can rigorously approach the ideas, the facts, the problems, but always in a light style, almost with a dance-like quality, an unarmed style" (Shor & Freire, 1987, p. 2).

The process of content coaching includes a preconference planning session and a postconference debriefing session. Dialog between coach and teacher may also occur during the enactment of the lesson. The nature of the dialog is one of curiosity, possibility, and support. The coach is genuinely interested in the teacher as a human being and as an educator with ideas, passions, beliefs, anxieties, and skills to be discovered and interwoven into the work. Skillful content coaches are authentically engaged in finding "mutual purpose" in relation to the work. They are *not* attempting to manipulate the teacher into using specific materials or a new practice or even a particular lesson, although all of these options may be discussed in the course of a coaching relationship. In other words, coaches are not invested in "convincing" teachers of anything. They are partners in exploring with teachers authentic concerns, issues, and hypotheses about teaching and learning. Conversations focus on the instructional core: the planning and implementation of lessons, reflecting on these lessons through the diagnosis of student talk and work, and designing interventions to improve student learning.

CONTENT COACHES
CONTRIBUTE THEIR EXPERTISE

The nature of the content coaching dialog is one of partnership and shared decision making. The coach's content knowledge and pedagogical expertise are acknowledged and used. Thus in this model of coaching, *the coach can have substantive input into the lesson.* This practice is different from some other models of coaching in which the coach mainly asks thought-provoking questions for the teacher to consider while the teacher essentially plans the lesson. When teachers' content knowledge is lacking or their instructional repertoire is limited or when they are inexperienced, they may not be ready to design sophisticated lessons without input from a more knowledgeable partner. In fact, the coaching process can be frustrating for the teacher if the coach only uses inquiry and never provides suggestions.

This approach is one that is used in athletic coaching. An athlete who hires a coach is doing so because the coach has insight that the athlete lacks. When the coach shares his or her insight about what is off in the athlete's golf swing, for example, and offers suggestions about how to correct it, then the athlete can "try on" the new practice and ask for additional feedback. The same is true for lesson design. When teachers are unsure about why their students are not learning or what the underlying "big idea" of a lesson is, for example, a coach can provide insight into the content of that lesson as well as the range of student understanding for teachers to attend to in their lessons. On the elementary level, it is often the case that teachers are not steeped in mathematics content and may have a fairly fragile understanding of the concepts they are being asked to teach. Content coaching seeks to scaffold a teacher's content knowledge during the planning process of a lesson by actively engaging the teacher in the mathematics from a "big idea" and "habits of mind" perspective. Then the coach and teacher step back to reflect on how mathematics is embedded in the selected activity. (Coaching is a valuable aid to the teacher but alone will not sufficiently develop robust content knowledge. Institutes, workshops, and coursework are also necessary and should be part of a menu of professional learning opportunities for teachers who need to deepen their understanding of the content they teach.)

The content coach can also assist the teacher in identifying central concepts and their underlying ideas. For example, in elementary school mathematics, it is important that students develop a robust and flexible understanding of the base-10 number system. Place value is a big idea in a network of related smaller ideas about our number system that when understood in relation to one another, lead to the capacity to work within the number system with confidence and skill. It is not easy for young students to begin to understand place value in any depth without many varied and contextualized experiences specifically designed to help them make sense of this system. The content coach will assist a teacher in identifying the network of big and small ideas at play and in selecting from available resources activities that give students access to these concepts. For example, one idea in the network of ideas related to place value is that a digit immediately to the left of the decimal point is 10 times greater than the one to the right. This multiplicative relationship is much more difficult to comprehend than is the activity to "circle the number in the tens place." Because a student can correctly circle a digit in a specific "place" does not necessarily mean the student understands the multiplicative relationship in place value.

A content coach will help a teacher see the levels of understanding students may have when grappling with the "big ideas," such as place value. In doing so, the coach is building the teacher's capacity to analyze student understanding; predict student responses; and plan lessons that address the range of student needs in any given class. (I use mathematics examples because my main focus in the field is mathematics, but content coaching is applicable to any academic domain; see Resources A and B.)

AN INQUIRY STANCE IN ACTION

The content coach also takes an inquiry stance, eliciting the teacher's goals, concerns, observations, questions, and beliefs—an inquiry that should be done with great humility and respect. Sometimes, especially in elementary schools where teachers are responsible for several subjects, the teacher may lack content knowledge in a given domain. Skillful questioning by a coach can uncover weaknesses in understanding and alert a coach to the kinds of support the teacher needs. The coach knows, however, that the teacher has knowledge of his or her own classroom that the coach may lack and that the teacher's own ideas are a good starting point for discussion. Often the first question a coach asks the teacher is, "What is your plan?" or "What ideas do you have?"

Questioning is an art. In our culture, questions are often seen as disguised judgments, interrogations, or manipulations to trip us up. People know by a person's attitude when a question, although asked in identical words, is sincere and when it is judgmental. "What were you thinking?" could mean, "I'm really curious about your thinking," or it could mean, "What kind of stupid move was that?" It is essential that a content coach set the stage for robust questioning that exhibits genuine curiosity and caring. Questioning is a two-way street with both coach and teacher free to ask what they will without fear of being judged. It is our genuine questions, not our preconceived answers, that lead to new insights.

Content coaches understand in the very core of their being that all human beings are natural learners who have wonderful ideas, dreams, and goals of their own. They see their job as taking a journey with the teacher in which both people will become smarter about teaching and learning as they both explore authentic questions about the impact of their lessons on student learning. They use the specifics of lesson planning to consider the philosophy and epistemology of teaching and learning in practice.

THE PRECONFERENCE IS KEY

We emphasize the preconference planning session because the planning session is designed to help ensure a successful lesson. It also helps to ensure that the conversation will be focused and specific rather than general. It is specificity in lesson design that makes all the difference. This emphasis is different from that of some models of coaching which emphasize the debriefing dialog. While we advocate for *both* opportunities for conversation in a coaching cycle, we have found that the planning session is key for transference to practice (see Figure 10.3).

Planning dialogs are considered the most important part of the process as they immerse the practitioner into robust habits of planning that eventually become internalized and over time result in "habits of planning" which, in turn, result in richer lessons. It is often the case that when teachers have been working with a coach for a few months, they

Figure 10.3   Conferencing: Benefits of the Preconference

Over the years, due to restraints on teacher time, we have had to choose between the postconference and the preconference. Experience has lead us to believe that if we must choose, the planning time is more useful then the debriefing time, especially for less experienced teachers.

- Collaborative planning sessions are more likely to ensure that the lessons presented to students will revolve around important big ideas or essential questions.
- Preconferencing allows for crisp articulation of the lesson goals and careful design of instructional strategies.
- Preconferencing focuses the teacher's attention on student learning and asks for deliberate pedagogical decisions designed to foster student understanding.
- Preconferencing encourages the teacher to take an analytical stance toward the written curriculum and empowers the teacher to actively engage with the curriculum.
- Preconferencing provides the coach a window into the teacher's thinking and needs. The coach can identify the following:
  - Issues important to the teacher
  - The learning theory which underpins the teacher's beliefs
  - The teacher's level of content knowledge and confidence
- Preconferencing allows the coach's postconference feedback about the lesson to be based on the shared lesson plan and its implementation.
- If postconference is not possible, feedback can be in the form of notes or e-mail, as the lesson plan and lesson enactment were shared experiences.

SOURCE: Staub, West, and Bickel (2003).

will report that when working alone, they can hear the coach's voice "over their shoulder" asking them the kinds of questions asked during a coaching session. This internalization process is necessary for transference to independent practice to take place.

In the preconference dialog a genuine belief in the power of collaborative lesson planning is at play, and the coach strives to empower the teacher to take an active role in the planning process. It is also understood that through probing and provocative questioning, we often deepen our understanding and invent new solutions to our dilemmas (knowledge creation). Thus the content coach inquires into the teacher's choices and the reasoning behind those choices. Together they design the lesson, and responsibility for its success is shared. But, the *teacher* has the ultimate decision-making voice. It is the teacher who chooses to take or leave a coach's suggestion. Teachers are the clients and they decide what "serves them." The lesson is jointly designed and the *responsibility for its success is shared*. If the teacher doesn't fully own and agree with the lesson design, he or she will not be able to artfully execute it (note: if the coach is teaching the lesson, then the final decisions rest with the coach with input from the teacher). Checking for teacher understanding and commitment to the choices made during the preconference is one way to ensure a successful lesson.

A CONTENT FOCUS

In each session, the coach works to ensure that the academic content of a lesson is worthwhile, important, and relevant. The intent is to create lessons that ensure that every student has access to the lesson, and the lesson is rich enough conceptually to challenge even the most informed in the group. Thus, content coaching tackles head-on the ubiquitous question, "How do I address the range of needs of *all* the learners in my class?"

Content plays a key role in our coaching conversations. In a mathematics coaching conference, for example, the coach always ask questions like, "What is the mathematics we want to teach? What are the concepts, strategies, and skills we want students to understand?" In a mathematics coaching session, for example, it is not sufficient to answer, "I'm teaching multiplication," as that is too general. It is also not sufficient to answer, "I'm teaching the facts," as this is not only too vague but also lacks a conceptual frame. Instead, the coach might suggest that we create a lesson that brings the commutative property of multiplication to the fore for students to understand how this powerful property allows them to learn twice as many facts. The ensuing conversation would concern how this property might be made visible and more concrete for students. What context can give them a way to conceptualize the idea that 4×5 and 5×4 both equal 20? What is the same and what is different in the meaning of the number sentences $4 \times 5 = 20$ and $5 \times 4 = 20$? An area model of multiplication might be considered, along with contexts that make meaning of this model. In addition, this exploration might be seen as a way to help students learn their multiplication facts, as they realize that two numbers multiplied together always result in the same answer, no matter their order.

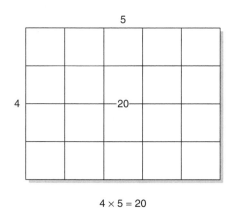

$4 \times 5 = 20$

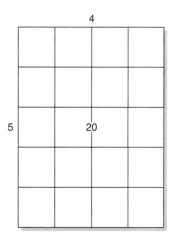

$5 \times 4 = 20$

CORE ISSUES OF LESSON DESIGN

The questions a content coach asks center around a set of research-identified core issues of lesson design (see Figure 10.4). When these issues are routinely and adequately addressed in lesson planning, the result is not only lessons that promote greater student understanding, but also development of robust habits of planning among practitioners, habits that naturally lead to the capacity to differentiate a lesson to meet the needs of a range of students, habits that question why something is taught in a particular sequence and at a particular pace, habits that seek out evidence of student understanding or lack thereof and that lead to the development of diagnostic and intervention strategies to assist student learning. When mindful lesson design is practiced systemically, everyone gets smarter.

Figure 10.4   Abbreviated List of Core Issues in Lesson Design

- Lesson goals
- Lesson plan and design
- Students' relevant prior knowledge
- Relationship between the nature of the task and the activity on one hand and the lesson goals on the other hand
- Strategies for students to make public their thinking and understanding
- Evidence of students' understanding and learning
- Students' difficulties, confusions, and misconceptions
- Ways to encourage collaboration in an atmosphere of mutual respect
- Strategies to foster relevant student discussion

SOURCE: West and Staub (2003).

These overarching issues have been turned into "guiding questions" in our main planning tool, the Guide to Core Issues in Lesson Design (see discussion that follows).

THE FRAMEWORK FOR LESSON DESIGN

The Framework for Lesson Design (see Figure 10.2) attempts to situate the core issues into the big picture. It shows the variables that impact lesson design: resources, policies, tools, theories, beliefs, and student prior knowledge. These variables all impact the what, how, why, and who of lesson design (Staub, West, & Bickel, 2003):

- What is the curricular content to be learned by the students?
- How is this content to be taught?
- Why is this specific content to be taught? Why will it be taught in this way?
- Who is the lesson designed to teach?

These basic questions can be discussed and addressed in myriad ways in relation to the curriculum materials, standards, or other tools in a teacher's toolbox and to the particular students in a class. That is to say, they are not dependent on a given program. All the materials and programs available to teachers and schools are understood to be tools, not scripts or panaceas. Learning is contextual and teachers must design lessons that take into consideration the prior knowledge of their students. Resources are only as effective as the skill level and beliefs of the people using them.

When some practitioners focus on the *what* aspect of lesson design, they ask, "What's the next lesson in the scope and sequence, curriculum, or textbook?" The *how* becomes, "What materials need to be gathered and what does the book tell us we should say or do?"

These versions of the "what and how" questions are different from the ones we are thinking about in content coaching. A focus on what comes next in the book or scope and sequence is often symptomatic of a mechanistic approach to teaching, an approach which can never address the following oft-heard lament: "There is such a big range of learners in my class, how can I possibly address all their needs? Many of my students are still struggling with the ideas in the previous lessons in the book. How can they possibly deal with this lesson? Yet, if I don't move on, what am I going to do with those who could understand this lesson in five minutes?" Mechanistic approaches have resulted in narrow lessons aimed at some imagined middle-of-the-spectrum student and do not serve the majority of children. They have also resulted in rhetorical stances that divide rather than inform the field. Rarely do practitioners seriously ponder the *why* questions proposed earlier in any depth beyond statements such as the following: "its important for the test," "so students can get into college," "for the next grade," or "for the work world." Often these clichés are used to justify practices that are ineffective and lead to trivial pursuits in classrooms. Content coaching encourages practitioners to question deeply the *how, what,* and *why* of their lessons and work to design lessons that go beyond testing requirements toward the development of robust habits of learning and thinking as well as deeper understanding of content.

Content coaches ask practitioners to consider the *who.* Who are the specific students and what do they already know, want to know, and need to understand to not only succeed on "the test" but in life; to not only get a good job, but to participate in a healthy democracy and a rapidly changing global reality?

FROM MECHANISTIC TO MINDFUL PLANNING

Content coaching seeks to upgrade the whole nature of lesson planning in this country. Lesson planning is part of the skill set that should distinguish teachers as professionals. When lesson design is done thoughtfully by well-informed teachers, the result is lessons that give all students access to important content and encourage habits of reasoning and discourse germane to a given domain. Presently, the common mindset (and policies that emerge from this mindset) that "anybody can teach as long as they stay a few pages ahead of the students in the textbook" is difficult to combat because the kind of planning many teachers do is exactly that of staying a few pages ahead in the book. In addition, many districts exacerbate this tendency by imposing rigid pacing calendars. Both tendencies imply a mechanistic view of teaching and learning that perpetuates the idea that teaching is a simple act of dispensing information that students might just as easily acquire in a book or online. It seems that we often confound the gathering and regurgitating of information and the capacity to follow directions with real learning. Learning is different from and in addition to simply accumulating information. Among other things, learning requires us to question critically even what may seem obvious (e.g., the status quo, policies or practices or procedures we do not understand or find meaningful or suspect are even detrimental), to analyze and synthesize information, and to process new information in the light of what we already think we understand. Furthermore, the process of learning differs from person to person, and these differences must inform us.

There is a history of attempting to create "teacher-proof" materials on the premise that teaching is a mechanistic act and anyone can teach as long as they follow the pacing guide and are familiar with the standards. Anyone who has ever attempted to teach knows the fallacy of this premise. Yet many policymakers and authors of curriculum materials continue to try to mandate or manipulate effective teaching through implementation of scripted programs. Content coaches acknowledge this history and work to transform practice through meticulous lesson design.

> Lesson-design takes place at the intersection of *what* and *how*. What is the relationship between curriculum and teachers' work in the classroom? In the United States, curriculum is most often thought of as an "organizational framework;" a "curriculum-as-manual," containing the templates for coverage and methods that are seen as guiding, directing, or controlling a school's, or a school system's, day-by-day classroom work (Westbury, 2000, p. 17). In other words, these manuals set forth *what* to teach and *how* to teach it. For a time, it was even hoped that a "technology of teaching" would lead to fully specified curricula that would guarantee effective teaching no matter who the teacher happened to be. The aim of constructing "teacher-proof" curricula, however, has turned out to be out of reach and based on a naïve conception of what effective teaching involves. Even when curriculum materials specify lessons in some detail, a competent teacher still needs to adapt a given lesson to the context of the particular classroom and to the individual

characteristics, needs, and backgrounds of the learners in it. (West & Staub, 2003, p. 6)

The standards movement has attempted to define "what" content should be taught. This movement has been contentious, sprouting "math and phonics wars" and endless arguments about what matters in a subject and how it should be taught. Often the standards are reduced to a laundry list of skills and concepts that must be "covered." Most textbooks are constructed to meet the various and sundry laundry lists of standards, which differ for all 50 states. This results in the cliché, "curriculum is a mile wide and an inch deep." It also results in needless and endless repetition from year to year because various states require similar concepts at different grade levels, and when teachers follow a textbook, they are often repeating as much as 70% of what was taught in the previous year. The common lament, "We don't have enough time to cover the curriculum," is a catch-22 because the tools that teachers are often using are part of the problem. There have been many attempts since the beginning of the standards movement to create more coherent curriculum materials in both math and literacy, with mixed results.

TEACHER CONTENT KNOWLEDGE AND LESSON DESIGN

Another job of the content coach is to encourage thorough examination of the "big ideas" in an academic domain so that the content (or the *what)* to be taught comes from a perspective of understanding that can lead students to develop the habits of mind associated with that academic domain. The fact that some teachers lack a firm handle on the conceptual underpinnings and organizational structure of content is one reason they have difficulty planning rigorous lessons around "essential questions" or "big ideas" and must, therefore, rely heavily on texts as scripts. This lack of a comprehensive content knowledge breeds in turn an insecurity that prevents them from allowing students to investigate a subject like math or science from an inquiry perspective. The worry is that the teacher might not be able to answer questions posed by students, especially precocious students. Teachers fear they will say the wrong thing or not be able to identify fledgling understanding of important ideas expressed by students who may not be expressing themselves precisely in the language of the domain.

Part of the problem seems to be that our present understanding of planning continues to be largely a mechanistic one. We read our teacher's guide, gather the prescribed materials, ask the questions proposed, and assign students the task suggested. While this basic approach to planning is not entirely without merit, it is insufficient to meet our oft-stated goal of taking all students to high standards. This insufficiency is slowly changing, but it is still prevalent.

Content coaches seek to assist practitioners in building a repertoire of powerful and nuanced instructional strategies to be used purposefully and specifically as appropriate (the how), the effectiveness of which are measured by evidence of student learning, one piece of which could include test scores. Content coaching is advocating something dramatically different and much more powerful than mechanistic, programmatic approaches to teaching and learning.

THE GUIDE TO CORE ISSUES IN LESSON DESIGN

The Guide to Core Issues in Lesson Design is a tool that invites coach and teacher to engage in a dialog that results in skillfully designed lessons that will engage students at all levels.

The guide was created by Fritz Staub, a visiting scholar from Switzerland, myself, and colleagues in Community School District 2, New York City, as well as at the Institute for Learning at the University of Pittsburgh. Fritz brought a European perspective and teaching theory to the work as well as a researcher's eye. During the birthing phases of content coaching, I was the principal investigator of a National Science Foundation Teacher Enhancement Grant which supported a mathematics initiative in Community School District 2 in New York City. District 2 was a lighthouse district studied widely because of its innovative and far-reaching professional learning opportunities. At the time, I was coaching both teachers and coaches and mysteriously getting remarkable results. Fritz and I videotaped dozens of coaching sessions. We were interested in finding out the specific things that coaches did that resulted in identifiable improvement of instruction. Fritz also often accompanied me during my own coaching sessions. He and I pondered questions of lesson design, enactment, coaching moves, and the impact coaching was having on teacher practice. Fritz was then able to hone a theory based on principles of learning and on European ideas about teaching, a theory that informs our book, *Content-Focused Coaching: Transforming Mathematics Lessons* (West & Staub, 2003).

Fritz and I spent many hours studying the coaching sessions and the lessons connected to the sessions. Through this process Fritz named the coaching moves that positively impacted lessons as evidenced by student learning and transference to instructional practice. Out of our observations and dialog with each other and teachers and coaches in the field, Fritz developed the Guide to Core Issues in Lesson Design as a tool for informing content coaching conversations (see Figure 10.5).

To drill deeply into the specifics of a lesson and develop robust habits of skillful lesson design, content coaches use the Guide to Core Issues in Lesson Design as a kind of map of the terrain of the possible issues that could be considered during a planning session. The guide we developed for a mathematics lesson is shown in Figure 10.4. Resources A and B contain some samples of guides that others have created from the original for literacy or science using the mathematics guide as a template.

Figure 10.5   Guide to Core Issues in Lesson Design—Mathematics

What are the goals and the overall plan of the lesson?

- What is your plan?
- Where in your plan would you like some assistance?

(Based on the teacher's response, the coach makes tentative choices about which of the following ideas to focus on.)

What is the mathematics in this lesson? (i.e., make the lesson goals explicit)

- What is the specific mathematics goal of this lesson?
- What are the mathematics concepts?
- Are there specific strategies being developed? Explain.
- What is the skill (applications, practice) being taught in this lesson?
- What tools are needed (e.g., calculators, rulers, protractors, pattern blocks, cubes)?

Where does this lesson fall in this unit and why? (i.e., clarify the relationship between the lesson, the curriculum, and the standards)

- Do any of these concepts or skills get addressed at other points in the unit?
- Which goal is your priority for this lesson?
- What does this lesson have to do with the concept you have identified as your goal?
- Which standards does this particular lesson address?

What are students' prior knowledge and difficulties?

- What relevant concepts have already been explored with this class?
- What strategies does this lesson build on?
- What relevant contexts (money, for example) could you draw on in relation to this concept?
- What can you identify or predict students may find difficult or confusing or have misconceptions about?
- What ideas might students begin to express and what language might they use?

How does the lesson help students reach the goals? (i.e., think through the implementation of the lesson)

- What grouping structure will you use and why?
- What opening question do you have in mind?
- How do you plan to present the tasks or problems?
- What model, manipulative, or visual will you use?
- What activities will move students toward the stated goals?
- How does this lesson engage students in thinking and activities that move them toward the stated goals?
- In what ways will students make their mathematical thinking and understanding public?
- What will the students say or do that will demonstrate their learning?
- How will you ensure that students are talking and listening to each other about important mathematics in an atmosphere of mutual respect?
- How will you ensure that ideas that are being grappled with will be highlighted and clarified?
- How do you plan to assist those students whom you predict will have difficulties?
- What extensions or challenges will you provide for students who are ready for them?
- How much time do you predict will be needed for each part of the lesson?

SOURCE: West and Staub (2003).

This tool is *not* a script. It includes far too many questions to discuss in any one coaching session. (It could be used in its entirety if one is engaged in a full "lesson study" over several sessions on the order of the Japanese model. See Lewis, 2002, and Wang-Iverson & Yoshida, 2005, for more information on Japanese Lesson Study.)

The purpose of this tool is to map the terrain for the core variables affecting teaching and learning and to carefully consider them in lesson design and instructional practices. If you study the guide you will note that there are several questions that revolve around content and others that focus on finding out what students think and still others that encourage the teacher to be planful about attending to the inevitable range of understanding in any group of students. These questions can also be considered in light of the principles of learning collected by Resnick and colleagues (Resnick, 1995; Resnick & Hall, 1998, 2000; Resnick & Nelson-Le Gall, 1997), and the work of various others (Dweck, 2002). For example, embedded in the following question from the guide is an acknowledgement that it is expected that students will inevitably have to work through confusions or misconceptions: "What can you identify or predict students may find difficult or confusing or have misconceptions about?" There are other questions in the guide that consider how to encourage students to expose their thinking through the development of classroom discourse or "accountable talk," such as the following: "What ideas might students begin to express and what language might they use?" "In what ways will students make their mathematical thinking and understanding public?"

In my experience in working with teachers of Grades K–12 in mathematics, the content questions in the guide are not easy to answer. When we ask teachers, "What is the specific mathematics goal of this lesson?" or "What are the mathematical concepts?" it is fairly common to hear them say things like, "I'm teaching lesson 2.5 today" or "I'm teaching multiplication." When we probe a bit deeper and ask, "What about multiplication are you teaching?" many teachers cannot adequately answer the question.

Answers tend to be too general (multiplication), too narrow (memorizing facts), or nonexistent (a workbook page from the text). This scenario might play out similarly in a literacy class. The question, "What are you teaching today?" might be answered with, "writing" or "essay writing," rather than, "the distinguishing features of essay writing." Examples like these show a lack of specificity or conceptual focus in the planning habits of many teachers and are reported to be the case by coaches in all content areas when teachers do not have a firm handle on the big ideas of the content they want to teach and a tendency to define a topic by the formats or procedures employed in the domain (e.g., the whole class writing in the form of haiku one day and rhyme the next). Without a clear, articulate, and rich enough content goal, lessons generally flounder or fall flat. The guide is designed to get teachers and coaches to drill down to the very core of the "what, why, how, and who" of the lesson. Just the act of asking the questions begins a journey to more reflective teaching.

MEASURING SUCCESS

Content coaching measures success through the lens of *evidence of student learning* as opposed to the implementation of specific curriculum materials, pedagogical strategies, or use of technology. Evidence of learning is an ongoing inquiry for content coaches. The question, "What constitutes evidence of learning?" is one that is interwoven through the planning sessions, the enactment of the lesson, and the debriefing sessions. Together we wonder how we might know to what degree students understand the content at hand and what we can do about improving or deepening student understanding. Example questions from the guide include the following:

- What can you identify or predict students may find difficult or confusing or have misconceptions about?
- In what ways will students make their mathematical thinking and understanding public?
- What will the students say or do that will demonstrate their learning?
- What ideas might students begin to express and what language might they use?
- How will you insure that ideas that are being grappled with will be highlighted and clarified?
- How do you plan to assist those students whom you predict will have difficulties?
- What extensions or challenges will you provide for students who are ready for them?

Content coaching is an attempt to deepen the conversation beyond the mere rhetoric of beliefs about teaching practices, or about the nature of learning, and toward the use of evidence of student learning as a focal point for informing teaching decisions. When we focus on evidence of learning, we reveal to ourselves whether our deeply held beliefs are worth holding onto or need to be let go in light of new information. Changing our cherished beliefs is one of the most difficult of human endeavors. Thus, rather than advocating a handful of teaching strategies as "best practice," why not hold all teaching strategies to the test of results? When teachers say, "I've been doing it this way for years," we could invite them to reflect on whether their way of doing things has resulted in 100% of their students demonstrating robust understanding. If not, we could wonder together about the impact of particular instructional strategies on the learning of specific students. Teachers might be willing to note that some students don't seem to learn the material deeply. Their present rationale may be that the students have "special needs" or are "second language learners" or have "poor home environments." The content coach might nudge teachers into acknowledging that, while any and all of that may be true, they have no control over those variables. The one thing teachers can do is be willing to try out additional instructional strategies and diagnose the resulting student work as well as student discourse for insights into how that strategy might be working to make content more accessible. Through dialog and inquiry into "what works," we might discover that there is a place for every teaching strategy ever contrived—at least some of the time with particular learners. On the other hand, we might discover that our ideas about who benefits from our preferred instructional style are mistaken and there are strategies and tools that would serve some students better.

Teaching and learning are complex acts. Finding evidence for what people are actually learning is what underpins the assessment movement, and the search for this evidence has resulted in some misguided and overzealous standardized testing practices. Content coaching is advocating that we pause and reflect collaboratively as explorers with wide-eyed curiosity and a healthy dose of skepticism into the question, "What counts as evidence of student (or teacher) understanding?" Content coaches engage with teachers to find out day-to-day, moment-to-moment what our students (teachers) are thinking about and how deeply they understand the content under study, so that we might adjust and adapt our lesson designs to meet the "differentiated" needs of our students (teachers).

WORKING TOGETHER DURING THE LESSON

Content coaching is a practice-based approach to upgrading instruction and learning. Like most coaching models, the coach spends time in the teacher's classroom engaged in teaching or in observing lessons. The role that the coach will play in any particular lesson is negotiated between the coach and the teacher prior to the lesson. The coach may teach the entire lesson with the teacher observing either a specific instructional practice or the talk and actions of students. The teacher and coach may coteach the lesson either as a team or in tandem, or the teacher may teach the entire lesson while the coach observes through an agreed-upon lens.

One of the more controversial practices of content coaching is that the coach might intervene during a lesson when the teacher is teaching. This is done with the teacher's prior consent. It is also done judiciously and never with the intent of "correcting" the teacher. The interventions are not done in a critical manner, but in more of a supportive one. Interventions are done sparingly and for a purpose. In all of my experiences with this practice, there is only one incident that I can recall that was "uncomfortable" for the teacher I was working with. The teacher's discomfort provided an opportunity for coach and teacher to dialog and become clearer about their relationship and the work.

Interventions are made for a number of reasons:

1. *A student expresses an important (mathematical) idea that is relevant to the lesson and the teacher does not notice or realize its relevance.* In this case the coach might suggest that the student repeat the idea, with the permission of the teacher. The coach might then ask a question of the students related to that idea, which allows the teacher to then pursue the concept and facilitate the discourse.

2. *The teacher's questions may be inhibiting student thinking.* For example, a primary teacher I worked with was asking students to come up with two addend combinations for the number 11. When students made suggestions, she put out counters and asked the class to count with her. She counted each addend and then she counted from 1 to 11. Several of her students were able to compute the sum without counting three times. They knew that 5 and 6 were 11. By having students count three times, this teacher was inadvertently guiding them to use the most primitive strategy for finding sums. In this instance, the coach might intervene and ask students how they might know that 5 plus 6 is 11 without having to count all the pieces. Some students might then share a counting-on strategy while others might share a doubles-plus-one strategy. The teacher, on hearing her students' more sophisticated strategies, might realize that she can ask questions that are designed to make public such thinking.

3. *The coach can "highlight" a moment that the teacher and coach can unpack during the postconference dialog.* Perhaps a student made a comment or asked a question that revealed a misconception or partial knowledge that can be addressed more fully in a future lesson. The coach may want to "highlight" that moment to help the teacher recall it during the postlesson coaching conversation.

In addition to the types of interventions described earlier, content coaches assist teachers as they work with individual students or small groups of students during the work period of a lesson. In this coaching practice, we do not "divide and conquer," we "stick together." What I mean by this is that the coach rarely works with one group of students while the teacher works with another. Instead they travel from student to student or group to group as a team. One or the other may take the lead when interacting with a particular student or group while the other listens. Then the teacher and coach might step off to one side and have a brief dialog about what occurred. The coach might invite the teacher to try a questioning strategy or suggest that he or she listen for a specific approach that is being demonstrated. This "over the shoulder" coaching is an "apprenticeship" model through which the teacher gradually builds a repertoire of intervention or facilitation skills. This practice addresses the "transfer to practice problem" that plagues so many professional development practices.

The reader may think it seems more practical for the coach to work with a subset of students while the teacher works with others. While there is merit in this thinking in terms of the short-term benefits to a small group of students, content coaches do not usually agree to work directly with students when the teacher is not present. Content coaching is aimed at upgrading the teacher's skills. How will the teacher's skills improve if he or she is not even present to observe when the coach is engaging with the students?

THE POSTCONFERENCE

After a lesson, the coach and the teacher spend time together discussing the lesson through any of several lenses or combination of lenses. They may study student work or reflect on student discourse. To reflect on student discourse, the content coach takes copious and verbatim notes of what was said in the classroom during the lesson. This skill takes practice and is often challenging for coaches to master. It is essential to have verbatim notes to inquire into the various levels of understanding, confusion, misconceptions, and partial knowledge that students reveal when engaged in rich problems and robust discussion. Verbatim notes also allow the coach to be very specific in his or her feedback. Specificity is critical to powerful coaching. Specific feedback coupled with an agreement to try on a new practice or look through a new lens is what promotes growth.

The coach and teacher might discuss the questions that were raised during the lesson. They might wonder about the visuals that were or could have been employed to provide better access for struggling students. In other words, they will revisit the core issues in the guide and this time reflect on what aspects of their design worked and what aspects need to be refined, discarded, or modified.

The most important goal of the postconference is to consider the focus of the next lesson in light of their reflections, particularly their examination of student work and comments. The follow-up lesson may or may not be the next lesson in the book or pacing calendar. The variable that will most strongly influence the next lesson will be the evidence of learning demonstrated by the students. This is often difficult for teachers to fully embrace in today's high-stakes, fast-paced climate. Content coaches attempt to assist teachers as they grapple with the tensions and paradoxes of the art and science of teaching and learning in a high-stakes testing environment. It may be necessary to slow down in order to speed up and dive deep to broaden understanding. The more specific we can be when diagnosing the work of a few students who represent the range of understanding in the class, the more likely we will be able to address the needs of the whole group. The more we design lessons in response to student understanding, the more likely that student understanding will increase. The more student understanding increases, the more test scores rise. The more attention to detail in the lesson design, the more we can let go of the plan and respond to the students as they engage in the messy process called learning.

ONE LAST THING

My work has evolved separately from the work of the Institute for Learning, from District 2, and from the work of Fritz Staub. What is written in this chapter is my perspective and does not necessarily represent the views of anyone else. The way I see it, content coaching is a dynamic and evolving practice. If one is focusing on the conceptual content of a lesson, taking an effort-based stance in relation to teaching and learning, and engaging in robust, frank, and detailed conversations about evidence of learning at both the adult and student levels, then one is probably engaging in content coaching. All of the tools offered in our book, *Content-Focused Coaching: Transforming Mathematics Lessons* (West & Staub, 2003), and herewith, are works in progress. They are tools to be adapted and reworked by practitioners who engage with them. Our goal in creating the tools was to provide a starting place, a framework, an entry level to the practice of robust, responsive lesson design and collaborative planning.

When done well, content coaching is a powerful strategy for upgrading the teaching profession and cocreating vibrant, collaborative, learning organizations where all members thrive. Content coaching is one strategy for transitioning to new schools sensitive to the demands of an ever-changing, complex world.

Resource A
Guide to Core Issues in Lesson Design—Science

What are the goals and the overall plan of the lesson?

- What is your plan?
- Where in your plan would you like some assistance?

(Based on the teacher's response, the coach makes tentative choices about which of the following ideas to focus on.)

Making explicit the lesson goals: What is the science content in this lesson?

- What is your goal?
- What are the science concepts?
- Are there specific strategies being developed? Explain.
- What is the skill aspect of this lesson (applications, practice)?
- What tools are needed (e.g., graduated cylinders, thermometers)?

Clarifying the relationship between the lesson and the curriculum: Where does this lesson fall in this unit and why?

- Do any of these concepts and/or skills get addressed at other points in the unit?
- Which goal is your priority for this lesson?
- What does this lesson have to do with the concept you have identified as your goal?
- Which standards does this particular lesson address?

(Continued)

(Continued)

What are students' prior knowledge and difficulties?

- What relevant concepts have already been explored with this class?
- What strategies does this lesson build on?
- What contexts could you draw on in relation to this concept that would be relevant to your students?
- What can you identify or predict students may find difficult or confusing or have misconceptions about?
- What ideas might students begin to express and what language might they use?

Thinking through the implementation of the lesson: How are students assisted during the lesson in reaching the lesson goals?

- What grouping structure will you use and why?
- What opening question do you have in mind?
- How do you plan to present the tasks or problems?
- What model, manipulative, or visual will you use?
- How does this lesson engage students in thinking and activities that move them towards the stated goals?
- In what ways will students make their scientific thinking and understanding public?
- What will the students say or do that will demonstrate their learning?
- How will you insure that students are talking and listening to each other about important mathematics in an atmosphere of mutual respect?
- How will you insure that ideas that are being grappled with will be highlighted and clarified?
- How do you plan to assist those students whom you predict will have difficulties?
- What extensions or challenges will you provide for students who are ready for them?
- How much time do you predict will be needed for each part of the lesson?

NOTE: This was adapted by Megan Roberts, Region 9, New York City.

Resource B
Guide to Core Issues in Lesson Design—Writing Workshop

What are the goals and the overall plan of the lesson?

- What is your plan?
- Where in your plan would you like some assistance?

(Based on the teacher's response, the coach focuses on one or more of the following ideas.)

What is the writing in this lesson?

- What is the specific writing goal of this lesson?
- Are there specific strategies being developed?

Where does this lesson fall in this unit of study and why?

- Do any of these elements, strategies, or skills get addressed at other points in the unit?
- Which goal is your priority for this lesson?
- What does this lesson have to do with the elements, strategies, and/or skills you have identified as your primary goal?
- Which standards and/or Principles of Learning does this particular lesson address?

What are students' prior knowledge and difficulties?

- What relevant concepts have already been explored with this class?
- What strategies does this lesson build on?
- What relevant contexts (i.e., other genres, oral language, craft elements, etc.) could you draw on in relation to this concept?
- What can you identify or predict students may find difficult or confusing or have misconceptions about?
- In what ways might students begin to express their ideas? What forms (written lists, oral stories, memories, etc.) might the students choose?

How does the lesson help students reach the goals?

- What grouping structure will you use? Why? When?
- What opening statement do you have in mind?
- How do you plan to present the tasks?
- What activities will move students toward the stated goals?
- In what ways will students make their writing, thinking, and understanding public?
- What will we see in the students' writing that demonstrates their learning?
- How will you ensure that students are talking with and listening to one another in an atmosphere of mutual respect?
- How will you be sure that your teaching point is clear to the students (not increase confusion)? Do you have a clear focus with one teaching point?
- How do you plan to assist those students who you predict will have difficulties?
- What extensions or challenges will you provide for students who are ready for them?
- How much time do you predict will be needed for each part of the lesson?

SOURCE: Reprinted with permission from *Content-Focused Coaching* by Lucy West and Fritz Staub. Published by Heinemann, Portsmouth, NH. All rights reserved.

NOTE: This draft was rewritten by Level III Writing Institute participants and Susan Radley Brown.

REFERENCES

Allington, R. L. (2000). *What really matters for struggling readers: Designing research-based programs.* Boston: Allyn & Bacon.

Costa, A., & Kallick, B. (2000). Discovering and exploring habits of mind. Alexandria, VA: Association for Supervision & Curriculum Development.

Dweck, C. S. (2002). *Messages that motivate: How praise molds students' beliefs, motivation, and performance (in surprising ways)*. New York: Academic Press.

Elmore, R. F. (2004). *School reform from the inside out: Policy, practice, and performance.* Cambridge, MA: Harvard Education Press.

Fullan, M. (2004). *Leadership and sustainability: System thinkers in action.* Thousand Oaks, CA: Corwin Press.

Lewis, C. (2002). *Lesson study: A handbook of teacher-led instructional change.* Philadelphia: Research for Better Schools.

National Research Council. (2005). *Choose effective approaches to staff development.* Retrieved April 29, 2008, from www.nas.edu/rise/backg4b.htm.

Resnick, L. B. (1995). From aptitude to effort: A new foundation for our schools. *Daedalus, 124,* 55–62.

Resnick, L. B., & Hall, M. W. (1998). Learning organizations for sustainable education reform. *Journal of the American Academy of Arts and Sciences, 127,* 89–118.

Resnick, L. B., & Hall, M. W. (2000). *Principles of learning for effort-based education.* Pittsburgh, PA: University of Pittsburgh.

Resnick, L. B., & Nelson-Le Gall, S. (1997). Socializing intelligence. In L. Smith, J. Dockrell, & P. Tomlinson (Eds.), *Piaget Vygotsky and beyond* (pp. 145–158). London: Routledge.

Saphier, J. (2005). *John Adams' promise: How to have good schools for all our children, not just for some.* Acton, MA: Research for Better Teaching.

Senge, P. M. (1990). *The fifth discipline: The art and practice of the learning organization.* New York: Doubleday.

Shor, I., & Freire, P. (1987). *A pedagogy for liberation: Dialogues on transforming education.* New York: Bergin & Garvey.

Staub, F. C. (1999). *Reflection on content-focused coaching dialogues.* Pittsburgh, PA: University of Pittsburgh, The Institute for Learning.

Staub, F. C. (2001). Fachspezifisch-padagogisches coaching: Forderung von Unterrichtsexperties durch Unterrichtsentwicklung [Content-Focused coaching in teaching: Fostering teaching expertise through long-term classroom-based assistance in design and enactment of lessons]. *Beitrage zur Lehrerbildung, 19*(2), 175–198.

Staub, F. C., West, L., & Bickel, D. D. (2003, August). *Content coaching.* Paper presented at the meeting of the European Association for Research on Learning and Instruction, Padua, Italy.

Stiegler, J. W., & Hiebert, J. (1999). *The teaching gap: Best ideas from the world's teachers for improving education in the classroom.* New York: Free Press.

Wang-Iverson, P., & Yoshida, M. (Eds.). (2005). *Building our understanding of lesson study.* Philadelphia: Research for Better Schools.

West, L., & Staub, F. C. (2003). *Content-Focused coaching: Transforming mathematics lessons.* Portsmouth, NH: Heinemann.

Westbury, I. (2000). Teaching as a reflective practice: What might Didaktik teach curriculum? In I. Westbury, S. Hopmann, & K. Riquarts (Eds.), *Teaching as a reflective practice: The German Didaktik tradition* (pp. 15–39). Mahwah, NJ: Lawrence Erlbaum.

Wheatley, M. J. (2001). *Leadership and the new science: Discovering order in a chaotic world.* New York: Berrett-Koehler.

11

Cognitive Coaching

Jane Ellison and Carolee Hayes

WHAT IS COGNITIVE COACHING?

Cognitive Coaching supports individuals and workplace cultures that value reflection, complex thinking, and transformational learning. Arthur Costa and Robert Garmston developed the process in 1984 as a way for principals to support teachers' thinking and self-directedness. Their intention was to move beyond a behaviorist philosophy that often focused on installing behaviors into a teacher's daily practice. At the time, monitoring and evaluation was based on compliance with desired behaviors. Checklists were common as principals, with clipboard in hand, checked off teacher behaviors. Teacher's words and actions were commonly scripted followed by a conversation where the principal praised the correct behaviors and talked to the teacher about the missing behaviors. Cognitive Coaching was a breath of fresh air to professional practice. It is grounded in the belief that the thought processes of the teacher are what drive practice. Instead of seeking compliance, Cognitive Coaching develops thoughtful professionals who are self-directed. The Cognitive Coaching process is not rote or directive, but instead uses structures for

AUTHOR'S NOTE: The following chapter contains content from the book *Effective School Leadership: Developing Principals Through Cognitive Coaching* (Ellison & Hayes, 2006b). Reprinted with permission of Christopher Gordon Publishers, Inc.

supporting the teacher's own planning, reflecting, and problem resolving. It is a set of tools designed specifically to enhance performance by supporting the teacher's internal thought processes.

As Cognitive Coaching became more widely used in educational institutions, it was clear that the skills and methods had application beyond teacher supervision. Teachers realized that the process works well with students and enhances their thought processes. Principals found that Cognitive Coaching can be used in meetings to assist groups in working at higher levels and being reflective in their practice. The skills of Cognitive Coaching also are useful with parents in conferring about their child's progress. Cognitive Coaching is a process that assists any group or individual in becoming more self-managing, self-monitoring, and self-modifying. These applications are described in the book *Cognitive Coaching: Weaving the Threads of Learning and Change Into the Culture of an Organization* (Ellison & Hayes, 2006a).

The term *Cognitive Coaching* is service-marked, which means whenever the term is used, it should refer to Costa and Garmston's work. The term *coaching* is generic and can refer to many different models; Cognitive Coaching is specific to one model. Cognitive Coaching becomes not only an interactive strategy intended to enhance the self-directedness of others; it becomes internalized into a way of being and an important part of an individual's identity. It is this unique attribute of Cognitive Coaching that makes the work so powerful and as many people have reported, so life changing.

RESEARCH ON COGNITIVE COACHING

Over 20 years of research on coaching teachers using this methodology has shown significant results (Edwards, 2005):

- Cognitive Coaching was linked with increased student test scores and other benefits for students.
- Teachers grew in teaching efficacy.
- Cognitive Coaching impacted teacher thinking, causing teachers to be more reflective and to think in more complex ways.
- Teachers were more satisfied with their positions and with their choice of teaching as a profession.
- School cultures became more professional.
- Teachers collaborated more.
- Cognitive Coaching assisted teachers professionally.
- Cognitive Coaching benefited teachers personally.
- Cognitive Coaching benefited people in fields other than teaching.

This chapter provides a framework for the basic constructs of Cognitive Coaching. Those who choose to embrace this way of working will benefit from taking more extensive training that will guide them in becoming knowledgeable and skillful with the principles and practices of Cognitive Coaching (www.cognitivecoaching.com).

THE MISSION OF COGNITIVE COACHING

Cognitive Coaching is a model that guides a person's actions and provides a process for working from the following mission:

> The mission of Cognitive Coaching is to produce self-directed persons with the cognitive capacity for high performance both independently and as members of a community. (Costa & Garmston, 2002, p. 16)

Missions define our purpose and reason for existing. Each word in the mission statement clarifies a way of working with intentionality.

The verb *produce* suggests that educators must be results-oriented with a focus on outcomes for the individuals with whom they work. Cognitive Coaching focuses on impact by assisting in identifying the results one is striving for and clarifying the success indicators and strategies for doing so. Additionally, the Cognitive Coach assists the coachee in examining data, reflecting on their meaning, and committing to action for the future.

Self-directed persons are one of the outcomes of a person who holds the mission of Cognitive Coaching in the forefront of his or her mind. Costa and Garmston (2002) define self-directedness through three distinct yet intertwined qualities—*self-managing, self-monitoring,* and *self-modifying.* Self-managing people are able to articulate their goals and intentions. They hold a clear vision for their own achievements and are strategic in planning for goal achievements. *Self-management* includes specificity about indicators of success. People with skill in self-management are deliberate about considering prior knowledge and experiences. They are careful to control the tendency to leap to action and instead gather information and consider options and relevant data. *Self-monitoring* requires constant vigilance of oneself and one's environment. Self-monitoring people gather data as an ongoing process. They draw on self-knowledge as a checkpoint for attending to what is working and not working. Self-monitoring is a process requiring attention to one's metacognition as well as external cues. In self-monitoring, an individual is constantly comparing the current conditions to the intended plan. To be truly self-monitoring requires attention to alternatives and choice-making in the moment. It demands focus through attentive listening and observing. To be *self-modifying,* an individual must evaluate his or her actions and decisions against intentions and goals. Self-modification requires reflection and introspection. A disposition toward continuous growth serves the self-modifying person. That disposition includes constructing meaning from experience and commitment to make changes based on the new learning. Self-modification draws from the self-monitoring process to focus forward and deliberate on future actions.

The phrase in the Mission Statement, *cognitive capacity*, differentiates Cognitive Coaching from other models of coaching or supervision. The unique focus of this work is to develop an individual's ability to engage in higher levels cognitive functioning (e.g., evaluating, analyzing, inferring). The concept of capacity assumes that the cognitive abilities can be developed. Cognitive functions are not mutually exclusive of emotions. Each is part of a system of biochemically interdependent responses incorporated into one singular system (Damasio, 1994). Cognitive Coaching addresses the intertwined nature of the cognitive and affective systems. Leaders who are coached have increased capacity for complex thinking and for addressing their own emotions and those of others. Cognitive Coaching draws on the research on teacher cognition and supports increased capacity for planning, reflecting, and problem resolving. Additionally, Cognitive Coaching supports the development of emotional and social intelligence as defined by Daniel Goleman.

In his most recent book, Goleman (2006) states that as human beings, we are wired to connect with each other. "Neuroscience has discovered that our brain's very design makes it *sociable*, inexorably drawn into a brain-to-brain linkup whenever we engage with another person" (Goleman, 2006, p. 4).

Cognitive Coaching expands the traditional work of an educator to include developing internal cognitive, social, and emotional capacities within others. When individuals are coached, they have a richer understanding of how to develop those capacities in others, and they simultaneously have their cognitive and affective capacities expanded. The mission of Cognitive Coaching describes cognitive capacity as a means for high performance in two domains—*independently* and *in community*. Cognitive Coaching draws on the concept of holonomy, the study of wholeness (Costa & Garmston, 2002). Central to the mission is a focus on the duality of human existence. Each of us lives an autonomous life with our own thoughts and emotions, unique talents and skills, and a personality unlike anyone else's. Simultaneously, we live as members of systems, be those family systems or organizational systems. We are influenced by the systems in which we live and concurrently, as individuals, influence the systems. The self and system are interconnected, interdependent, and inseparable. However, the dual nature of this reality creates tensions between our internal self and the systems self. Those tensions have been defined as tensions of holonomy (Costa & Lipton, 1996).

Resolving the tensions allows us to rise to the challenges of human growth and development and to live more productive lives, serving others and ourselves. Through Cognitive Coaching, individuals become

---

Tensions of Holonomy

Ambiguity and Certainty

Knowledge and Action

Egocentricity and Allocentricity

Self-Assertion and Integration

Inner Feelings and Outer Behaviors

Solitude and Interconnectedness

SOURCE: Costa, A., & Lipton, L. (1996). *Holonomy: Paradox and promise.* Unpublished manuscript. Reprinted with permission of Art Costa.

more skillful in resolving the inherent tensions within themselves and their jobs. The Cognitive Coach is intentional in providing assistance in finding resources to balance and manage the tensions. Those resources are called *States of Mind.*

FIVE STATES OF MIND

Cognitive Coaching draws on an impressive list of many well-respected researchers, including the following: Lev Vygotsky, Richard Bandler and John Grinder, Carl Jung, Richard Shavelson, David Berliner, Carl Glickman, Arthur Koestler, Reuven Feuerstein, Albert Bandura, Gregory Bateson, Noam Chomsky, John Dewey, Robert Goldhammer and Morris Cogan, Antonio Damasio, Carl Rogers, and Abraham Maslow. At the core of the work, and unique to this model, is the concept of States of Mind. This is the original work of Costa and Garmston. The States of Mind describe and illuminate the resources necessary to become intentionally holonomous and self-directed. They are abstractions that provide a conceptual framework for understanding the internal drives within each of us. The five States of Mind that are central to the work of a Cognitive Coach are efficacy, flexibility, consciousness, craftsmanship, and interdependence.

1. Efficacy

Teacher and school *efficacy* are among the most highly researched aspects of educational literature. Albert Bandura (1997) describes self-efficacy as belief in one's capabilities to organize and execute the courses of action required to produce given attainments. In an educational setting, efficacy is an internally held sense that one has the knowledge and skills to impact the learning processes in the school to attain desired results. Efficacy exists within individuals and for schools. For example, with high efficacy, a teacher knows her actions make a difference across the school community. Each interaction contributes to the overall learning of the community. High teacher efficacy means teachers hold a belief that their actions will result in student learning. Ongoing efforts will pay off with results. When a person has low efficacy, there is a strong external locus of control, often manifesting itself as blame and victimization; for example, "These kids come from such deprived homes," or "I had such better results when I had a different population of students."

Efficacy is a foundational State of Mind, being a resource that gives us a sense of motivation, hope, and a belief in our own ability to influence and change our world. Research on efficacy has shown to have consistent findings (Tschannen-Moran, Woolfolk Hoy, & Hoy, 1998):

- Efficacy is self-fulfilling. With increased efficacy, teachers make greater effort resulting in improved results. With lower efficacy, less effort is expended leading to fewer results and decreased efficacy.

- Efficacy leads to openness to new ideas and experimentation to support learning.
- Efficacy increases resilience and the willingness to persist in efforts in light of challenges.
- Efficacy decreases criticism of students when they are not successful and draws up their planning and organization
- Efficacy decreases the likelihood a teacher will make a special education referral.
- Efficacy increases a teacher's enthusiasm for teaching.
- Efficacy at the school level relates to a healthy organizational climate.
- School efficacy relates to an orderly and positive environment and more classroom-based decision making.

The process of Cognitive Coaching in and of itself builds efficacy.

2. Consciousness

Consciousness leads to self-awareness and allows for examination of other States of Mind. It requires attention to one's own metacognition. Highly conscious people listen to their own listening. In working with others, they notice biases interfering with their ways of understanding, they think about how their preferences affect their perceptions, and they track the processes of their thinking. The following are examples of the kinds of internal questions a conscious person might ask. Such consciousness provides capacity for reflection before, during, and after an experience:

- Am I being logical or emotional?
- How is my prior knowledge of this situation affecting my thought processes?
- What judgments am I making?
- How can I gain another perspective on this?
- What might I do to become more data-based?

In addition to internal attention, the conscious person is monitoring external cues and data in an ongoing manner. In working with a teacher, the coach pays attention to the subtle, nonverbal cues in addition to the words being spoken. The principal observing a classroom is aware of the need to attend to both the teachers and the learners. Focus is given to both types of data. Every experience is lived at two levels, one with attention to self and one with attention to others. The executive capacity to manage both simultaneously is a sign of highly developed consciousness. In addition, the conscious person makes connections between past and present experiences, seeking patterns and connections. The ability to do that kind of thinking is what distinguishes us from other species and mammals (Damasio, 1994).

3. Craftsmanship

Craftsmanship is an internal drive toward personal and group excellence. It manifests itself behaviorally in a drive for continuous improvement. It is not about becoming a perfectionist, but instead focusing on clear criteria for quality. It is about measuring one's performance against a standard and seeking ongoing means for moving toward a higher standard. Craftsmanship is data-driven. The teacher with high craftsmanship invites the use of data in determining areas of growth for her students. She pushes the envelope, always holding higher and higher expectations for students. She models her value on growth in her actions and expectations. She commends successes by giving specific feedback on the sources and examples of striving for higher performance. Simultaneously, she analyzes cause and effect before setting future goals. Craftsmanship is not judgmental, but seeks ongoing self-assessment using criteria for excellence. From the self-assessment stage, craftsmanship leads us to examine our actions and their outcomes with an intention to refine them for development and growth toward even more successful performance and outcomes.

4. Flexibility

Flexibility is the State of Mind that allows us to move beyond our natural tendencies toward egocentricity. Egocentricity is necessary for survival; it allows us to monitor our internal states, knowing when to withdraw from a situation and even telling us when we need to take shelter and food. However, egocentricity simultaneously limits our ability to see and understand our world beyond our internal frameworks and lenses. Low flexibility is the source of low creativity and high rigidity. We are trapped by our egocentricity, becoming blind to new and different ways of seeing. Margaret Wheatley (2005) describes listening for flexibility:

> There are many ways to sit and listen for the differences. Lately, I've been listening for what surprises me. What did I just hear that startled me? This isn't easy—I'm accustomed to sit there nodding my head as someone voices what I agree with. But when I notice what surprises me, I'm able to see my own views more clearly, including my beliefs and assumptions. (p. 212)

The flexible teacher is open to understanding the multiple perspectives of his or her students and embracing the diversity. As Wheatley (2005) states, "It's not the differences that divide us. It's our judgments that do. Curiosity and good listening bring us back together" (p. 212). Taking those multiple perspectives enhances a leader's ability to unite diverse factions. Flexibility is a doorway to interdependence.

Flexibility is also a touchstone for creativity and problem solving. A flexible person explores multiple alternatives, viewpoints, and possibilities.

We spoke with a participant in Tennessee whose school was struggling with tardiness. Many efforts had been tried, including student consequences and appeals to parents. Thinking flexibly, the principal purchased alarm clocks for students that were distributed with talks about self-management and self-monitoring. Behaviors began to change. The flexible position moved from blaming and punishing to inviting alternative behaviors.

5. Interdependence

Interdependence is a resource that allows us to move beyond a self-centered view of the world to a view that assists us in seeing ourselves as part of something larger. Interdependence assists us in moving between egocentricity (self-centered), allocentricity (other-centered), and macrocentricity (system-centered). Interdependence draws on our ability to see the nature of our relationships instead of thinking in isolation:

> Those of us educated in Western culture learned to think and manage a world that was anything but systemic or interconnected. It's a world of separations and clear boundaries: jobs in boxes, lines delineating relationships, roles, and policies describing what each individual does and who we expect them to be. (Wheatley, 2005, p. 100)

> The recognition that individuals need each other lies at the heart of every system. From that realization, individuals reach out, and seemingly divergent self-interests develop into a system of interdependency. Thus, all systems form through collaboration, from the recognition that we need another in order to survive. (Wheatley, 2005, pp. 102–103)

Mutuality and reciprocity are critical attributes of the State of Mind of interdependence. Interdependent people see themselves inside a system and appreciate the flow of resources. They understand the need to contribute to the system and appreciate the value they receive from the system.

Given the growing body of research on the importance of building collaborative cultures to impact student achievement, effective educators will move beyond a hierarchal and authoritarian structure of leadership. To do so, they will need to have their own internal resource of high interdependence with their staff and the school district. Equally important, they will have a skill set for creating increasing interdependencies within their school.

So how do coaches utilize their knowledge of States of Mind to support self-directed learning? Cognitive Coaches listen closely to the thoughts of the coachee. As they listen, they are not only hearing the content of the words being delivered, but at a deeper level, they are listening for what the words say about the person's States of Mind. As the coaches explore the States of Mind, the thinking of the coachee deepens, expands, and takes on new dimensions. The direction is unknown to the coaches because the new thinking is created inside the coachee. The coaches deftly use States of Mind as a means to create new possibilities, new thinking, and new resources for the people being coached.

ASSUMPTIONS OF COGNITIVE COACHING

Cognitive Coaching is grounded in the assumption that humans seek learning and growth as inherent parts of their being. It presumes resourcefulness and sufficiency in others. Cognitive Coaching is a process that provides conditions for maximizing the individual's drive for self-directedness.

A toddler illustrated this to his grandmother. The grandmother was observing her young grandson struggle with a puzzle. Wanting to see him succeed, she offered her assistance. In his innocent way, with his limited language, he responded to her offer with these words: "Grandma, I do it I-self." What a powerful spoken message early in life about the natural drive to be self-directed. The grandmother wisely listened to her grandson's words and backed away, observing him work tirelessly to make the puzzle pieces fit. After much ado, he had some successes and some frustration with the more complex aspects of the puzzle. As he reached the point of maximum effort with low success, he shifted his posture with his grandmother by saying, "Grandma, I need some help." This story illustrates the faith in human capacity within Cognitive Coaching. We are naturally self-directed, striving for a sense of freedom as a learner. We are equally dependent on our environment to support our need to go beyond our current capacity. Cognitive Coaching allows for the human nature within us to find its place in a nurturing environment. It provides support for managing the tensions of autonomy and community.

Cognitive Coaching is a mental model for cognitive development. It assumes that when thinking is mediated, cognitive growth will occur. The word *mediation* is derived from middle, like the word *median*. The mediator, using a set of coaching skills, intervenes between a person and a task or between a person and an experience. When a person faces a task or problem to be solved, the mediator or coach uses Cognitive Coaching maps and tools to assist the person in thinking clearly about his or her goals and resources. In mediating between a person and experience, the coach assists the person in reflecting on available data about the experience, analyzing the meaning of the information, and constructing new learning that will lead the person forward to future applications. The same process occurs in reflection. The coach intervenes between the person and the experience and invites analysis and new insight. From the reflection, the individual is able to project the learnings into future applications. The intention of the coach is to assist the learner in clarifying, developing, and modifying his or her internal schema (Costa & Garmston, 2002). That is the process for creation of new learning. Without mediation of thinking, there is little likelihood that internal thought structures will be modified.

Robert Kegan's (Kegan, 1995; Drago-Severson, 2004) constructive-developmental theory illustrates how the processes of Cognitive Coaching influence adult development. The theory operates on a fundamental assumption that growth and development are processes that are ongoing and never-ending throughout life. If those growth processes are to be sustained, interventions to reshape and expand internal meaning-making structures are necessary. Kegan differentiates informational learning and transformational learning. Informational learning adds value to what a person knows and the skills he or she can demonstrate. Transformational learning changes the way a person knows. As ways of knowing shift, leaders develop in their ability to deal with greater complexities and challenges in their environment. Kegan names three stages of adult development, sometimes given different names: the Socializing, the Self-Authoring, and the Self-Transformational.

Adults at the Socializing level can be characterized as dependent on others as sources of their values. Experiences are tests of whether others value them. The environment is the source of well-being. Criticism and conflict are perceived as negative and become threatening to the self. Transition to the Self-Authoring level is evidenced by a stronger sense of values being internally developed, and an internal set of standards becomes a measuring tool for success. Self-Authoring people are constantly questioning whether they are living in a way that is congruent with their own values. At the Self-Transformational level, the adult is most capable of dealing with a world that is nonlinear, ever-changing, and highly demanding. Conflict is an inherent part of life and is seen as a source of deeper understanding and improvement. Most adults never reach the stage of becoming Self-Transforming. They remain trapped in earlier stages because they are not in an environment that mediates their development; instead it only adds skills and information to their repertoire.

Kegan assists us in having mental models for promoting transformational development (Kegan, 1995; Drago-Severson, 2004). Like children, adults need an environment that provides developmentally appropriate supports while simultaneously offering challenges. It is the critical combination of support and challenge that allows the adult to construct new ways of being and knowing. Without that environment, the conditions for development are nonexistent. Cognitive Coaching is a perfect match to developmental-constructivism. It supports teachers and principals with a listening, nonjudgmental ear. Additionally, it invites inquiry, a reshaping and reconstructing of one's thinking, and challenges the deep structures of a person's mental models, beliefs, values, and identity. Without this kind of intervention, educators become trapped in a professional development and support system that is informational only. True growth is limited rather than expanded. Cognitive Coaching can create conditions for transformational learning.

Cognitive Coaching is a constructivist model of learning. It rejects behaviorist notions that ignore the capacity of the human mind to create knowledge, examine the meaning of knowledge, and make decisions about how to act on knowledge. The coach intentionally structures human interactions to maximize productive analysis of one's work and environment to act more effectively as a professional.

As professionals, we have a responsibility to those we serve to be continuously learning. There is ample evidence (Joyce & Showers, 1995) to indicate that without coaching, educators have little likelihood of moving knowledge learned in training into important arenas of application. Cognitive Coaching is grounded in an assumption that explicit processes are required to facilitate learning. Learning is not linear, but it is also not haphazard. Attention to structures and processes for learning enhances the likelihood for results and capacity for forward momentum.

Cognitive Coaching is a nonjudgmental process. The person being coached makes his or her own judgments. The coach builds trust by being nonjudgmental. The coaching environment frees the person to take risks and examine long-held assumptions without fear. Cognitive Coaching is congruent with the body of research describing the importance of environmental conditions for thoughtful practice. Under stress, the brain reverts to old pathways that move the actor toward fight or flight. Those patterns are counterproductive for the conditions and needs of today's educators. By contrast, Cognitive Coaching enhances the environmental conditions necessary to sustain the neural capacity to work at the neocortical or higher level thinking part of the brain. If we want to be thoughtful, reflective practitioners, we have a responsibility to provide systems of support to make that happen. The skills of the Cognitive Coach enhance and support the most basic neural needs to develop our most exquisite capacities.

FOUR SUPPORT FUNCTIONS

Costa and Garmston (2002) have developed a model of four functions for professional support: Cognitive Coaching, collaborating, consulting, and evaluation. These functions allow those who are supporting others to be clear about the purpose of their interactions and to apply functions to their work based on need rather than some prescribed process. Costa and Garmston refer to this as a capability: "Know one's intentions and choose congruent behaviors" (p. 64). All four support functions are intended to support growth and development, but they do so in very different ways. Although all four have a place in systems of support, Cognitive Coaching has the greatest potential for transformational learning. It is an ongoing process whereby the coach invites regular reflection based on the needs of the coachee, thus increasing capacity with the coachee's internal resources. It is a constructivist-developmental process, one of the most compatible of the four support functions with transformational learning.

Evaluation is probably the most familiar in educational settings. It refers to making judgments about one's performance based on a well-understood set of external standards. While evaluation is an important accountability measure for districts, it has little potential for transformational growth as it is externally imposed and rarely constructivist in nature. The implementation most often relates to personnel systems rather than growth.

Consulting is also a familiar form of support in the world of schools. Consultants work to support others by providing expertise and knowledge to them with the intention to expand their informational learning. This is often seen in the form of mentor programs where others are assigned to teachers and principals to share their knowledge and experiences. The mentors help their mentees "learn the job" and problem solve with them. While very helpful, without an added Cognitive Coaching component, these are not effective in transformational learning, the most effective source of adult development.

Another support function, collaboration, allows a team or pair of educators to work together to plan, problem solve, or inquire together. The notion of collaboration is about a community of learners, sharing their ideas and creating learning together.

A key feature that differentiates the four support functions is the source of judgment in each. In Cognitive Coaching, the judgments are made by the coachee, for example, "I was not happy with the meeting today because . . ." In collaboration, the judgments are shared by the collaborators, for example, "We seem to agree that by disaggregating our data, we are becoming more effective in addressing learner deficits." The consultant provides judgments about the criteria for performance using his or her expertise to define them, for example, "When you can document that you are spending 30% of your time on learning walks, you can expect to see some gains from the process." In evaluation, the criteria are set through defined standards and the evaluator makes judgments about the person's performance in relation to the data, for example, "Your work is a level 3 on our performance criteria for Instructional Leadership. Here are the data I am using to make that rating."

COGNITIVE COACHING CONVERSATION MAPS

Cognitive Coaches are guided in their interactions by three coaching maps. When we think of a roadmap, we think of a symbolic representation of some territory we might like to explore. It serves as a guide for assisting us through some terrain, focusing us on staying on course and getting where we want to go. We know the map is only a depiction and that we have to make midcourse corrections as we traverse the territory. Cognitive Coaching maps serve a similar function. They give us templates for conversations for planning, reflecting, and problem resolving. They are not scripts, but guides through the territory of the teacher's thinking. They serve to focus the conversation, keeping it on course and supporting productive use of time. The maps reflect research on effective planning, reflecting, and problem resolving. As coaches internalize the maps, it frees them to focus fully on truly listening to the internal maps of the teacher's mind, revealed in their conversations. Further it gives the coach guidance in patterns of questioning that build capacity for self-directed learning. The Cognitive Coaching model is based on three maps, each with different purposes.

The Planning Conversation Map serves to assist a teacher in preparing for an upcoming event. It is generic and can be used for multiple purposes (e.g., planning a staff meeting or lesson, preparing for a parent conference, long-range planning related to school improvement). This map has two focuses—one on the event and one on the person doing the planning. It ends with a reflection on the coaching. The first three regions of the map focus on the event. In doing so, the planner has the opportunity to mentally rehearse the event, gaining greater clarity and craftsmanship about the event's desired outcomes and the ways of assessing those outcomes. The teacher anticipates effective strategies and considers ways to monitor and adjust as the event progresses. The fourth region, the personal learning focus, shifts the teacher's thinking from the event to an internal focus. The teacher is asked to identify areas of learning and growth. This region may be the most critical region of the map as it is the source of an internal focus and goal setting for learning. Without this element, the map is shallow, providing only thinking for the event, but no deeper commitment to professional growth and meaning-making from the experience. The final region of the map invites reflection on the conversation, providing thinking to synthesize for the teacher and feedback to the coach.

The Reflecting Conversation Map serves the teacher in analyzing and learning from experiences. It invites a person to move from a significant experience to making meaning of the experience in a manner that leads to transferring learning into the future. Without reflection, teachers are doomed to repeat patterns of behavior. Contrasted with the common educational practice of planning, few educators are given the opportunity to reflect and few have internalized the processes of reflection. This map provides a structure that moves teachers from focusing on events (episodic thinking) to gleaning key learnings and generalizations from experiences. In doing so, the map is compatible with how human brains remember. We do not remember specifics, but instead store generalizations and guiding principles: for example, inclusion is a key factor in decision making; budgeting is something that is often misunderstood by staff. Those larger frames inform us in the future. Smaller frames (e.g., that was a challenging staff meeting because three teachers were upset about how the final decision was made) do not inform us for the future. They only cause us to recycle an event over and over.

In the reflecting conversation, the coach is careful to not invite storytelling, a simple reiteration of the experience. Instead the coach supports the reflector in linking impressions with data that support those impressions. The critical focus of this map is on analyzing causal factors. The coach supports high consciousness by assisting the thinking about each decision and each part of the experience. As those are analyzed, the teacher begins to construct new learning about factors that contributed to the outcomes, successes, and failures in the experience. From that analysis, the reflector is able to gain new insights that lead to generalizations for future application. The final region of the map, reflect on the process, is the same as in the Planning Conversation.

The Problem-Resolving Map draws on brain research about the human mind under stress. It is a map a coach might use with teachers who are seemingly low in resources and unable to find forward direction. Examples might be as follows:

- A teacher is uncertain about how to implement a new program.
- A teacher is having a difficult relationship with his assistant.
- A difficult parent issue seems without resolution.
- A teacher is discouraged by the pressure to deliver improved test scores.

The Problem-Resolving Map differs from the other maps in that it is more conceptual and less focused on specific steps to explore. The States of Mind are the source of questions in all of the three maps, but especially critical in this map. The coach is attuned to the emotional and cognitive needs of the coachee, balancing the two.

The map first attends to an acknowledgement of the existing state, that is, what is the current reality for the coachee. This is important because, under threat, the brain experiences neurochemical changes causing loss of cognitive capacity. The structure and processes of the map support enhanced cognition. The map begins with a process called pacing which paraphrases the existing state of the person. Attention is given to both emotion and content of the existing state, for example, "You're hurt because your boss is not seeing your contributions."

The map's structure leads the coach to refocus the coachee's energy toward the desired state. The coachee begins to envision a better future, for example, feeling valued. The increase in the brain's neurotransmitters occurs when language is given to creating an image of something more positive. The coach uses language to assist the problem resolver in expressing a more desirable way of being. Finally, using the States of Mind as sources of energy, the coach questions the problem resolver to develop internal resources related to the desired state.

Skilled coaches develop flexibility in using the maps. They sometimes use only some of the regions of the map in their mediation of the teacher's thinking. Other times they modify the sequencing of the maps to align with the needs of the teacher. Coaches use the maps both formally and informally. A short conversation in the hall might cover just a few elements of the map and the coach could leave the teacher with a question to ponder. Such conversations do not bring closure to a coachee's thinking. The brief hallway conversation is still coaching and leaves the person more resourceful. The coach knows that work can continue with the coachee in future conversations. The focus of coaching is on serving the needs of the person in the moment, not on completing the maps.

COACHING TOOLS

Cognitive Coaches work from a toolkit of effective communication skills that support creating an environment of trust. If the coach is to grow transformationally, there must be challenge *and* support. The coach's toolkit is congruent with those intentions. One teacher called her coaching sessions her, "brain massage." When you think of the qualities of a skilled massage, there is an opportunity to tune out other stimuli and focus on self. The atmosphere is relaxed and slowed in pace. However, with deep massage, like deep thinking, there is often some pain and challenge.

Rapport skills allow the Cognitive Coach to create comfort in the moment and let the coachee know that the coach is truly present and listening intently. The kind of listening that is seen when the coach attends fully, using verbal and nonverbal skills, is rarely seen in an educator's day. The rapport is intended to create optimal conditions for thinking.

Cognitive Coaches are knowledgeable in response behaviors designed to mediate thinking. Those behaviors include pausing, paraphrasing, and probing for specificity. Our culture has come to equate speed with intelligence. Similarly we equate productivity with speed (Wheatley, 2005). The pause provides time to think for both the coach and the teacher. It allows for space to engage in the behaviors of complex thinking and reflection. Pausing has been shown to create an increased level of cognitive functioning in students. It is our experience that the same is true for adult learners.

Paraphrasing, well executed, is a fundamental tool for mediating thinking. When people hear their own words reflected back in a rephrased manner, it is often the first time they attend to the meaning of their own thinking. It is the social construction of placing one's thinking in the middle between the coach and teacher and examining it with one's own words and then examining it a second time through the coach's paraphrases that causes a reshaping and deeper examination of the internal thought processes that may have been previously unexpressed. Without language being put to the inner thoughts, they remain inaccessible and cannot be modified. Cognitive Coaches use a variety of paraphrasing types to cause teachers to hear their own feelings, key concepts, and generalizations. The most complex paraphrases give teachers access to their inner beliefs, values, assumptions, goals, and mental models.

Probing for specificity is one way a coach increases the teacher's precision and craftsmanship. Words are simply an externalization of thinking. When words lack specificity it is often a reflection of lack of clarity in thinking. Take for instance a teacher who says, "It's important to me that my students collaborate." If the teacher is to genuinely target student collaboration, he or she will need to have a clear picture about the meaning of collaboration. Does it mean that teachers share texts, coplan, examine student work, or use common assessments? The Cognitive Coach would assist the teacher in moving toward clarity by following, "It's important to me that my students collaborate," with a probe such as, "If your students were genuinely collaborating, what might be some of the behaviors you would expect to see?" Another probe might be, "What does collaboration mean to you?" Probes bring focus and clarity to words that allow us to move them to action.

Inquiry is another tool a coach uses. Inquiry differs from probing in that it has the intention to broaden thinking to more divergence. The coach, speaking to a teacher about his or her value around collaboration, might inquire by asking, "What might you anticipate happening for student thought processes if they were to collaborate?" or "As you envision a more collaborative classroom, what possible downsides might there be?" Effective inquiry is open-ended and has no agenda. It is an invitation to explore. Inquiry has intellectual risk embedded in it as it may cause one to think about things that one had not considered before, or it may make visible things which are uncomfortable, challenging, or even threatening. This is the heart of using Cognitive Coaching for transformational learning. Inquiry moves the person into the territory of challenge. In pairing inquiry with the other coaching tools, it also creates a sense of support. When people are invited to think through inquiry, they begin to internalize the process of inquiry and become more self-directed in developing a professional identity as an inquirer.

IDENTITY AS A MEDIATOR OF THINKING

The thinking of Cognitive Coaches distinguishes them from other types of coaches. The focus on self-directed learning requires that Cognitive Coaches think about their role as neutral and nonjudgmental about the topic of conversation. Although Cognitive Coaches are unbiased about *what* the person is thinking, they are biased that the person *is* thinking.

The metacognition of Cognitive Coaches is based on their identity as mediators of thinking. Our identity is who we believe we are and is usually held unconsciously. Although it may be unconscious, it is reflected in all our words and actions and is apparent to all those with whom we live and work. Our identity influences our perceptions, interactions, choices, and ultimately the way we fulfill our roles and responsibilities in life.

The term *mediator* comes from the work of Reuven Feuerstein (2000) and refers to mediated learning experiences. Feuerstein describes a mediated learning experience as one in which a person processes the experience at deeper levels because a mediator is interposed between the event and the learner. Such mediated learning experiences lead to deeper, more pervasive change.

Costa and Garmston (2002) explain mediator in the following way:

> The word *mediate* is derived form the word *middle*. Therefore, mediators interpose themselves between a person and some event, problem, conflict, challenge or other perplexing situation. The mediator intervenes in such a way as to enhance another person's self-directed learning. (p. 56).

When one's identity is that of a mediator of thinking, one believes that he or she is someone who can be neutral and nonjudgmental in supporting another person's thinking toward being self-directed. A mediator of thinking does not solve other people's problems for them because that would be robbing them of an opportunity to grow. Metaphorically, a mediator shines a spotlight of awareness on the other person's thinking. Ultimately, mediators of thinking believe in the human capacity for continual growth, in themselves and in others, and also in their capacity to empower others.

It is as a mediator of thinking that each of us holds the greatest potential for supporting growth and development of another person. When a coach mediates a teacher's thinking, the teacher's learning is enhanced, and there is an increased likelihood of change. From these mediated learning experiences, teachers are able to more fully develop their potential for success as leaders.

METAPHORICAL ORIENTATIONS

Costa and Garmston (2002) contrast four metaphorical orientations that people sometimes take when they are not being a mediator of thinking. The metaphorical orientations are parent, expert, friend, and boss. As metaphors, they serve to help us understand the presuppositions and goals we have when we are not engaging neutrally without judgments. For many coaches it is the orientation of expert that is problematic to developing one's identity and capacity as a mediator of thinking. Past experience and positive reinforcement for offering advice and suggestions often interfere with becoming a mediator of thinking. In fact, the job title "consultant" communicates to others that you are an expert, someone to be consulted on designated topics.

People who have an expert orientation place high value on their ability to help others by sharing their expertise. Their sense of self-worth is based on how much they know and how much they can share that knowledge and skill with others. Oftentimes they have been promoted and sought out in an organization as a person to call on to have things "fixed." Letting go of an expert orientation as a default position must happen before a coach can develop the identity of a mediator of thinking. It doesn't mean that the coach will never share his or her expertise. When the decision is made to share expertise, it will be based on the coachee's need to receive it and not the coach's need to share it.

The expert orientation is the basis for the support function of consulting. If a coach begins a conversation in the consulting support function, he lowers the efficacy of the person and builds dependency on the coach. Given the percentage of time that teachers will spend with coaches, versus the amount of time they will spend on their own, the coaches who enter conversations as consultants are not doing all that they can to build the self-directedness of the coachees.

Entering a conversation from a neutral, nonjudgmental perspective enables coaches to determine whether Cognitive Coaching is the most appropriate support function to support self-directedness. Additionally, it enables coaches to determine what information they might need to offer while collaborating, consulting, or evaluating. When one's identify is that of a mediator of thinking, he or she defaults to the support function of Cognitive Coaching. Just as a computer defaults to a certain font when you turn it on, mediators of thinking default to the support function of Cognitive Coaching when they enter into an interaction with another person. It is from this neutral perspective that one can make decisions about other ways to support the teacher.

THE COGNITIVE COACHING PROCESS

Every human interaction is an opportunity to mediate another person's thinking. We do not choose to mediate in every interaction, but the choice is always available. In viewing coaching as ongoing, we begin to view our work as a process of continuous improvement and development. Although most educators come to their work with skills, the job is organic, changing, and evolving. Effective educators seek opportunities to reflect on practice and broaden and deepen their thinking and internal thought structures. Without a coaching process, opportunities for reflection and focused thinking become infrequent. Cognitive Coaching provides a structure for and expectation of reflective practice. Cognitive Coaching is not a process of evaluation. Evaluation exists to make judgments about performance. It is a key feature of effective human resource management, but it is generally ineffective in developing professionals with increased capacity for rich cognition and self-directedness. The process of Cognitive Coaching institutionalizes the expectation that educators will be supported as growing professionals.

REFERENCES

Bandura, A. (1997). *Self-efficacy: The exercise of control.* New York: W.H. Freeman.

Costa, A., & Garmston, R. (2002). *Cognitive Coaching^SM: A foundation for renaissance schools.* Norwood, MA: Christopher-Gordon.

Costa, A., & Lipton. L. (1996). *Holonomy: paradox and promise.* Unpublished manuscript.

Damasio, A. (1994). *Descartes error: Emotion, reason and the human brain.* New York: HarperCollins.

Drago-Severson, E. (2004). *Helping teachers learn.* Thousand Oaks, CA: Corwin Press.

Edwards, J. (2005). *Cognitive coaching research.* Highlands Ranch, CO: Center for Cognitive Coaching.

Ellison, J., & Hayes, C. (2006a). *Cognitive coaching: Weaving threads of learning and change into the culture of an organization.* Norwood, MA: Christopher-Gordon.

Ellison, J., & Hayes, C. (2006b). *Effective school leadership: Developing principals through cognitive coaching.* Norwood, MA: Christopher-Gordon.

Feuerstein, R. (2000). Mediated learning experience. In A. Costa (Ed.), *Teaching for intelligence II: A collection of articles* (p. 275). Arlington Heights, IL: Skylights.

Goleman, D. (2006). *Social intelligence.* New York: Bantam Dell.

Joyce, B, & Showers, B. (1995). *Student achievement through staff development* (3rd ed.). Alexandria, VA: Association for Supervision and Curriculum Development.

Kegan, R. (1995). *In over our heads: The mental demands of modern life.* Cambridge, MA: Harvard University Press.

Tschannen-Moran, M., Woolfolk Hoy, A., & Hoy, W. K. (1998). Teacher efficacy: Its meaning and measure. *Review of Educational Research, 68*(2), 202–248.

Wheatley, M. J. (2005). *Finding our way: Leadership for an uncertain time.* San Francisco: Berrett-Koehler.

Partnership Communication

Chapter 12

Creating Learning Conversations

Jim Knight

I love communicating with people. I love making people feel good about themselves and what they teach. This is the perfect job to make people feel good about themselves, to feel good about their profession, and to help kids learn.

—Lynn Barnes, instructional coach,
Jardine Middle School

CHAPTER OVERVIEW

The success or failure of a coaching program hinges on the coach's ability to communicate clearly, build relationships, and support fellow teachers. A coach who struggles to get along with others will likely struggle to be successful. This chapter introduces six aspects of effective communication: (a) understanding the communication process, (b) employing authentic listening, (c) understanding our audiences, (d) recognizing stories, (e) interpreting nonverbal communication and facial expressions, and (f) building relationships through emotional connection. Coaches who learn and apply these aspects of communication to their professional and personal life should be better prepared to connect with people in meaningful, healthy relationships.

CREATING LEARNING CONVERSATIONS

We face a crisis of communication. Although we may talk with dozens of people every day, we can go through entire weeks or longer never having a single, meaningful conversation. Margaret Wheatley, author of *Turning to One Another: Simple Conversations to Restore Hope to the Future* (2002), describes our situation as follows:

We have never wanted to be alone. But today, we are alone. We are more fragmented and isolated from one another than ever before. Archbishop Desmond Tutu describes it as "a radical brokenness in all of existence." (p. 4)

On those occasions when we work up the courage to share a few honest words, we often find that things fall apart. We try to make a simple point, to express a well-thought-through opinion, and find ourselves silenced, or ignored, or inadvertently offending someone whom we meant no harm, or offended by someone who meant us no harm. In a time when many people long for more intimacy, we struggle to find a common language to make meaningful conversation possible. For many, the only place where intimate conversations exist is on the Internet, with strangers.

Communicating an important message can be one of the most authentic, rewarding experiences in life. When we communicate, we learn; we share thoughts, experiences, and emotions; we become colleagues, friends, and soul mates. Words and language, messages sent and received, can build a tie between people that is deep, strong, and even lifelong. Effective communication can enable the kind of faithful relationship that we build our lives around. Unfortunately, words can also destroy relationships. A simple, innocent comment can do damage that may take years to repair, or damage that may never be repaired. Getting our messages through is a messy business.

Our common struggle to communicate is doubly important for ICs (instructional coaches). The ability to communicate effectively stands at the heart of what ICs do, not just inside the walls of a school, but inside every important relationship in which they live. An IC who is a highly effective communicator is well on the way to a successful career. An IC who struggles to communicate effectively, however, faces a world of challenges. We may not be far off the mark if we say that ICs cannot be effective in their profession unless they understand how to be effective communicators.

Lynn Barnes, an IC at Jardine Middle School, believes that communication and relationship building lie at the heart of being an effective coach. "You have to build a relationship before you can do anything. You have to truly care about the individuals and students you are working with. At all times, you have to be compassionate, empathetic, patient and understanding. There's no place for sarcasm with kids or adults."

Lynn Barnes

Lynn Barnes, an IC at Jardine Middle School, has a total of 35 years of teaching experience. Of the 35 years, she has been an IC for 6 years and taught language arts for 15 years. Lynn won Topeka's Middle School Teacher of the Year Award and is certified as a Strategic Instruction Model Content Enhancement Professional Developer, a Strategic Instruction Model Learning Strategies Professional Developer, and a Professional Developer for Randy Sprick's Safe and Civil Schools program.

THE COMMUNICATION PROCESS

Understanding the communication process can help us see why communication frequently falters and fails. As the figure below illustrates, communication of any sort is more complicated than meets the eye (or ear, I suppose, depending on the way the message is shared) and the process of communication involves several components.

Figure 12.1   The Communication Process

- Speaker
- Message
- Listener
- Interference
- Perceived Message
- Feedback

Components of the Communication Process

Communication usually begins with an intended message, that is, an idea, thought, opinion, or statement that someone wishes to communicate to another person or persons. The person who expresses the idea, thought, opinion, or statement we call the *speaker*, and the person(s) receiving the message we call the audience. As simple as this sounds, a funny thing happens to the message on the way from the speaker to the audience, however. Interference messes with the message. Like static on the radio, interference is anything that stands in the way of us sending or receiving our message.

Consequently, the audience receives a modified version of the intended message—we call this the perceived message. Unfortunately, the perceived message can be quite a bit different from the intended message, but the audience doesn't know that and believes the perceived message is real. Since interference hinders the transparent communication of ideas, a speaker has to evaluate the reaction of his or her audience to ascertain whether or not the intended message has made it through the interference. This reaction, which we call feedback, can be spoken loudly and obviously (laughter, shouts, smiles) or transmitted so subtly as to be almost imperceptible (a momentary look away).

The moment the audience arches an eyebrow, smiles, or breaks into tears, the audience becomes a speaker sending a new message. Indeed, even if the audience didn't intend to send a message, nothing still communicates something, and any reaction can be understood to convey countless additional perceived messages. Such is the way communication proceeds, with speakers and audiences sending out messages all with the goal of getting the message through interference.

Interference can occur in a multitude of ways. Interference can literally be some real noise that makes it difficult for an audience to perceive a message. If Pandora Radio is playing loudly when your daughter is talking about her applications to college, and you find it difficult to hear her over the music on the computer speakers, obviously the sound is causing interference. If you're leading a two-hour workshop exploring a complicated teaching practice and the school secretary has a riotous time sending out messages over the PA, the sound of the PA would be interference.

Interference is manifested more subtly as well. If your friend applies for an important position in an executive firm and shows up for the interview wearing a Sex Pistols T-shirt, her clothing might interfere with her audience's ability to perceive her intended message that she really is qualified for the job (though there may be one or two settings where that T-shirt might communicate that she is the perfect person for the job).

Interference frequently is invisible, existing in our audience's preconceptions, competing priorities, experiences, prior knowledge, or lack of prior knowledge. Our thoughts, perceptions, beliefs, values, emotions, and prior knowledge can keep us from being effective audiences for others' important messages.

The art of effective communication is finding ways to get around interference so that the message we want to communicate more or less becomes the message that is perceived by our audience.

Partnership Principles and Communication

ICs who ground their actions in the partnership approach find it easier to send and receive messages effectively. If they believe that they are partners with others and that everyone has something to teach them, they are more inclined to be respectful and open to the people with whom they interact. Respect, equality, and openness are good starting points for learning conversations. Lynn Barnes believes that the respect inherent in the partnership approach makes it much easier for her to connect with teachers: "Teachers know that if they tell me something, I won't get upset. I accept their opinions, and as a partnership, we just value each other's opinion, and we are more accepting of each other. They're willing to share ideas; they're willing to meet with me, and they share their kids with me. They don't share their kids if they don't believe and trust you."

EMPLOYING AUTHENTIC LISTENING

If you pick up just about any book on communication, leadership, relationships, or self-help, there is a good chance you will find several pages or chapters dedicated to the art of listening. Many authors have emphasized the importance of this skill. For example, Robert K. Greenleaf, who first described the concept of servant leadership (1998), states that "the inability to listen may be the most costly of the human relations skills to be without" (p. 71). Douglas Stone, Bruce Patton, and Sheila Heen (1999) observe that "listening well is one of the most powerful skills you can bring to a difficult conversation. It helps you understand the other person. And, importantly, it helps them understand you" (p.163). Margaret Wheatley (2002) even goes as far as stating, "I believe we can change the world if we start listening to one another again" (p. 3).

We need to listen better. We know it, and yet we do not do it. We zone out of conversations, we argue with others before we fully hear what they have to tell us, and we turn the focus back to us when we should be focused on those with whom we are talking. We want to listen, but we just do not seem to be getting much better at it. Or we are blithely unaware of how poorly we listen. And the people around us don't seem to be very good listeners either. If only they'd listen, things could be so much easier.

How Misconceptions Keep Us From Listening

Of course, the problem usually isn't the other person. The problem is that we frequently misjudge our ability to listen. To paraphrase R. D. Laing, if we don't know we're not listening, we think we're listening. If the other person isn't listening well, maybe our best solution is to listen to them. Over time, I have learned that when I listen with great care, the person I'm speaking with almost always becomes a much better listener.

So why is it so difficult to listen? William Isaacs explains that "if we try to listen we find it extraordinarily difficult, because we are always projecting our opinions and ideas, our prejudices, our background, our inclinations, our impulses; when they dominate, we hardly listen at all to what is being said" (1999, p. 84). Our memories, especially, interfere with our ability to listen. For example, an IC who remembers he was criticized by a teacher in a team meeting a month ago may find that memory interfering with his ability to listen objectively in the here and now. Even if the teacher makes a positive statement, the IC's memory might make it difficult to hear the positive comments.

We also struggle to listen simply because we may not want to hear what others are saying. We are usually drawn to those messages that confirm our hopes or affirm our assumptions about ourselves. Even after years of communication training, for example, many find it easier to listen to praise than criticism. David Bohm (2000) explains that if someone examines the way they listen,

> if one is alert and attentive, he can see, for example, that whenever certain questions arise, there are fleeting questions of fear, which push him away from consideration of these questions and of pleasure, which attract his thoughts and cause them to be occupied with other questions . . . can each of us be aware of the subtle fear and

pleasure sensations that block his ability to listen freely? Without this awareness, the injunction to listen to the whole of what is said will have little meaning. (p. 4)

Attentiveness

In a now famous quotation, Woody Allen reportedly once said, "Eighty percent of life is just showing up." I think that much the same can be said about listening. More than anything else, the defining characteristic of effective listening is being attentive. An IC who truly wants to listen better has to make the effort. Listening is an act of will as much as it is a skill or an art, and no matter how many coaching books ICs read, they won't be effective listeners unless they decide to roll up their sleeves and stay focused on the person with whom they're speaking. Susan Scott (2002) explains the importance of attentiveness as follows:

Think for the moment about the kind of attention you bring to your conversations. While someone is talking, where are your thoughts? When you are face-to-face, do you look at the individual in front of you or do your eyes roam in a sort of perpetual surveillance? While you're talking with someone on the telephone, do you scan your email? And can you tell when someone is scanning his? (p. 95)

IC Lynn Barnes works very deliberately to pay attention to collaborating teachers when she listens.

Sometimes when they come with their stories, and there are 15 other things I have to do, I have to tell myself, "put your pencil down, give them eye contact, put yourself in their shoes." I've had the experience happen to me when I was talking to someone and they were typing an email or doing something else, and it was like they could care less about me being with them. I need to value each moment that a teacher wants to be with me. I make sure when someone comes to my office, I make sure that I'm really listening, all there. I'm not thinking about what pressing engagement I have to do. I can't have that distraction. I'm needed. I try to think of them first.

Self-Awareness

Aside from attending to "the kind of attention" brought to listening, coaches should also consider whether or not they are listening in a biased manner. Are they only hearing information that confirms their assumptions? Are their memories biasing them as they listen? William Isaacs (1999) explains, "You can begin to listen by listening first to yourself and to your own reactions. Ask yourself, 'What do I feel here? Or how does this feel?' . . . To learn to be present, we must learn to notice what we are feeling now" (p. 92).

In order to be better listeners, ICs need to learn to distinguish between experiencing and evaluating during conversation. We need to ask, are we listening through the filter of our personal biases? Do we judge as we hear? Or, when we experience a conversation, do we focus our attention on simply hearing exactly what the other person is saying? ICs who listen effectively do not paint the words of others with their biases; they simply focus on understanding fully what the other person says.

Honesty and Authenticity

No matter how many listening techniques ICs learn, they will not be effective listeners unless they honestly want to hear what others have to say. As Stone et al. (1999) have observed,

> Scores of workshops and books on "active listening" teach you what you should do to be a good listener . . . The problem is this: you are taught what to do and how to sit, but the heart of good listening is authenticity. People "read" not only your words and posture, but what's going on inside of you. If your "stance" isn't genuine, the words won't matter . . . If your intentions are false, no amount of careful wording or good posture will help. If your intentions are good, even clumsy language won't hinder you . . . Listening is only powerful and effective if it is authentic. Authenticity means that you are listening because you are curious and you care, not just because you are supposed to. The issue, then, is this: Are you curious? Do you care? (p. 168)

Empathy and Respect

Stephen Covey (1989) has been very articulate in describing the importance of empathy in the act of listening. "Empathic listening gets inside another person's frame of reference. You look out through it, you see the world the way they see the world . . . The essence of empathic listening is not that you agree with someone; it's that you fully, deeply, understand that person, emotionally as well as intellectually" (p. 240). Without empathy, little true listening takes place. However, with empathy, deep communication, nourishing humanizing communication is possible.

What must we do to be empathetic? I believe that we begin to be empathetic when we begin with humility. The goal of empathy, what Covey refers to as *empathic listening,* is to silence ourselves and attend to others. We need to teach ourselves to put our personal concerns aside, and to concern ourselves with whomever we are speaking to. This may mean that we learn to duck, metaphorically speaking, when we are criticized or attacked, or that we put our opinions or agendas aside temporarily to hear others. To really listen to others, we have to learn to keep our personal needs for attention, self-defense, prestige, or power from interfering with our ability to hear what is being said.

An empathic response is also a powerful way to demonstrate respect. William Isaacs (1999) reminds us, "Respect is not a passive act. To respect someone is to look for the spring that feeds the pool of their experience . . . it involves a sense of honoring or deferring to someone. Where once we saw one aspect of a person, we look again and realize how much of them we have missed. This second look can let us take in more fully the fact that before me is a living, breathing being" (p. 111). To respect is to commit fully to the belief that each other person carries within him or her a humanity that must be recognized, validated, and listened to.

Isaacs (1999) suggests that one way we can increase respect is to remind ourselves, "This, too, is in me," when we hear something that provokes in us an un-listening reaction. Isaacs explains that "we may be tempted to say that a given behavior is all 'theirs'—I do not have anything like that in me! Maybe so. But the courage to accept it as not only 'out there,' but also 'in here,' enables us to engage in the world in a very different way" (p. 124). Isaacs goes on to say that we can build respect by demonstrating "the willingness to forgive that which we see in another and come to the point where we can accept it as being in us" (p. 124).

The kind of respect Isaacs describes is central to the partnership approach. We believe that the others with whom we interact are equal to us, that our voice is no more important than theirs, and that they have something to teach us. Even more fundamentally, we believe that it is a moral necessity to see the value in those with whom we interact. We don't tell them what to do or make their decisions; we respect them as fellow human beings traveling a road very similar to our own.

Listening Strategies

Developing inner silence
Listening for what contradicts our assumptions
Clarifying
Communicating our understanding
Practicing every day
Practicing with terrible listeners

Some Listening Strategies

Developing inner silence. We can improve our ability to listen by training ourselves to silence thoughts we have that lead us to judge rather than simply experience the comments of others.

Listening for what contradicts our assumptions. Since we are frequently attracted to messages that reinforce our biases and predispositions, we can improve our listening if we direct our brain to listen for messages that contradict our assumptions.

Clarifying. An obvious but frequently overlooked listening strategy is to check with our colleagues to ensure that we understand what they are saying. Clarifying might take the form of a paraphrase ("let me tell you what I'm hearing you say, and you tell me if I've got it right") or might simply involve asking our colleague to slow the pace of conversation or to repeat an idea that we missed the first time it was spoken.

Communicating our understanding. Being a good listener does not mean that we sit silent and frozen like a rock. Good listeners ask questions, clarify, and communicate that they understand what is being said. We can communicate our understanding verbally or nonverbally. The important thing is that we communicate that we understand, and thus encourage the speaker to keep talking.

Practicing every day. Listening, Stephen Covey (1989) reminds us, "is something you can practice right now" (p. 258). I find it most effective to plan specific times or situations when I will work on my listening skills. Like other healthy habits, we become better listeners the more we practice.

Practicing with terrible listeners. Stone et al. (1999) assert that "the reason why the other person is not listening to you is not because they are stubborn, but because they don't feel heard" (pp. 166–167). To prove their point, the authors suggest a simple test: "Find the most stubborn person you know, the person who never seems to take in anything you say, the person who repeats himself or herself in every conversation you ever have—and listen to them. Especially, listen for feelings, like frustration, or pride or fear, and acknowledge those feelings. See whether that person doesn't become a better listener after all" (p. 167).

UNDERSTANDING OUR AUDIENCE

Becoming an effective listener is a great start for one of the most important communication strategies—learning how to present information so that it can be understood easily by an audience (in this case collaborating teachers). A coach's best intentions, a coach's communication goals, or a coach's obvious intended message doesn't matter a whit if the collaborating teacher doesn't hear it. The message that matters is the one in the teacher's mind, not the one in the coach's mind. For that reason, coaches who are effective communicators structure every message so that it can be accurately perceived by their audience. If coaches start by understanding their audience, they then can frame their message so that it will be heard.

What Questions Can Instructional Coaches Ask to Focus on Their Collaborating Teachers?

What are my collaborating teacher's most pressing concerns?
What does my collaborating teacher know about this topic?
What are my collaborating teacher's learning preferences?
What are my collaborating teacher's values?

ICs communicate better with their teachers if they first ask a few questions. An IC might start working with a teacher by asking these questions in an actual learning conversation, or an IC might consider these questions on her own as she prepares for a future conversation with teachers.

1. *What are my collaborating teacher's most pressing concerns?* The importance of this question might seem obvious, but far too many of us have shown up with ideas to share with a teacher without really ever knowing what is on that teacher's mind. As Lynn Barnes explains, "I have to meet their needs, when they need it." Put another way, ignorance of what is most important to a collaborating teacher can interfere with a coach's ability to have an impact. If a teacher is really concerned about classroom management, and I fail to address that when I meet with her, I may or may not be able to create a sustained relationship focused on professional learning. However, if I can respond to a teacher's pressing concern that he needs to learn classroom management techniques quickly, and as a coach I hear that concern and provide the teacher with tools that help him keep his kids on task and learning, I can make a difference.

2. *What does my collaborating teacher know about this topic?* Chances are, all of us have been in learning situations where teachers misjudged what we knew about a topic before they started teaching us. On the one hand, if an IC assumes I know a lot about a topic and dives in full-throttle without checking to make sure I have sufficient background knowledge, the IC runs the risk of leaving me behind in the dust of her rapid-fire explanations. On the other hand, if an IC tediously explains a topic I already know well, the IC can be even more frustrating because she is wasting my precious time or, more problematic, appears to be patronizing me by teaching me something I know very well.

Effective ICs, then, must do their best to understand as fully as possible how much their audience knows about a topic. Coaches can start by making some assumptions based on their prior knowledge of a given teacher and others who hold similar positions in the school. However, as quickly as possible, the IC needs to check with the teacher to see if her assumptions are correct, asking a few quick questions to determine how much the teacher knows. Then, throughout future collaborative conversations with teachers, the coach should continually check to make sure that the explanations are sufficiently complete without being overly comprehensive.

Lynn Barnes says that the secret of assessing teachers' prior knowledge is to "ask questions. You find out what they know about this, if they've had training, if they really know it or not . . . you ask questions and you start formulating in your own mind an idea of how much they know."

3. *What are my collaborating teacher's learning preferences?* Asking this easily overlooked question can yield some very useful information. If we can get a better understanding of how our collaborating teachers prefer to learn, that can help us communicate more efficiently. Jane Kise's *Differentiated Coaching: A Framework for Helping Teachers Change* (2006) appears to be the definitive work on learning preferences and coaching. Kise compares several ways of explaining learning types but employs the Myers-Briggs Type Indicator tool (MBTI) to explain why coaches should understand learning types and how they can use that information when coaching teachers.

The MBTI is a self-reporting instrument that people can complete to better understand their learning preferences. The MBTI sorts our learning styles into four pairs of preferences: (a) judging and perceiving, (b) extraversion and introversion, (c) sensing and intuition, and (d) thinking and feeling. Kise's definitions of each preference pair are included in the tables below:

Judging and Perceiving: How We Approach Life	
Judging	"A preference for planning their work and working their plan. They are not more judgmental but rather prefer to come to judgment (closure) on things" (p. 86)
Perceiving	"A preference for staying open to the moment. They are not more perceptive but rather prefer to continue to perceive (gather) more information" (p. 86)

Extraversion and Introversion: How We Get Energy	
Extraversion	"Gaining energy through action and interaction, the outside world" (p. 89)
Introversion	"Gaining energy through reflection and solitude, the inner world" (p. 89)

Sensing and Intuition: How We Gather Information	
Sensing	*"First* paying attention to *what is,* to information you can gather through your five senses—the facts" (p. 93)
Intuition	*"First* paying attention to what *could be,* to hunches, connections or imagination—a sixth sense" (p. 93)

Thinking and Feeling: How We Make Decisions	
Thinking	"Making decisions through objective, logical principles" (p. 96)
Feeling	"Making decisions by considering the impact of each alternative on the people involved" (p. 96)

Since ICs can personalize learning experiences for each collaborating teacher, they seem uniquely capable of responding to teachers' learning preferences. An IC who recognizes that a collaborating teacher has a "judging" learning preference, for example, might take care to spend much more time collaboratively planning with that teacher. Similarly, an IC with an extroversion learning preference should be careful to adapt her communication when working with a teacher who gets energy from solitude. Extroverts who try to energize introverts can sometimes push them away if they do not recognize the introverts' learning style.

ICs can benefit by deepening their understanding of learning preferences by reading works such as Kise's *Differentiated Coaching.* However, even without extensive knowledge of learning types, coaches should be attentive to the unique learning preferences of those with whom they collaborate. IC Lynn Barnes observes that learning styles are important to consider when planning group presentations. "I think it's good to realize that we all have different learning styles, like students. In our trainings we have to incorporate multiple learning styles so that we meet the needs of all those styles in our trainings."

4. *What are my collaborating teacher's values and how do my own values affect my relationship with this teacher? What is most important to this teacher?* An IC who understands a teacher's values, that is, knows what a teacher considers to be important or valuable, has a significant advantage when it comes to communication. For that reason, coaches should do their best to understand each teacher's values so that they can communicate in the most efficient manner.

Consider, for example, the value teachers ascribe to standardized test scores. Some teachers are very concerned about the results their students and school achieve on standardized test scores, so when working with those teachers, ICs would be prudent to explain how particular interventions might help students do better on standardized tests. Other teachers view standardized tests negatively, believing they promote a narrow understanding of what education is and can be. When working with a teacher who ascribes a negative value to standardized tests, an IC would be prudent to explain how interventions address other aspects of education that the teacher values.

ICs also have to consider other values a teacher holds that might enhance or interfere with communication. Teachers' time, for example, is something that Lynn Barnes is very careful to respect. "Their time is valuable, and when you show them you understand that, that's important to the relationship." At the same time, Lynn also avoids topics that might put her at odds with collaborating teachers. "You know, the older I get, the wiser I get. I try to really be conscious of what I say, really conscious about the way I say it. I'm never flip with people. I could care less about persuading them to vote Democrat in the next election or persuading them to be a Protestant rather than a Catholic. I'm not at the job to talk politics. I'm there because I truly care about helping them in their profession and meeting the needs of those kids."

RECOGNIZING AND OVERCOMING INTERFERENCE

Effective communication, more than anything else, is all about getting the message through various forms of interference. If we are at a Yo La Tengo concert, for example, and the band is playing very loud, we may have to resort to sign language, touch, or notes to get our message through the interference of the music. Similarly, when we work with teachers, we have to employ strategies that help us get through the interference that keeps them from hearing what we have to say.

One common form of interference has been identified by Stone et al. in *Difficult Conversations: How to Discuss What Matters Most* (1999). The authors explain that when a conversation has implications for someone's identity, when it becomes what they refer to as an *identity conversation,* a person often finds it difficult to hear the intended message being communicated:

> The identity conversation looks inward: it's all about who we are and how we see ourselves. How does what happened affect my self-esteem, my self-image, my sense of who I am in the world? What impact will it have on my future? What self-doubts do I harbor? In short . . . the identity conversation is about what I am saying to myself *about me.* (p. 14)

Communication is difficult in schools when change leaders are insensitive to the identity implications of what they are proposing. Teachers don't resist new ideas as much as they resist the suggestion that they are not competent and they need to be helped or improved. When coaches clearly communicate their genuine belief that their collaborating teachers are competent and skilled, that is, when they take the partnership approach, there is a chance that those teachers will hear what their coaches have to say. However, when coaches communicate even ever so slightly that they are in the school to fix the "bad teachers," then teachers hearing that message will resist to protect their identity no matter how great the information is that a coach has to share. Simply put, to make sure people hear you, be careful not to start the conversation by attacking their identity.

A second form of interference exists inside ourselves. Our stories about events can also interfere with our ability to communicate. Over the past few decades, authors such as Michel Polanyi (1983), Thomas Kuhn (1970), and Peter Senge (1990) have shown that our ability to understand the world is limited or incomplete. What all these authors communicate, whether they discuss "the tacit dimension" of perception, or "paradigms," or "mental models," is that what we see, hear, and perceive is dramatically shaped by our prior knowledge (both conscious and unconscious).

An experience I had at a party for my son Geoff's hockey team helped me gain insight into just how incomplete our perceptions can be. Geoff and his young teammates were celebrating the end of a fun season. A kindly grandmother of one of the players had videotaped the final game. After all the food had been eaten, kids and parents herded into the basement recreation room to watch the video of the game. While at first everyone was excited to see the game, within a few minutes, the kids began to get restless. The proud grandmother had filmed every move of her grandson, whether or not he was involved in any action on the ice. During those moments when her grandson was in the midst of the play, everyone in the room was excited to watch. However, during those minutes (and to the children they seemed like very long periods of time) when her grandson was not in the action, the videotape of the boy standing on the blue line, back from the action, was, to say the least, disappointing to all the other players on the team. In short, the boys got to see a tape of the game, but because the tape focused on only one boy, the tape missed most of the game.

Our perceptions of the world are very similar to this grandmother's videotape. We only get a partial view of the action, and our personal interests tend to focus us on some things more than others. Patterson, Grenny, McMillan, and Switzler (2002) illustrate this phenomenon by discussing the impact of stories, stating that stories "are our interpretations of the facts. They help explain what we see and hear. They're theories we use to explain *why, how, and what*" (p. 99).

ICs must be careful not to let their personal stories interfere with their ability to understand what is really happening. On occasion, the stories we tell ourselves about reality shape our perceptions much more than the bare facts right in front of our faces.

When my colleague Mary Brieck came into our research center as our administrative manager a few years ago, every researcher at the Center breathed a sigh of relief. With someone carefully managing our office, we hoped, we would be able to spend more time working on what we felt mattered and less time on bureaucratic minutiae. At first, mind you, I was concerned that Mary was not helping at all. In her first few weeks on the job, Mary instituted several procedures that seemed to be anything but helpful. First, she instituted a policy that compelled all of us to sign out the center's state car if we wished to drive it—up until that point the car had had a nickname that I liked quite a lot, "Jim's car," and I had simply used it whenever I wished. Now I had to sign it out, and sometimes others signed it out ahead of me. Then Mary introduced a policy that she had to approve all grant-related purchases before the orders could be processed. I found myself writing time-consuming e-mails to Mary explaining why I needed a digital camera or why I needed to attend a particular conference. Worse than that, sometimes she wrote back to say I couldn't make the purchase.

As time went on, Mary's impact on my work life grew, and I wasn't happy about it. What was the point of all these new rules, I thought, except for making Mary feel like she was in control? Each week, I found myself increasingly frustrated, going home at night to complain to Jenny about how the new office administrator was a "control freak" who seemed determined to be a thorn in my side.

I got more and more frustrated with her policies and actions. Finally, my feelings and thoughts came to stand in the way of my ability to work with Mary, and I decided to confront her about her behavior. I knew what her problem was, and I was going to fix it, I reasoned. Fortunately, when I sat down and talked with her, I started by asking her to explain why she was doing what she was doing. I quickly discovered that my story was the problem, not Mary's actions. Mary tactfully explained that she was told when she was hired that her chief task was to create systems to organize the way we functioned and to increase our accountability. "My job here, and the way I will be evaluated," Mary said, "is whether or not I can create systems that make sure we don't do anything that will get us in trouble with our funding agencies."

Understanding how Mary perceived her actions made a world of difference to how I perceived what Mary did. Once I knew that she was only interested in ensuring that we were efficient and legal, our relationship changed. I realized that Mary wasn't someone intent on making my life difficult—she was intent on making sure I stayed out of jail. From that day on, when Mary e-mailed me to ask why I needed to make a particular purchase, I no longer saw her as a control freak, but as someone intent upon ensuring that we use our funds correctly and thereby ensuring we continue to get funding for our research. She wasn't against me; she was very clearly pulling for me, working on my side.

If ICs are not careful, they can make the same mistake I made with Mary and allow their personal stories to interfere with an accurate perception of reality. For example, a coach might come to believe that teachers are stubbornly resisting change when in reality they are simply taking time to balance competing demands on their time. If a coach writes off teachers as being resistant, hostile, or negative, they may dismiss teachers who might actually be open to change. By failing to inspect their own stories, coaches can do teachers and their students a real disservice.

Lynn Barnes told me a story that illustrates how she keeps herself from letting stories interfere with her ability to reach out to teachers. When Lynn first met "Alison" at her school, Alison brushed Lynn off, telling her, "I know all about graphic organizers, so you won't have to deal with me." Although tempted to take Alison at her word, Lynn said, "I continued to do what I do—greeting her in the hall, giving her positive notes, inquiring about her life, finding positive things about her as a person. It ended that she was all for our strategies. She didn't need me right away, but she was able to see the benefits of our strategies in her classroom. We should never dismiss teachers; there is always some way we can help them."

Patterson et al. (2002) identify what they refer to as "vicious stories" we tell ourselves that interfere with our ability to communicate. One such story is the story in which we paint another person as a villain. Thus, an IC might develop a story that an administrator who questions every intervention a coach offers is a bad person who is determined, for selfish or evil reasons, to destroy everything good that the coach is doing.

I spend a great deal of time in schools across the nation, and everywhere I go I hear educational leaders described as if they are villains (even one loving, dedicated coach I know, who seems to have a kind word for everyone, once referred to her administrator as a witch when the administrator failed to support her). The reality is that few people wake up in the morning determined to do evil to adults or children in schools. However, when coaches fall prey to the villain story, it is very difficult for them to reach out to those they consider villains. If I'm sure you're my enemy, I will find it difficult to listen to, empathize with, respect, or connect with you.

A second type of vicious story is the helpless story. Here, we create a story in which we convince ourselves that we are helpless in the face of some challenge. "How can I ever teach these students," a teacher might ask, "when they're not motivated, when their parents don't care, when the class size is far too big?" By telling ourselves that our situation is helpless, we create a situation where the only appropriate reaction seems to be to give up.

It is easy to understand why an IC might give in to helpless stories because at times the challenges of school improvement can seem overwhelming. I have indeed met many coaches who are seduced, momentarily at least, by the story that they cannot make a difference. But a primary message of this book, and a major conclusion to be drawn from our research, is that ICs are not helpless. Indeed, our data show quite clearly that ICs can have a profound impact on the way teachers teach and students learn. In fact, the ICs who are most helpless are those who choose to give in to the vicious story of their own helplessness.

The art of communication involves finding ways to get around interference that stands in the way of the transparent sharing of ideas. In some instances, the interference comes from within ourselves. Our stories about people can stand in the way of us understanding them. Thus, an IC who wants to connect with others needs to be aware of the ways in which his or her own preconceptions might block communication.

Just Talking Together

I had a meeting a while back that I thought was going to be awful. I got an e-mail from the principal, who wrote, "I'm not happy with how things are going. We need to talk." Sometimes it seemed as if the principal just didn't want me to help her with her kids, you know, and at first I didn't like that e-mail a bit. But I knew I couldn't ignore it. As it turned out, the next day was a day when teachers were out of the building, so I suggested we get together.

That night I thought a lot about how to handle the meeting. I decided that my main goal would be to listen. I wanted her to know that I got what she was saying. I wanted to see the world through her eyes and feel her feelings. When I went in she had a lot of criticisms, and I just listened. I didn't agree, but I didn't argue. I just said, "I can see why you feel worried. I can see why you might be concerned." I asked about her work, and the frustrations she was facing. She was overwhelmed and I was amazed that she could handle so many things at once. I told her that, too, and it seemed to help.

Something happened during the conversation. Somehow we shifted from her criticisms to talking about all kinds of things, her son, her new teachers, the new vice principal, our philosophies of life. It became a fun conversation, and I started to like her a lot more. In the midst of the conversation, I explained why I was doing what I was doing. My goal wasn't to trick her. We were just talking, and like never before, she understood me. Everything worked out that day. Sometimes you get lucky.

THE SUBTLE LANGUAGE OF COMMUNICATION: FACIAL EXPRESSIONS AND EMOTIONAL CONNECTIONS

When we think about communication, we might think about things that are fairly easy to see or hear, such as speech, e-mails, memos, letters, or touch. I would contend, however, that most communication is more subtle. When we communicate with others, much of what takes place in the interaction happens beneath the surface. We watch for nonverbal cues, we read body language, we look for eye contact, and we pay attention to how we feel as we talk with others. Furthermore, we often respond positively or negatively to a speaker for reasons that we can't really explain. We like someone, like the way they communicate, like their message. We often find it easier to hear the same message from one person than it is to hear it from another.

Facial Expressions and Nonverbal Communication

Most of us have read about, learned about, or studied nonverbal communication. The basics are well-known. The way we carry ourselves, the way we move and gesture, often communicates louder than words ever could. Nonverbal communication can reveal whether we feel affection for, are interested in, want to control, or trust those with whom we communicate.

Strategies for effective nonverbal communication include such tactics as (a) facing people when you speak with them, (b) making eye contact, (c) avoiding distracting gestures, (d) nodding your head in an encouraging way, (e) finding an appropriate place for communication, (f) paying attention to how close we sit with others, (g) choosing an appropriate tone of voice for the message we want to communicate, and (h) touching or not touching others appropriately depending on the situation. These are important, if well-known, skills every IC should master. In particular, it is important to ensure that what we communicate nonverbally reinforces the messages we intend to communicate verbally.

The most important part of nonverbal communication is facial expression. Paul Ekman and his colleagues have studied people's emotional responses worldwide (in primitive and modern cultures). They conclude that facial expressions represent a universal language that can be interpreted in the same way we interpret other forms of language. Ekman's Facial Action Coding System, developed in 1978, "is now being used by hundreds of scientists around the world to measure facial movements" (2003, p. 14).

Ekman (2003) explains that facial expressions often communicate in "micro expressions," "very fast facial movements lasting less than one-fifth of a second" (p. 15). Ekman suggests that our "micro expressions" can trigger emotions in others, or others' "micro expressions" can trigger emotions in us. Simply put, the communication of emotion happens in a flash, and we must be very conscious to recognize what others' facial expressions communicate to us. As Ekman observed, "As an emotion begins, it takes us over in . . . milliseconds, directing what we do and say and think" (pp. 19–20).

According to Ekman "seven emotions each have a distinct, universal, facial expression: sadness, anger, surprise, fear, disgust, contempt, and happiness" (p. 58). In *Emotions Revealed* (2003), Ekman describes the facial expressions for each of these emotions in detail, including illustrations that, in some cases, are difficult to look at given how evocative they are. ICs would be wise to study Ekman's work to gain a deeper understanding of the subtle way in which facial expressions can communicate messages that support or undercut what is being spoken. By watching facial expressions carefully, ICs can learn a lot about their collaborating teachers and can improve their ability to communicate clearly.

Over the years, Lynn Barnes has learned a lot about reading body language. When she meets with teachers, she says, she "pays attention to the obvious things, eye contact, their body stance, whether they're nodding." Lynn also looks at her collaborating teachers' nonverbals to determine whether the teacher is ready and willing to learn. "We need to take consideration that maybe they have something else pressing, they might be agitated, they might need to call a parent, and maybe we should meet at another time. A lot goes into it." Lynn goes on to say, "It's just about being aware and acting upon it."

BUILDING AN EMOTIONAL CONNECTION

Facial expressions and nonverbal communication are an important part of another part of the subtle side of communication—emotional connections. To be effective, ICs, we have found, must become masters at building emotional connections with their teachers. When I interviewed teachers who had collaborated with Lynn Barnes, they were quick to heap praises on their IC. Although the teachers said they appreciated the valuable tools and teaching practices Lynn had to share, more frequently they noted that they liked working with Lynn because they flat out liked her as a person. Hannah Waldy, for example, told me, "I think you picked the right person to do this job because she is smart, intelligent, with-it, and also has a very kind heart." Jim Edmiston said, "Lynn's got a very outgoing personality. She's an awesome listener, and I think what helps us most is she has an uncanny knack to sense when something is not going the way we expected and offer some suggestions." Linda Lake told me that Lynn is "such a comfortable person to be around." Others commented on Lynn's warmth, kindness, attentiveness, compassion, sense of humor, and positive nature. Jim Edmiston summed up the opinions of all of the teachers: "You could get somebody else to do that job, but it's the person in that job that makes the difference, and Lynn's that person."

These comments, as complimentary as they are to Lynn, might trouble the rest of us. Does an IC have to be born with a super personality? Can ICs learn to connect with teachers the way Lynn does? Fortunately, research conducted by John Gottman suggests that we do not have to be born perfect to be an IC. Much of what Lynn accomplishes can be learned. Gottman, who has spent his professional life studying people in relationships, describes the specific practices that shape relationships as follows:

> We have discovered the elementary constituents of closeness between people, and we have learned the basic principle that regulates how relationships work and also determines a great deal about how conflict between people can be regulated. That basic idea has to do with the way people, in mundane moments in everyday life, make attempts at emotional communication, and how others around them respond, or fail to respond, to these attempts. (Gottman & DeClaire, 2001, Preface)

Gottman describes "the elementary constituent of closeness between people" as an emotional bid: "A bid can be a question, a gesture, a look, a touch—any single expression that says, 'I want to feel connected to you.' A response to a bid is just that—a positive or negative answer to somebody's request for emotional connection" (2001, p. 4). People extend bids for emotional connection to others all the time, he contends, and in healthy relationships, both members extend and respond positively to these bids. Emotional bids can be obvious gestures, such as inviting someone out to dinner, or incredibly subtle, such as a second of sustained eye contact. Bids can be verbal or nonverbal, funny or serious, physical or intellectual. Bids for emotional connection can be questions, statements, or comments about thoughts, feelings, observations, opinions, or invitations.

When someone makes an emotional bid, Gottman argues, we can respond in one of three ways: (a) turning toward, (b) turning away from, or (c) turning against.

When we turn toward someone who offers us an emotional bid, we respond positively toward that invitation. If someone shakes our hand, we might pat them on the back. If we are invited out to dinner, we say yes, or acknowledge the thoughtfulness of the invitation. If someone smiles, we smile back.

Though she might not refer to them as emotional bids, Lynn Barnes does many acts that enhance her emotional connection with teachers in her school. "I find out their interests, personal things at home. I try to connect with them on things that are near and dear to their heart." Lynn tries to make a personal connection with each teacher every day. "My daily goal is to try to find something to do to validate each person. Recognition is what babies cry for and grown men die for. We need it for the good things we do."

When we turn away from a bid, we fail to respond to the bid for emotional connection. For example, an overwhelmed administrator might be too preoccupied by the countless work-related demands on her time and turn away by failing to notice or acknowledge a colleague's complimentary comments. Gottman observes that turning away "is rarely malicious or mean-spirited. More often we're simply unaware of or insensitive to others' bids for our attention" (2001, p. 5).

The impact of turning away can be devastating. Gottman reports that "When somebody turns away from a bid, the bidder loses confidence and self-esteem. In our observational studies, we see how people almost seem to 'crumple' when their partners turn away. The bidders don't get puffed up with anger; they don't get indignant; they just seem to fold in on themselves. On video we can see their shoulders sag slightly as if they've been deflated. They feel defeated. They give up" (2001, p. 47). Lynn Barnes is very aware of teachers who turn away from her during the school year. "If I go home and there is a person who has turned away, not wanting to make that emotional connection, I try to figure out a way to do something positive for them. You have to give them personal recognition."

When people turn against bids, they react in argumentative or hostile ways. If someone makes a bid by offering to cook dinner, for example, a person turning against might respond by saying, "Are you kidding? I've tasted your cooking." For me, the perfect example of a couple that turns against is George Costanza's parents on *Seinfeld.* Each conversation between George's parents proceeds like a verbal boxing match in which both partners throw disdainful comments at each other. When we watch these conversations on TV, we laugh, but when we experience them in our own lives, they can be far from funny—the results can be profoundly destructive. Lynn Barnes admits that teachers who turn against her can be difficult to handle. "I'm really working hard on not taking things personally," she says, "but it can take its toll. I have to respect their decision. I read a quotation a while back and I thought, I had to memorize it: 'respect those you want to silence.' I'm working on that. You've just got to respect them and go on."

ICs can increase their effectiveness if they are fully aware of how bids for emotional connection function, almost like an invisible undercurrent in any relationship bringing people together or keeping them apart. An IC who carelessly adopts a sarcastic tone may inadvertently turn against his or her colleagues' bids for connection.

ICs also need to train themselves to be very sensitive to the ways in which teachers extend emotional bids for connection, which Gottman refers to as mindfulness. ICs should be attentive to collaborating teachers' thoughts, emotions, and concerns, so they can recognize emotional bids for connection and respond in ways that enrich their emotional connection with others. If they miss their colleagues' emotional bids, they will likely have a more difficult time making a difference in their teaching practices. As Gottman has observed, "If you don't pay attention, you don't connect" (2001, p. 66).

Gottman's research should also be a caution to ICs to be careful not to misinterpret a colleague's behavior. On occasion, a loud, aggressive, or hostile manner can be a teacher's way of reaching out. If an IC is too quick to assume she will never build an emotional connection with a colleague, she runs the risk of writing off someone who might benefit from becoming more connected with the coach. Time and again I have found that my first impressions of people can be disproven if I work to build some kind of respectful common ground with them. Gottman observes:

If you can see past a person's anger, sadness, or fear to recognize the hidden need, you open up new possibilities for relation. You're able to see your coworker's sullen silence as a bid for inclusion in decisions that affect his job, for example. Or you can recognize that your sister's agitation says she's feeling alienated from the family. You can even see the bid in your three-year-old's temper tantrum: He not only wants the toy you can't buy for him, he wants your comfort in a frustrating situation, as well. (2001, p. 36)

HOW IT ALL FITS TOGETHER, SORT OF

The ideas, strategies, tactics, and concepts discussed in this chapter reinforce and overlap with each other frequently. For example, if we have carefully built an emotional connection with teachers, then we should find it easier to discuss topics that might come close to unearthing an identity conversation with teachers. If we become aware of our own "vicious stories" about others when they start to take root, we may find it much easier to build an emotional connection with people whom we might have otherwise avoided.

If we are aware of our own body language and become more adept at reading others' body language, we can become better listeners. Our listening skills can help us construct our message in a way that our audience can understand, and by listening we can also build connections, get around our own and others' stories, and make connections with others that make a difference. What's more, if we learn to share positive comments with others, we stand the chance of improving the kind of conversations that take place in our schools. We then can start to transform our schools into settings where respectful, supportive interchange takes the place of stories about villainy, helplessness, and victimization.

Underlying all of this is the importance of the partnership orientation. When we authentically see our collaborating teachers as equal partners, when we engage in dialogue and encourage reflection, when we focus on praxis, when we respect teachers' choices, when we listen to and encourage teachers' choices, when we expect to learn from others as much as they can teach us, we remove many of the barriers that interfere with communication. People resist our supportive efforts when they feel they are being tricked, manipulated, or bullied. When we treat others as partners, more often than not, they open themselves up to us as collaborators, as partners, and frequently, as friends.

ICs who adopt a partnership approach and who become fluent in many of the partnership communication skills described here will find themselves in healthier, more rewarding relationships, both inside and outside their schools. This ultimately is the great reward of the partnership approach. If it is true that we live in a time of communication crisis, perhaps ICs have, so to speak, something to say about that. By nourishing meaningful conversations in their day-to-day work, ICs may move all of us closer to a world where more intimacy between people becomes a reality. Coaches can shorten the gap between people one conversation at a time.

GOING DEEPER

John Gottman's *The Relationship Cure* (Gottman & DeClaire, 2001) is an accessible summary of his research suggesting that emotional bids are at the heart of personal relationships. Gottman and Silver's *Seven Principles for Making Marriage Work* (1999) relates the insights gained from his research to the specifics of marital relationships. Malcolm Gladwell's *Blink* (2005) offers another perspective on Gottman's work, along with many insights regarding the interrelationship of perception and interpretation.

Stephen Covey's *The 7 Habits of Highly Effective People* (1989) remains the best, most useful handbook on listening, in particular the chapter "Seek First to Understand, Then Be Understood," in which Covey introduces the concept of empathic listening.

Patterson and colleagues' *Crucial Conversations* (2002), Stone and colleagues' *Difficult Conversations* (1999), and Scott's *Fierce Conversations* (2002) introduce several communication strategies that enhance our ability to get around interference and deal directly with the most important issues. Stone and colleagues provide an especially helpful description of different types of difficult conversations that can very quickly disrupt our efforts at communication.

Paul Ekman's *Emotions Revealed* (2003) offers a thorough, well-researched discussion of facial expressions, what they mean, what they reveal about us, and what they can tell us about those with whom we are communicating.

Tony Jeary, who has written *Life Is a Series of Presentations* (2004), is a kind of modern-day Dale Carnegie, offering many practical tips on how to successfully deliver the many presentations we give each day—whether they are to an audience of thousands or to our 3-year-old son. The original Dale Carnegie's *How to Win Friends and Influence People* (1936) may seem a little dated, but it remains, in my opinion, a tremendously valuable work for anyone working with people—and that is pretty much anyone.

TO SUM UP

- The communication process involves a speaker, with a message, who tries to penetrate interference to communicate with an audience, who receives a perceived message, and whose reactions to the message function as feedback for the speaker.
- Effective communicators start by trying to understand their audience, and they shape their messages so that it is easier for their audience to perceive them.
- An authentic desire to listen to others may be our most important communication skill.
- How well a person connects or fails to connect emotionally with others profoundly affects the quality of relationships that person experiences. John Gottman refers to the essential constituent of emotional connection as a bid; people turn toward, turn away from, or turn against bids.
- Our personal stories, and the stories held by those with whom we communicate, can block our ability to build emotional connections and to communicate effectively.
- If we take a partnership approach, we frequently find it much easier to communicate transparently with others.
- ICs make the world safer for more meaningful communication, one conversation at a time.

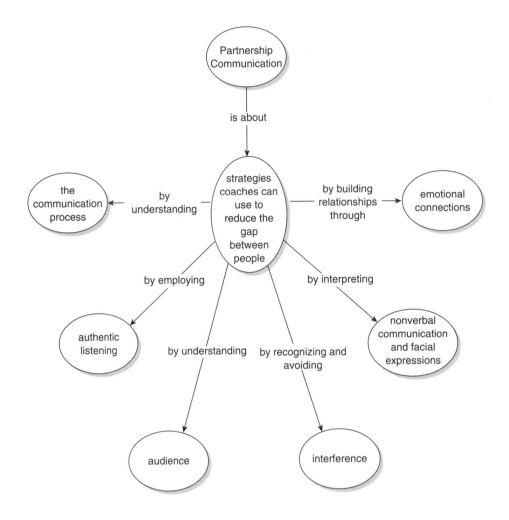

REFERENCES

Bohm, D. (2000). *On dialogue*. New York: Routledge.

Carnegie, D. (1936). *How to win friends and influence people*. New York: Simon & Schuster.

Covey, S. (1989). *The 7 habits of highly effective people: Powerful lessons in personal change*. New York: Simon & Schuster.

Ekman, P. (2003). *Emotions revealed: Recognizing faces and feelings to improve communication and emotional life*. New York: Henry Holt.

Gladwell, M. (2005). *Blink: The power of thinking without thinking*. Boston: Little, Brown.

Gottman, J. M., & DeClaire, J. (2001). *The relationship cure: A 5 step guide for building better connections with your family, friends, and lovers*. New York: Crown.

Gottman, J. M., & Silver, N. (1999). *The seven principles for making marriage work*. New York: Crown.

Greenleaf, R. K. (1998). *The power of servant-leadership*. San Francisco: Berrett-Koehler.

Isaacs, W. (1999). *Dialogue and the art of thinking together*. New York: Doubleday.

Jeary, T. (2004). *Life is a series of presentations: 8 ways to inspire, inform, and influence anyone, anywhere, anytime*. New York: Fireside.

Kise, J. (2006). *Differentiated coaching: A framework for helping teachers change*. Thousand Oaks, CA: Corwin Press.

Kuhn, T. S. (1970). *The structure of scientific revolutions* (2nd ed.). Chicago: University of Chicago Press.

Patterson, K., Grenny, J., McMillan, R., & Switzler, A. (2002). *Crucial conversations: Tools for talking when stakes are high*. New York: McGraw-Hill.

Polanyi, M. (1983). *The tacit dimension*. Gloucester, MA: Peter Smith.

Scott, S. (2002). *Fierce conversations: Achieving success at work and in life, one conversation at a time*. New York: Penguin.

Senge, P. M. (1990). *The fifth discipline: The art and practice of the learning organization*. London: Random House.

Stone, D., Patton, B., & Heen, S. (1999). *Difficult conversations: How to discuss what matters most*. New York: Penguin.

Wheatley, M. (2002). *Turning to one another: Simple conversations to restore hope to the future*. San Francisco: Berrett-Koehler.

13

Overcoming Obstacles and Reaping the Rewards

Kathleen Feeney Jonson

I love working with new teachers. I love working with enthusiastic and dedicated people. I learn from them and try to make them see that teaching is a learning process. I feel that, as a mentor, I am helping new teachers adjust to the rigorous life of a teacher, yet understand their importance in a child's life. I'm preparing them so that I can retire feeling that I'm leaving our schools in safe hands. Working with new teachers makes me have faith in the future of public education—most of them are great teachers!

—A mentor (Jonson, 1999b)

I f teachers in general are dedicated educators, mentors are optimally so. Not only are they competent teachers, but they are teachers who willingly extend themselves, continually helping others while seeking professional growth and personal rejuvenation.

A now-classic synthesis of the research on mentoring beginning teachers (Gray & Gray, 1985) revealed that exemplary mentors

- are secure,
- have power and expertise,
- are goal oriented,
- like and trust their mentees,
- take a personal interest in the careers of their mentees,
- encourage their mentees for their ideas, and
- help their mentees gain confidence and become self-directed professionals.

Many who have taken on the challenge agree that the decision to accept a mentorship role can lead to one of the most professionally rewarding experiences of a teacher's career. No matter how competent the individual teacher and how great the motivation, however, mentoring is ultimately a lot of work, requiring both time and commitment beyond the already significant time and commitment required of a teacher. If the mentor becomes caught up in one or more of several potential pitfalls associated with the position, the decision to serve as a mentor can lead to considerable frustration.

What are some of these potential pitfalls? How can a successful mentor overcome the obstacles? And why would a teacher take the position anyway? The pitfalls can be serious, but those who avoid them will find plenty of payoffs.

THE PITFALLS

Unless a protégé is explicit in the discussion of her learning, a mentor cannot always be sure what new ideas are being assimilated. I may come to the end of a mentoring relationship and be unclear about what has been accomplished. But I have learned that some ideas will not be absorbed until a future time. I may need to be satisfied with little things, such as a comment, a smile, a willingness to learn.

—Jane Fraser (1998, p. 51)

There are times when mentors may not be sure of what they are accomplishing or whether their long hours and exhausting efforts are bearing results. This is certainly one of the intangible, sometimes frustrating, aspects of the responsibility, which counters the many times when mentors can clearly see the results of their input. It is only one of many potential pitfalls, however. Behaviors associated with other pitfalls—some of which can be guarded against—fall into roughly four categories:

1. Overextending

2. Proceeding without clarification of the mentor's role
   a. From the administration
   b. From the mentee

3. Assuming too much responsibility for the mentee
   a. Who is less than qualified
   b. Who is unwilling

4. Underutilizing professional growth opportunities

FINDING TIME

To avoid the pitfall of overextending themselves, teachers need to be effective managers of their personal and professional lives—and, importantly, of their time. A survey in Marin County, California, asked five mentors for new teachers about their experiences and insights regarding effective mentoring (Smith, 1993, p. 10). All five were glad to be mentors (p. 16), they said, but they discussed "nonsuccesses" in their efforts as well as "successes." All of these mentors felt that they were spread too thin, that they didn't have enough time to do all they wanted to do, and that funds for accomplishing their goals were limited (p. 13).

Finding time can be a challenge for any mentor. Some programs are set up to help alleviate this problem; they release mentors from some or all of their other teaching responsibilities or hire retired teachers to serve as mentors. But in many programs, teachers are expected to combine their responsibilities as a mentor with their full-time teaching responsibilities. In these cases especially, the mentor needs to manage time well. Discussing time issues up front with the mentee and as needed throughout the relationship can help both parties keep perspective and focus on learning goals. Some of the following strategies might help:

- Begin the relationship with a frank discussion about time, the need to focus and use time well, and the need to come to meetings prepared so as not to waste time.
- For informal discussions, combine goals. For example, help mentees set up their rooms while also discussing their objectives for the year.
- Hold informal discussions over lunch, while on bus or cafeteria duty, or between sessions at school- or district-wide meetings.
- For formal discussions, schedule time in advance. Begin each discussion with a review or update of relevant information to regain focus, and then keep the focus throughout the discussion.
- For observations, obtain a videotape of a mentee conducting a lesson to be discussed at a convenient time.

- Use e-mail, fax, and telephone to answer brief questions. Be sure to set limits. For example, let mentees know when they may call and how soon they can expect a response to e-mail questions.
- Have the mentee keep a journal that can be reviewed for response at the mentor's convenience.
- Seek administrative assistance in scheduling common prep times or getting the help of a substitute for release time. Another teacher might be asked to cover the mentor's class during a prep period so that the mentor can observe the mentee, for example.
- With the permission of site administration, combine two classes for an activity or lesson; the mentor may then demonstrate a skill or observe the mentee in action.
- Form teams (Heller, 2004, p. 83). Have one teacher use a prep period to take another's class, for example, thus relieving the second teacher to observe a mentee.
- Dedicate paraprofessionals to the program (Heller, 2004, p. 83). These paraprofessionals could free teachers for observations, conferences, and other tasks.
- If progress seems slow, consider taking a time-out. A pause may give the mentee a chance to absorb new information and reflect on learning.
- Set priorities. Avoid committing to many other activities simultaneously.

This last point is particularly important. Many teachers have "caretaker personalities": they care for and give to others much more than they take care of themselves. Because of their professional commitment, teachers all too often find themselves saying "yes." They might join a text adoption committee, participate in curriculum planning, supervise a student group, and serve as a mentor. Unfortunately, some believe in the myth of a Super Teacher, a teacher who can do all that is asked—and do it perfectly. Mentors need not try to be superhuman; they need simply to strive and to care. To be available for the mentee, they must learn to choose a limited number of activities carefully and then simply say a professional "no" to other extra duties or committees. Teachers need to set realistic goals and standards and to focus on celebrating successes. They must learn to replenish and to receive in balance with their giving.

DEFINING THE ROLE

Also important for teacher-mentors is defining their role, clarifying just what they are expected to do. Of the five Marin County mentors surveyed, three expressed "a sense of confusion and anxiety because they were unclear what their jobs were and who they were accountable to" (Smith, 1993, p. 13). Mentors need to establish guidelines both with the administration and with the mentees themselves. Clarification of the role can come through training, through working with a mentor coordinator, and through ongoing communication.

Support From the Administration. Potential mentors should investigate school and district commitment to the program in terms of policy and procedure statements, budgetary allocations, and processes necessary to ensure the ongoing success of the project. Establishing clearly defined expectations between mentors and administrators is absolutely necessary. Consistent feedback and communication between these groups are also necessary, as is follow-up support.

"Remember to inform your principal of your plans," one experienced mentor advises (Jonson, 1999b). "List some ideas, activities, and other pertinent information you need to share with your principal." Supportive resources—such as additional planning time, materials, and technical assistance—do not magically appear at the onset of a mentor-teacher program. These types of continuing support, all too often absent, however, are crucial. "While training usually occurs before mentors take up their new responsibilities," writes Feiman-Nemser (1996), "mentors are more likely to develop their practice as mentors if they also have opportunities to discuss questions and problems that arise in the course of the work with novices" (p. 3).

Marin County mentors also expressed wariness about administrators who attempted to "make gray [the] line" between mentoring and evaluating; all agreed that they should not evaluate their mentees despite their administrators' wishes (Smith, 1993, pp. 13–14). In addition, all five of these mentors noted that other faculty members sometimes had negative feelings toward mentors. "I know there's all these hard feelings [that I got the job and others didn't]," one said. Mentor support groups might help combat this problem, one suggested.

Guidance From the Mentee. A beginning teacher may not clearly understand what to expect from the mentor. Is the mentor an arm of the administration? Will the mentor make unreasonable demands on the mentee's time? Can the mentor be trusted with professional concerns? Again, it is best to keep mentoring entirely separate from the teacher evaluation process and to reinforce this issue consistently with the beginning teacher.

In the Marin County survey, some of the mentors discussed nonsuccesses that were directly related to the mentees themselves. Mentors felt frustrated that the mentees were not always willing to take advantage of what was offered to them. One mentor called a meeting of new teachers in her district and was dismayed when only four came. "People said, well, I got your letter and I didn't have time to open it and it's still in my pile. . . . Or, I was going to come but I had to do this instead," the mentor reported (quoted in Smith, 1993, p. 12). All five of the mentors recognized that the new teachers were simply overwhelmed by their jobs (p. 12). One mentor also pointed out that mentees sometimes worried that others would see them as incompetent if they asked for help from a mentor (p. 13).

The mentor and the beginning teacher, then, must work together to establish the parameters of the mentor's responsibilities and expectations. One way to do this is by setting up an action plan. Working together on such a plan allows both parties to address their needs and concerns and helps them feel comfortable within their respective roles.

WORKING WITH DIFFICULT MENTEES

When mentors become overly involved with the beginning teacher, they may assume too much responsibility for the mentee and foster a relationship of dependency. The mentor may be overprotective or assume too many obligations to ensure the mentee's success. Some mentees are simply difficult to work with, and it is important in these cases that mentors have a clearly defined concept of facilitating as compared to defending. Mentors may also face the unwelcome reality that a beginning teacher has significant deficiencies or problems beyond the mentor's ability or authority to address.

Occasionally a mentor may feel an ethical obligation to report problems when mentees' actions are harmful to students in their care. The best approach in such a situation will depend on existing school policies and procedures. A decision to break confidentiality and seek assistance should not be viewed as failure on the part of the mentor, but more as a professional responsibility—one to be handled prudently and with sensitivity.

The Less-Than-Qualified Mentee. A mentor may on occasion work with a teacher who simply isn't qualified to be a good teacher. In some cases, the teacher has received an emergency credential without completing the usual course of study. There is an acute shortage of qualified mathematics and science teachers, for example, especially in low-income and high-minority schools, and this leads to the hiring of individuals who are not fully qualified. Some districts still view teachers as an expense and not as an asset and prefer to hire untrained teachers who cost less than qualified teachers with more education and experience. In other cases, a teacher has completed appropriate training but just doesn't understand how to work with children. In some of these situations, the mentor may need to accept that a mentee simply doesn't have the knowledge and skills necessary to become a qualified teacher.

Investing in teachers' professional knowledge and development can pay off, not only in the classroom but in the profession as a whole. But occasionally mentees who perform poorly may need be removed from their positions. This has legal ramifications, and in such situations, it is important for the mentor to turn the case over to the principal. Most principals were probably wary from the beginning about hiring an underqualified teacher, but in many cases the pool of qualified applicants was limited.

The Unwilling Mentee. At other times, a mentee may not want the assistance of a mentor or may seem to challenge the mentor at every opportunity. One teacher, Sophie, for example, often seemed not to listen to discussions, refused to stay focused, and neglected to meet deadlines for review of her work (Shulman & Sato, 2006, pp. 171–185). The mentor working with this new teacher wondered if she should continue to try to help the teacher or if it would be better for the teacher to become discouraged and leave the profession. The mentor continued to help but also set boundaries; when Sophie asked for assistance after a deadline had passed, the mentor refused to give it.

In dealing with a difficult mentee such as Sophie, it is important to be specific about expectations concerning the relationship. The mentor should make clear that information shared will be confidential, thus encouraging open discussion. Expectations for participation in discussions should also be explained clearly. For example, mentors might tell the new teacher that they will stop a discussion that becomes heated and revisit the issue later if it seems appropriate.

In a discussion about how to lead workshops, Portner gives tips for dealing with difficult questions. Several of his suggestions apply to mentor-mentee situations as well (2006, p. 45). He suggests the following:

- Anticipate awkward questions. Think about good ways to answer them before being put on the spot.
- Listen carefully when the mentee asks questions. Take care to hear the entire question before responding.
- Be willing to admit that you don't know the answer to a question.
- Avoid doing all of the talking. Continue attempting to get the mentee to participate actively.

UNDERUTILIZING PROFESSIONAL GROWTH OPPORTUNITIES

One major misconception is that teaching is relatively simple and easy to learn. In the psychological and developmental literature, however, it is widely recognized that novices do not learn simply by copying or modeling what experts do. Instead, professional growth in teaching has an emerging quality and takes a substantial amount of time. Furthermore, complex understandings and skills follow developmental patterns similar to those of other complex learning endeavors.

To assist beginning teachers in their route from novice to expert, the mentor must not only understand these precepts but also be able to facilitate the beginner's professional growth through a variety of methods and techniques. Mentors must incorporate into their professional repertoire various skills, including working with adult learners, conducting observations and data collections, problem solving, demonstrating empathy, and providing constructive criticism. It is incumbent that mentors take advantage of professional growth opportunities not only to enrich themselves but also to better enable their mentees' growth.

Any effective mentoring program incorporates training components for both mentors and beginning teachers. Unfortunately, because of poor communications and lack of program support or for various other reasons, teachers participating in district-sponsored mentoring programs sometimes find that obtaining release for training is confusing and difficult at best. Essential opportunities and resources are not always available. Again, mentors need to communicate with administrators and clarify specific details and procedures for the program before assuming the mentor role.

> Take care not to let your added responsibilities eclipse your own personal and professional growth and development. You can't give what you don't have.
>
> —A mentor's advice

THE PAYOFFS

> I like helping people. I like being validated for my skill and being paid as a professional. I get to see what other teachers are doing, and I use their ideas as well. Those teachers also serve as a resource for future mentees who might benefit from their expertise.
>
> —A mentor (Jonson, 1999b)

So why *do* teachers agree to be mentors? They do so because the payoffs are many and generally, for dedicated mentors, exceed the pitfalls. These payoffs include, but are not limited to, the satisfaction of helping strengthen the profession, the enrichment that comes with professional sharing, the satisfaction of helping the novice grow, the possibility of receiving cutting-edge training in relation to the position, visibility within the educational community, an expanded career role, personal rejuvenation, heightened prestige, and basic appreciation from the mentee (see Figure 13.1). Credit for advancement on the salary schedule and release time from other responsibilities are two other potential payoffs.

Lortie (1975) classifies possible incentives and rewards for educators into three groups: extrinsic, ancillary, and intrinsic. *Extrinsic* rewards include things that come from the outside—things such as money and prestige. *Ancillary* rewards remain constant and are considered part of the job—in teaching, these might include unpaid summer vacations, professional conferences, and tenure. *Intrinsic* rewards, such as recognition and self-satisfaction, are more personal (internal) and vary among people (Orlich, 1989, p. 72). Among mentors, intrinsic rewards play a large role as incentives, with extrinsic rewards also playing a part.

As a less tangible reward, mentors are likely to improve their own teaching in the process of helping the mentee improve. In fact, Moran (1990)

Figure 13.1   The payoffs

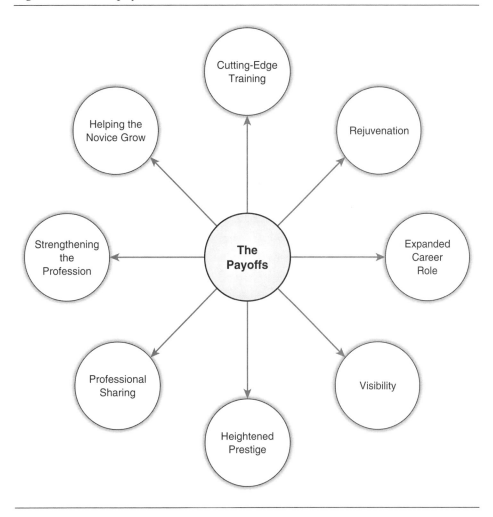

suggests, "It may even be true that the greater professional development accrues to the experienced teacher, who benefits from giving voice to philosophy and practice" (p. 212). Mentors are likely through their work to become more aware of their own development as teachers and of the rationale for their teaching strategies. They may come to appreciate the diverse styles of other teachers as well (Smith, 1993, p. 9). A mentee may even demonstrate a particular technique new to the mentor.

Affecting the practice of experienced educators is an important benefit of new teacher-mentoring programs. Mentors who have participated in training programs on standards-based professional development share a common language in discussing what constitutes effective teacher practice. A survey of Connecticut special educators who were trained as mentors and portfolio scorers showed that 83% of participants made at least moderate changes in their own classroom practices as a result of the training.

One teacher in Connecticut's BEST Program commented, "Going through the portfolio process has reminded me to include conscious reflection on lessons to target what worked and what needs to change" (Alliance for Excellent Educators, 2004).

In Tangipahoa Parish, Louisiana, mentors praised the new teacher induction program as a way to improve their own teaching skills. One mentor explained, "Being a mentor has kept me in touch with what's new in the field and has kept me fresh and motivated. I have been able to help the teachers that I work with, but they have also benefited me." Sentiments like these were echoed throughout teacher evaluations of the Tangipahoa FIRST program.

Another indirect payoff is increased professionalism. In Toledo, Ohio, the new teacher induction program has formed teachers into a community of learners over the years. According to Dal Lawrence of the Toledo Federation of Teachers, "The Toledo Plan began to change the way in which teachers think about their practice and each other's practice, as well as their accountability and responsibility for overall competence and excellence. We didn't see that happening when we started out, but it definitely exists now." Creating a culture of educators who take responsibility for themselves and their colleagues is no small feat. Participation in a culture such as this makes it possible for teachers to grow and thrive.

In a study of 158 mentors of student teachers from the University of California, Irvine, beginning in 1991, mentors filled out questionnaires regarding the benefits they saw from working with mentees (Clinard & Ariav, 1998). Although the mentees in this study were student teachers, the issues explored are relevant to any mentor working with a beginning teacher. Researchers were interested in learning the following:

1. What benefits do mentors gain from working with student teachers?

2. Is the mentoring experience having any effect on the mentors' practice (with their students)?

3. Is the mentoring experience having any effect on the mentors beyond the classroom (as professionals and as private individuals)?

Participants ranked benefits in each of these three categories after working with their mentees. See Tables 13.1 through 13.3 for their responses.

Ultimately, as Bruce Joyce and Beverly Showers (1995) suggest, a powerful incentive for any staff development activity is simply "the clear understanding that it produces success" (Orlich, 1989, p. 74). And although collegial relationships among teachers are valuable in general, the results of mentor-mentee projects are particularly impressive. See Box 13.1 for mentors' comments about their experiences.

Table 13.1   Benefits Gained From Working With Student Teachers

Benefits	UCI Mentors Average[a]	Rank
Enthusiasm	3.50	1
Opportunity to collaborate	3.34	2
Knowledge of subject matter	2.93	3
Reflective mirror	2.90	4
Innovative strategies for teaching	2.90	4
Technology expertise	2.76	5
Insights about individual students' background	2.54	6
Assessment strategies	2.34	7
Sheltered language insights	1.68	8
Bilingual skills and strategies	1.20	9
Working with mainstreamed students	—	—

SOURCE: Clinard, L. M., & Ariav, T. (1998, Table 1). What mentoring does for mentors: A cross-cultural perspective. *European Journal of Teacher Education, 21*(1), 91–108.

a. Scale in questionnaire was from 0 ("very little contribution") to 4 ("great contribution"). N:89 (out of 158 participating mentors).

Table 13.2   Impact of Coaching Experience on Mentors' Work in Their Own Classrooms

Practice Areas	UCI Mentors Average[a]	Rank
Reflecting more often on planning and implementation	3.02	1
Using cognitive coaching techniques with students in the classroom	2.56	2
Reassessing classroom management and discipline strategies	2.56	2
Using instructional technology more frequently and effectively	2.44	3
Collaborating more with other teachers	2.27	4

SOURCE: Clinard, L. M., & Ariav, T. (1998, Table 2). What mentoring does for mentors: A cross-cultural perspective. *European Journal of Teacher Education, 21*(1), 91–108.

a. Scale in questionnaire was from 0 ("very little contribution") to 4 ("great contribution"). N:89 (out of 158 participating mentors).

Table 13.3   Impact of the Coaching Experience Beyond the Classroom

	Average[a]	Rank
Professional Life		
More committed to quality teacher education	3.26	1
Validation as a colleague working with university/college	3.07	2
Renewed enjoyment of/enthusiasm about teaching	3.06	2
Increased respect for university/college faculty	2.89	3
More motivated to invest in the profession	2.37	4
Considering teacher education as a future career	1.89	5
Private Life		
Experienced sense of pride as an individual	2.90	1
More effectively helping people do their own thinking/problem solving	2.80	2
Demonstrating more respect in relationships	2.52	3
Communicating/interacting with others more confidently	2.50	4
Changed attitudes in dealing with family members	1.22	5

SOURCE: Clinard, L. M., & Ariav, T. (1998, Table 3). What mentoring does for mentors: A cross-cultural perspective. *European Journal of Teacher Education, 21*(1), 91–108.

a. Scale in questionnaire was from 0 ("very little contribution") to 4 ("great contribution"). N:89 (out of 158 participating mentors).

BOX 13.1

From the Mentor's Mouth

The following quotations are from teachers experienced with mentoring programs. As these teachers indicate, mentors gain as much or more from their participation as do the beginning teachers.

When teachers share their unique talents, there is a sense of electricity in the air. The Mentor Program provides an environment for this excitement to occur. It brings teachers together to share and grow professionally.

I consider it a privilege to work with my colleagues in an exciting, innovative program for teachers.

Teachers learn from students and from each other. I find mentor work stimulating, and it keeps teaching interesting. The stipend for conferences and educational materials keeps me on top of the latest methods, trends, and ideas in teaching.

More than anything, I want to see teachers stay in the profession so they, too, can enjoy the same benefits without the feeling of being lost, or alone, as I did starting out.

The exchange of ideas helps my teaching. Intellectual discussions with a colleague are stimulating. In helping mentees, I learn more, stay more current. Also, I enjoy the status.

I enjoy working with teachers—they're like your best students—but even more dedicated and appreciative.

I learn new techniques. It's very beneficial being paired with a recently trained teacher.

I was a new teacher and received tremendous support even though I was very overwhelmed. I truly believe that a support system can help teachers succeed and deal with all the demands of being a new teacher. . . . Collaboration keeps me engaged, interested, and motivated, and I hope to provide that for others.

I am interested in seeing the curriculum that I've developed over the past 25 years continue as a legacy to that mentee and future generations of her students.

I find it very rewarding to work with other teachers [with various levels of experience]. Also, I am dedicated to education, and mentoring offers a unique opportunity to help new teachers.

I get reenergized by working with beginning teachers. I get new ideas and try out new approaches.

SOURCE: Jonson (1999b).

CONCLUSION

When teachers have the autonomy, opportunity, time, and resources to participate in their own and their colleagues' professional growth, instructional improvement is the obvious consequence. The collegial nature of the mentoring relationship, and of the larger mentoring program, means that all involved contribute to its growth and reap its benefits.

Being concerned for others is an important stage in career development. At the utilitarian level, mentors help their own careers by helping others. At the altruistic level, one mentor expressed the feeling well in saying, "I sleep better at night because I do for others what I wish had been done for me!" Another mentor explains,

Being a mentor keeps me current. When I have to answer my mentee's questions, it makes me ask, "Why am I doing what I'm doing?" In discussing philosophy, problems, or techniques with this new teacher, I find out what I really believe. That makes me a stronger person and a better teacher (Gordon & Maxey, 2000, p. 34).

REFERENCES

Alliance for Excellent Education. (2004, June 23). *Tapping into potential: Retaining and developing high-quality new teachers.* Washington, DC: Author.

Clinard, L. M., & Ariav, T. (1998, Spring). What mentoring does for mentors: A cross-cultural perspective. *European Journal of Teacher Education, 21*(1), 91–108.

Feiman-Nemser, S. (1996). Teacher mentoring: A critical review. *Peer Resources.* Retrieved November 30, 2001, from www.islandnet.com/~rcarr/teacher mentors.html

Fraser, J. (1998). *Teacher to teacher: A guidebook for effective mentoring.* Portsmouth, NH: Heinemann.

Gordon, S. P., & Maxey, S. (2000). *How to help beginning teachers succeed.* Alexandria, VA: Association for Supervision and Curriculum Development.

Gray, W. A., & Gray, M. M. (1985). Synthesis of research on mentoring beginning teachers. *Educational Leadership, 43*(3), 37–38.

Heller, D. A. (2004). *Teachers wanted: Attracting and retaining good teachers.* Alexandria, VA: Association for Supervision and Curriculum Development.

Jonson, K. (1999a). Parents as partners: Building positive home-school relationships. *The Educational Forum, 63,* 121–126.

Jonson, K. (1999b). [Survey of 28 mentor-teachers in the San Francisco Unified School District]. Unpublished raw data.

Joyce, B., & Showers, B. (1995). *Student achievement through staff development.* White Plains, NY: Longman.

Lortie, D. C. (1975). *Schoolteacher: A sociological study.* Chicago: University of Chicago Press.

Moran, S. (1990). Schools and the beginning teacher. *Phi Delta Kappan, 72,* 210–213.

Orlich, D. C. (1989). *Staff development: Enhancing human potential.* Boston: Allyn & Bacon.

Portner, H. (2006). *Workshops that really work: The ABC's of designing and delivering sensational presentations.* Thousand Oaks, CA: Corwin Press.

Shulman, J. H., & Sato, M. (Eds.). (2006). *Mentoring teachers toward excellence: Supporting and developing highly qualified teachers.* San Francisco: Jossey-Bass.

Smith, R. D. (1993). Mentoring new teachers: Strategies, structures, and successes. *Teacher Education Quarterly, 20*(4), 5–18.

Coaches as Leaders of Change

Jim Knight

I think that most teachers see their teaching as an art and when you're messing with their art, they can become really angry. And it's really hard not to take it personally. But I keep moving forward because I'm bringing better methods, and once I've given lots of backup, once they've started using it, once they see growth in their kids, they're OK.

—Jean Clark, instructional coach,
Bohemia Manor Middle School

Chapter 14

COACHES AS LEADERS OF CHANGE

The temptation is to avoid the leadership challenge altogether. Isn't it enough, we might ask, if ICs perform all the components of coaching (enroll, identify, explain, model, observe, explore, support, and reflect) in efficient and validating ways? Certainly a coach who does each of those tasks well is doing important and valuable work. The problem is that the complex challenges that require leadership refuse to leave coaches alone. ICs, sometimes on a daily basis, are thrown into situations where they will not be effective unless they lead. ICs need to shape team norms, facilitate schoolwide implementation of interventions, promote more constructive styles of professional discourse, motivate unmotivated teachers, raise thorny issues, negotiate resolutions to the conflicts that those thorny issues stir up, and stand in opposition to any action or attitude that is not good for children. Whether they like it or not, effective coaches must be effective leaders.

The concept of leadership carries with it many preconceptions. When we think of a leader, we often conjure up Hollywood images of men (usually) who exhibit heroic fortitude, courage, discipline, determination, and focus as they whip a bunch of losers into shape and overcome obstacles to fight the battle, take the flag, score the points, win at all costs, and beat the enemy. Clearly, that notion of leadership is at odds with the partnership approach proposed for ICs.

When it comes to instructional coaching, a different concept of leadership is more appropriate. In line with recent studies of leadership, ICs need a paradoxical mix of humility and ambition (Collins, 2001), a desire to provide service that is at least as powerful as the drive to succeed (Greenleaf, 1998), a deep understanding of the emotional components of leadership (Goleman, Boyatzis, & McKee, 2002), and a recognition that a good leader must first be an effective teacher (Tichy, 2002). The reality is that instructional coaching usually demands leadership. The good news is that there are tactics (strategies or methods) that coaches can learn and employ that will increase their ability to lead change. This chapter focuses on eight high-leverage leadership tactics that coaches can employ to lead change in schools.

TACTIC 1: STAY DETACHED

Before she became an IC at Bohemia Manor Middle School in Cecil County, Jean Clark, one of the first winners of the Cecil County Teacher of the Year Award, was respected as a highly successful teacher. In fact, she was brought to Bohemia Manor by her principal, Joe Buckley, because he had personally experienced how effective she was. Nevertheless, despite her personal warmth and professional pedigree, Jean's first year at her new school was not all smooth sailing.

Jean came to Bohemia Manor excited about introducing Content Enhancement Routines and other research-based teaching practices to her teachers. An energetic and driven professional, she found it difficult to hide her enthusiasm for the teaching practices, and she fully expected her colleagues to see the value of focused planning and explicit teaching. Unfortunately, some teachers were not so quick to catch Jean's enthusiasm. In fact, not long after she started talking with staff, Jean observed that teachers were starting to avoid her in the halls, disparage her in the staff lounge, and going to great lengths to get out of her way. This wasn't easy for Jean to accept.

Talking about her experiences, Jean observed that "the decision to step forward and become a leader can be difficult because both professionally and personally you're moving away from your colleagues, and that's a very difficult thing—there's a lot of self-doubt and fear."

Jean Clark

Jean Clark is an IC at Bohemia Manor Middle School in Cecil County, Maryland. She became an IC in 2004, but she says that she feels she has been a change agent for most of her professional life. Jean taught English for many years, and was one of the first Cecil County Teachers of the Year. Jean is a certified Strategic Instruction Model Content Enhancement Professional Developer, a writer, and a poet.

Unfortunately, the resistance and personal attacks that Jean experienced are not uncommon. Ronald Heifetz and Marty Linsky, in their book *Leadership on the Line: Staying Alive Through the Dangers of Leading* (2002), observe that

> adaptive [complex] change stimulates resistance because it challenges people's habits, beliefs, and values. It asks them to take a loss, experience uncertainty, and even express disloyalty to people and cultures. Because adaptive change forces people to question and perhaps redefine aspects of their identity, it also challenges their sense of competence. Loss, disloyalty, and feeling incompetent: That's a lot to ask. No wonder people resist. (p. 30)

When people are nervous about change, they can feel compelled to resist, and can give voice to that resistance by attacking the person promoting the change. By standing for a new vision of what a school or individual can be, by standing for change, ICs can inadvertently put themselves in the line of fire. And attack can be a very effective way to resist change. According to Heifetz and Linsky (2002),

> Whatever the form of attack, if the attackers can turn the subject of the conversation from the issue you are advancing to your character or style, or even the attack itself, it will have succeeded in submerging the issue. (p. 41)

Jean Clark found that teachers were inclined to attack her even after they had seen success. In her role as an IC, Jean reminded teachers of how they were falling short in their commitment to help children. Jean explains,

> Teachers might be using the Unit Organizer and the course map and starting to see kids that normally don't respond, responding. Even with that, they'll use it for a while and then stop using it because they need a lot of support or because they're very busy at home, and eventually they revert to the old way of take out your book and let me do round-robin reading. Then they become angry because I suspect they know that's not what they really want to be doing. And here comes Jean Clark and I'm going to throw a pallet at her.

If coaches aren't attacked personally, they may find that their interventions come under attack. Even when programs are going well, when results are unmistakable, people in a school may find reasons to criticize a program. Unfortunately, what frequently occurs in schools is a vicious cycle that ensures that new teaching practices never get implemented—an "attempt, attack, abandon cycle" that prevents any real change from taking hold in schools. During the "attempt, attack, abandon cycle," someone introduces a new practice into a school, and teachers make a half-hearted *attempt* to implement it. Then, before the program has been implemented effectively, and before it has been given sufficient time to be fully implemented, various individuals in the school or district begin to *attack* the program. As a result, many of the teachers implementing the program now begin to lose their will to stick with it. Inevitably, even though the practice was never implemented well, leaders in the district reject it as unsuccessful, and *abandon* it, only to propose another program that is sure to be pulled into the same vicious cycle, to eventually be attacked and abandoned for another program, and on and on. Thus, schools stay on an unmerry-go-round of attempt, attack, abandon, without ever seeing any meaningful, sustained change in instruction taking place (Knight, 2006).

Figure 14.1   The Attempt, Attack, Abandon Cycle

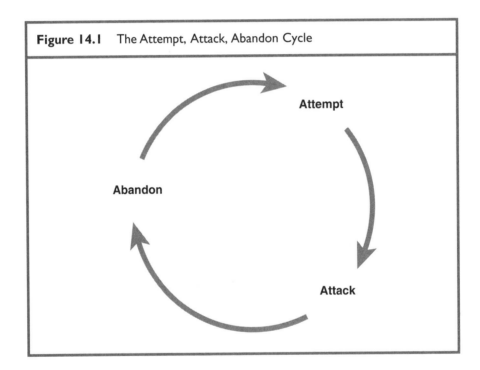

The Attempt, Attack, Abandon Cycle

What should coaches do when they come under attack? Jean Clark is unequivocal about how difficult it can be to encounter resistance: "I've been really depressed at times because I can't stand being the enemy." After interviewing Jean and other ICs across the nation and observing many coaches in action, I've come to believe that ICs have to "stay detached" to stay effective. If coaches become too personally involved in their change initiatives, if they see every attack on their program as an attack on themselves, they may find the personal consequences devastating. Jean says that she's "getting tougher" and learning to detach herself from each teacher's individual struggle to change and improve. "I'm getting tougher to where I can say, hey, let them go, this is the change stuff that you're seeing; you're seeing them blow up, it's a loss right now and they're grieving over a lot of stuff. Just get out of the way."

I suggest four strategies ICs can employ to maintain a healthy distance when they are leading change.

1. *Use partnership communication.* This suggestion may seem paradoxical, or even contradictory. If partnership communication is all about building an emotional connection, how can ICs stay detached while also staying connected? In reality, it is paradoxical. The partnership approach grounds any act of communication in the belief that everyone's point of view should be listened to because everyone is equally valuable. Partnership communication helps us listen more effectively, empathize, and rethink communication from the perspective of the listener as opposed to our own point of view. ICs taking the partnership approach consciously build relationships by extending and turning toward others' emotional bids, and they are very aware of how their personal stories or the stories held by a listener can interfere with and sometimes stand in the way of any effective communication.

By taking the partnership approach, ICs can detach themselves by, first, proactively eliminating many of the time bombs that can blow up during interpersonal communication. Simply put, when teachers feel respected, when they are aware that their IC listens authentically, and when they feel an emotional connection with their IC, they are much less likely to attack the coach or the program. Paradoxically, therefore, the first step in staying detached is to reduce the number of attacks you might experience by taking the partnership approach.

2. *Change your thinking to create distance.* When Linda Stone, a former senior Microsoft executive, wrote out the most important lessons she'd learned in her life, she offered advice that seems highly pertinent to coaches trying to stay detached. Stone wrote, "Whenever we feel defensive, hurt, personally attacked, confused, or afraid, we have a choice—we can get very curious. Rather than saying, 'I never would have said that,' we can say, 'I wonder what these people heard me say? I wonder what their perception is?'" (Jensen, 2005, p. 63). Coaches can stay detached by reconceiving the attack as an opportunity to learn and better understand the people with whom they work.

3. *Keep it from being personal.* Perhaps the chief strategy ICs can use to stay detached is to be sensitive to the emotional undercurrents at work in any interchange. Then, if they notice an interaction turning negative,

they can stay detached by recognizing what is happening and by telling themselves to keep their distance. William Ury, more than two decades ago, referred to this tactic as "going to the balcony" (Ury, 1985). He suggested that whenever we feel a conversation turning negative and personal, we can detach ourselves by imagining that we are watching the interaction from a balcony. Ury describes "going to the balcony" as follows:

> When you find yourself facing a difficult negotiation, you need to step back, collect your wits, and see the situation objectively. Imagine you are on a stage and then imagine yourself climbing onto a balcony overlooking the stage. The "balcony" is a metaphor for a mental attitude of detachment. From the balcony you can calmly evaluate the conflict almost as if you were a third party . . . Going to the balcony means distancing yourself from your natural impulses and emotions. (1985, pp. 37–38)

The simple trick of imagining that we are physically distanced from the conversation can help us feel psychologically distanced from the interchange and help us avoid responding in ways we will later regret. One IC stays detached when things get heated simply by thinking, "Wow this looks like one of those conflict situations; I wonder if I can use my communication techniques to keep this from escalating." The simple act of naming the situation as one with potential for conflict somehow provides the distance necessary for this coach to stay detached.

Coaches also need to ensure that their program or activities are not seen as their personal pet project. An additional part of "keeping it from being personal," then, is to ensure that we keep the focus on instruction and students and not on us. Although we want to build an emotional connection and want our colleagues to enjoy working with us, we do not want them to work with us out of personal obligation. If teachers try our practices merely because they feel they owe it to us, rather than because they believe it is good for kids or for them, eventually, they will grow tired of spending their energy pleasing us. Coaches must resist the temptation to use their friendship as a leverage point for motivating colleagues, and continually turn the focus of conversations to how strategies or teaching practices can help students.

4. *Take the long view.* Staying detached is not synonymous with being apathetic about results. In truth, it is just the opposite. If ICs are too personally involved in their project, they may find the unsuccessful days emotionally devastating. Furthermore, if the teaching practices proposed are tied too closely to the IC, that perception can further inhibit the spread of ideas in schools.

We believe that by staying detached, ICs increase the likelihood that interventions will catch on in a school. To effectively lead change, ICs sometimes need to consciously stand back from the potentially distressing moments of resistance that might keep them up late into the night. A better strategy is to take the long view, recognizing that research is quite clear that a well-organized coaching program should lead to widespread implementation and improvements in student achievements. By staying detached, by seeing beyond the momentary lapse and keeping the long-term goals in view, ICs can be more effective leaders of change.

TACTIC 2: WALK ON SOLID GROUND

ICs who are uncertain of their principles, goals, priorities, or practices may be unprepared for the turbulence and waves of resistance they may encounter in a school. ICs must be clear on what they stand for, if they want others to stand with them in improving instruction for students. Henry Cloud, in his book *Integrity: The Courage to Meet the Demands of Reality* (2006), writes about the importance of being clear on who we are and what we stand for:

> People who do best in life have a well-defined *identity* on a number of fronts. They are secure in their boundaries, they know what they like and don't like, what they believe in and value, and they love and hate the right things. They are not wishy-washy and what psychologists call identity diffused, wondering who they are or what they are about, or thinking that they are everything. You get a good definition of who they are just from being around them. (p. 144)

A starting point for walking on solid ground is for ICs to work out their beliefs about the partnership principles of equality, choice, voice, dialogue, reflection, praxis, and reciprocity. ICs need to deeply understand these principles, first, so that they can decide whether or not they will ground their actions in them. If they do not agree with some of the principles, ICs should reflect and determine the principles that they will use as a foundation for action. Inevitably, ICs will be called upon to act in ways that are inconsistent with these principles (leading a change initiative that doesn't allow any room for teachers' choices, for example), and if they are unsure of their principles, they will have a harder time resisting such suggestions. They may also act in ways that will end up unsuccessful.

Jean Clark experienced the importance of walking on solid ground first-hand. When the program Jean was leading at Bohemia Manor Middle School began to gain momentum, administrators and teachers around the district started to ask her for the quick-fix version of Content Enhancement. She was invited to give a one-hour presentation to large groups of teachers, and to send materials to teachers without providing any kind of follow-up professional development. Jean's clarity about what she stood for, and her commitment to praxis and dialogue, helped her to say no. Because she knew what she stood for as a leader of professional learning, Jean was able to advocate for more effective forms of professional learning and keep the "attempt, attack, abandon cycle" from occurring, at least for the moment.

To stay grounded, coaches also need to stay fully conscious of the moral purpose that is at the heart of the work they do. As Michael Fullan observes, "Moral purpose, defined as making a difference in the lives of students, is a critical motivator for addressing the sustained task of complex reform. Passion and higher order purpose are required because the effort needed is gargantuan and must be morally worth doing" (2003, p. 18). One way for coaches to walk on solid ground is to remind themselves—perhaps every day, hour, or minute—that the primary purpose of their work is to make life better for children.

To stand on solid ground, coaches also need to understand fully their long-term and short-term goals. Lynn Barnes, a coach at Jardine Middle School, sets goals for every week, making plans, for example, to speak briefly to three non-implementers every five days. A useful practice for ICs before any meeting with a teacher or administrator is to ask, "What are my short-term goals for this interaction?" An IC's short-term goal with a teacher might be as simple as trying to enhance a relationship or as ambitious as getting someone on board to help lead a schoolwide reading program. When meeting with an administrator, a coach might set the short-term goal of always explaining a research-based teaching practice or explaining what someone should watch for while observing a teacher implement a new teaching practice.

As important as short-term goals are, an IC's long-term goals are even more important. Long-term goals provide focus and help ICs set priorities. Coaches who take the time to set long-term goals, and who monitor their progress, are better prepared to use their time efficiently. Simply put, coaches will lead change more effectively if they know their top priorities and have a clear understanding of the outcomes they hope to achieve. To lead teachers and schools in a given direction, coaches need to be clear on their destination.

Let me add a final word: being sure of what you stand for is an essential part of being a leader, but steadiness is not the same thing as stubbornness. In our studies of ICs, we have found that having too firm a ground to stand on can be problematic if coaches become impervious to new ideas. Michael Fullan offers some excellent advice: "beware of leaders who are always sure of themselves" (2001, p. 123). Coaches need to remain open to new ideas, to learning from the teachers and administrators with whom they collaborate, or their lack of flexibility may keep others from working with them. Indeed, when coaches have reflected on and clarified what it is that they stand for, they may actually find it much easier to open their mind to other ways of understanding.

TACTIC 3: CLARIFYING YOUR MESSAGE

In addition to being clear about short- and long-term goals, ICs also need to be clear about the information and vision they want to share with teachers. Noel Tichy, whom *BusinessWeek* has rated as one of the "Top-Ten

Management Gurus," considers such clarity to be an essential attribute of effective leaders. "Leaders," Tichy observes, "must be able to share their experience. And in order to do that, they must externalize the tacit knowledge within them. They must draw lessons from their experiences, and then convey those lessons in a form so that others can use it" (2002, pp. 74–75). Leaders intent on creating such learning conversations require what Tichy refers to as a *Teachable Point of View* (TPOV). A TPOV is a "cohesive set of ideas and concepts that a person is able to articulate clearly to others" (2002, p. 74). Roger Enrico from PepsiCo has said that "a Teachable Point of View is worth 50 IQ points" (Tichy, 2002, p. 97).

Tichy describes four basic building blocks of a TPOV. First, a TPOV is built on central ideas. Ideas "enable the leader to create dynamic and engaging stories that detail where the company is, where it is going, and how they will get there" (p. 75). Second, a TPOV must include values that leaders can articulate explicitly to shape support for ideas. Third, a TPOV must be energizing, including "a clear set of beliefs and actions for motivating others" (p. 76). Finally, a TPOV involves what Tichy describes as "edge," "facing reality . . . and making tough decisions" (p. 76).

When Jean Clark began as an IC, she spent a great deal of time developing her own TPOV—though she likely wouldn't have used that terminology. Jean was determined to find effective ways to explain Content Enhancement—and that took time. "In the beginning," Jean said, "this stuff didn't make any sense." So, to "make sense" of Content Enhancement, Jean spent many hours reading through instructor's manuals, paraphrasing materials in her own mind, drawing semantic maps, and taking notes until she felt she knew the material. Jean also practiced teaching routines in the classroom so that she was fully aware of how it felt to teach students how to master concepts using the Concept Mastery Routine (Bulgren, Schumaker, & Deshler, 1993) or how to organize their units using the Unit Organizer Routine (Lenz, Bulgren, Schumaker, Deshler, & Boudah, 1994).

Jean found that "the smartest thing" was to take time to learn "a piece at a time." According to Jean, "You can't take this really quickly, you have to think about it." However, Jean's determination to get clarity about Content Enhancement is paying off: "I'm definitely changing as a result of this, and I'm really starting to get the big picture with Content Enhancement and the whole model, the whole Strategic Instruction Model." As she gets clearer, Jean finds she has become more capable of getting other teachers to implement the model. Jean reports, "Other people are having 'aha's'! All you need is one person to have an 'aha' every now and then; that's enough."

TACTIC 4: MANAGING CHANGE EFFECTIVELY

Buckingham and Coffman (1999), who studied more than 80,000 managers from different industries, suggest that a large part of effective leadership is effective management. These researchers sifted through literally millions of data sets, sorting and resorting until they synthesized the essence of effective management into six critical questions. These questions help us understand how ICs can perform many management tasks of leading change.

The Big Six

1. Do I know what is expected of me?

2. Do I have the materials and equipment I need to do my work right?

3. At work, do I have the opportunity to do what I do best every day?

4. In the past seven days, have I received recognition or praise for doing good work?

5. Is there someone at work who cares about me?

6. Is there someone at work who encourages my development?

Let's take a look at each of these questions as they apply to instructional coaching.

Do I Know What Is Expected of Me?

Teachers who do not understand what they have to do to implement a teaching practice may be quick to drop that practice when they find out it is not what they expected. Consequently, if ICs are unclear about what teachers need to do in order to implement practices, they run the risk of severely damaging a relationship they may have spent months or years developing. For example, a teacher trying out a new approach she learned from a coach who is blindsided by a time-consuming demand to grade learning sheets may quickly reject the approach or, perhaps even worse, reject the coach when she realizes the additional grading is more than she can handle.

To be effective, ICs have to be careful to explain exactly what teachers can expect why they try something new. Among other concerns, ICs should explain (a) what additional demands, if any, will be made on teacher time; (b) how much class time a given teaching practice will take; (c) how students might be expected to respond; (d) how the intervention fits with the district or state curriculum; and (e) what else may have to change for the practice to be implemented.

Do I Have the Materials and Equipment I Need to Do My Work Right?

Teachers tell us that one of the main reasons why they often do not implement new teaching practices is that they do not have the time or desire to put together all the materials necessary to try something new. ICs in Topeka and Baltimore have gotten around this barrier to implementation by giving teachers a cardboard box called "strategy in a box," filled with every item a teacher might need to implement a strategy or routine, including printed overheads, handouts or learning sheets for students, reading materials, or whatever else might be necessary for implementation. As IC Irma Brasseur has commented, "Part of our goal is to release teachers from burdensome, mundane things so they can spend time thinking about being a learner, to make changes to bring out critical teaching behaviors."

At Work, Do I Have the Opportunity to Do What I Do Best Every Day?

Although coaches usually have little or no say in who teaches what classes, an IC can collaborate with teachers to make it possible for them to do their best every day. Most important, when coaches and individual teachers work together to identify instructional practices, they must be careful to identify interventions that build on the teacher's unique strengths. Teaching practices are not generic; what works well for one teacher might not work as well for another. The art of coaching is working together with a teacher to identify interventions that respond to the teacher's most pressing need while also taking advantage of the teacher's greatest strength.

In the Past Seven Days, Have I Received Recognition or Praise for Doing Good Work?

Recognizing and praising each teacher each week may be a stretch goal for some ICs, but that doesn't mean that it isn't a worthy one. As we've explained throughout this book, a coach is often much more effective if she can build an emotional connection with fellow teachers, and this includes recognizing, praising, and supporting teachers whenever possible. For Jean Clark, recognizing teachers also provides an opportunity for follow-up and dialogue: "If you don't have the follow-up and you don't have the opportunity to continually reuse it and talk about it and dialogue about it, it's not going to stick."

Is There Someone at Work Who Cares About Me?

Can a coach be successful if he doesn't care about fellow teachers? I don't think so. Coaches who are truly collaborative can't help but find themselves in caring relationships with collaborating teachers. Interviews I've conducted with coaches across the nation have shown again and again that an important aspect of coaching is simply being available as a listener or a friend to fellow teachers. As IC Devona Dunekack has observed, being a coach is "more than PD [professional development]. Every week, several times, people come and see me, shut the door and let go. They might talk about something personal, or something in the school. I'm just a good listening ear, and after we've talked, they can get up and do the job that is extremely important to do."

Is There Someone at Work Who Encourages My Development?

Ultimately, this is what an IC's primary work is, to continually encourage each teacher to develop, to be a better professional, to reach and encourage and support more children. As such, an effective IC contributes in immeasurable ways to the continual progress of the school. By facilitating the professional growth of their colleagues, coaches help teachers stay alive, stay growing, and stay effective shapers of children's lives.

Buckingham and Coffman's questions bring into focus some of the tactics, strategies, and perspectives an IC should employ, and the questions also demonstrate that having an IC in a school can be a powerful way to accelerate professional learning and, indeed, enable people to realize their potential and live meaningful lives. But managing is only part of leadership. To really lead change, you need to go further.

TACTIC 5: CONFRONTING REALITY

The most obvious leadership challenge may also be the most difficult: confronting reality. According to Bossidy and Charan (2004), who literally wrote the book on this topic, *Confronting Reality: Doing What Matters to Get Things Right*, "to confront reality is to recognize the world as it is, not as you wish it to be, and have the courage to do what must be done, not what you'd like to do" (pp. 6–7). But, recognizing and acting on the world as it is, is not always easy for ICs. When working one-to-one with teachers, for example, coaches may find it difficult to candidly discuss instructional practices since the way people teach is so intertwined with the way they define themselves. As a result, if I present an unattractive picture of the way a teacher delivers a particular lesson, for example, I may be criticizing an act that is at the heart of who that person is. To talk about teaching practice is to talk about one of the most personal parts of a teacher's life.

Recently, flying home from a work visit in Michigan, I had an experience that brought home to me just how difficult it can be to confront reality with others. When I sat down on the plane, I found myself sitting beside a fascinating man from the East Coast. We quickly found ourselves talking about his work and his life, and I was impressed by the man's intellect, sense of humor, and wisdom. There was just one problem. His breath was terrible. Even though I really wanted to listen to this interesting man, I just couldn't get past the fact that his breath was so bad.

Always the coach, I began to be concerned about the many problems his breath might be causing. "I wonder," I thought, "if I should tell him about his problem. If this breath is a common problem, I wonder if this fellow is losing customers just because they can't stand the aroma emanating from his smiling face? I wonder what impact it has on his marriage and family? What does his wife think about this? I really should tell him about this problem so he can do something about it!" But I didn't say anything. The risks of upsetting this nice man, or getting him angry with me, seemed too great, and I just sat there listening—more concerned with getting along with him or avoiding conflict than I was with giving him some information that might have been very important.

My challenge on the plane is the challenge coaches face every day. ICs struggle to share information that is unpleasant at the same time that they work to maintain a healthy relationship with collaborating teachers. What is difficult one-to-one, where we are able to build strong, supportive bonds with individuals, is even more difficult at the group level. When we surface difficult truths in larger organizations like schools, not only do we have to address the personal issues that are an unavoidable part of confronting reality, we also have to deal with the other contingencies of life in organizations, such as incomplete data sources, misinformation arising from failure of internal communication, individuals who hide from their own professional failures, and so on. It's no wonder that Bossidy and Charan (2004) conclude that "avoiding reality is a basic and ubiquitous human tendency" (p. 26).

Despite the seductive appeal of avoiding the truth, the fact is that schools won't move forward, and students' lives won't improve, unless ICs and other educational leaders ask some core questions about the teaching and learning that occurs in every classroom:

- What is it like to be a student in this classroom or school?
- How do the students feel in this class?
- Is this teacher using "hi-fi" teaching practices?
- Does the teacher appreciate, enjoy, and respect students?
- Are students engaged in this class?
- Are students experiencing meaningful learning experiences or are they simply completing tasks that fill the time?
- Does this class increase or decrease students' love of learning?
- Will students remember this class?

Along with questions about individual classes, coaches and educational leaders can confront reality by asking questions about the school and school culture:

- Are our teachers focused on becoming better teachers or are they focused on making excuses?
- Is our school improving or declining?

- Do our teachers focus on students and teaching during team meetings, or do they focus on blaming, excuse-making, or finger-pointing?
- Are our leaders supportive and positive?
- Do our leaders encourage our teachers to meet high standards?
- Do our leaders walk the talk?

Confronting reality in most schools is tough, but failure to confront reality is much worse because it ensures that no meaningful improvement takes place. ICs can help a teacher or school face facts by asking some or all of these truth-seeking questions.

TACTIC 6: UNDERSTANDING SCHOOL CULTURE

More than two decades ago, researcher Susan Rosenholtz made the rather startling (to me at least) claim that "reality is socially constructed and maintained through everyday organizational life" and that "teachers shape their beliefs and actions largely in conformance with the structures, policies and traditions of the workaday world around them" (1991, pp. 2–3).

Rosenholtz identified shared goals, teacher collaboration, teacher certainty, learning enrichment opportunities, and teacher commitment as important attributes of effective schools. She adapted organizational theorist Rosabeth Moss Kanter's description of "stuck" and "moving" institutions to distinguish between effective and ineffective academic social organizations:

> The stuck feel no sense of progress, growth or development and so tend to lower their aspirations and appear less motivated to achieve. They shy away from risks in the workplace and proceed in cautious, conservative ways. The moving, by contrast, tend to recognize and use more of their skills and aim still higher. Their sense of progress and future gain encourages them to look forward, to take risks, and to grow. (Rosenholtz, 1991, p. 149)

The implications of Rosenholtz's research are provocative, suggesting that a teacher's effective or ineffective teaching practices result as much from where the teacher teaches as much as they do from who the teacher is. Thus, if you moved teachers from a stuck school to a moving school, just by virtue of where they worked, Rosenholtz suggests, they would in many cases become better teachers. When I share this research with educators, 25 years after Rosenholtz conducted it, these ideas still ring true.

Whether they fully agree with Rosenholtz or not, ICs need to attend to Rosenholtz's lesson: school culture can accelerate or inhibit change in numerous ways in schools. In a sense, culture functions like gravity, no one can see it, but it keeps things in place. In workshops, I often talk about the culture of the elevator. Somehow, most people in North America have mysteriously learned that that there are certain rules to being in an elevator. You know the rules: (a) don't talk, (b) face the door with your back to the wall, (c) look at the numbers. When I was an undergraduate student at the University of Ottawa in Canada, a young poet purposefully broke these rules, by standing with his back to the door, facing the other passengers in the elevator. Usually some people riding along became genuinely uncomfortable just by the way he stood in the elevator. It was as if these people were thinking, "Doesn't he know what the rules are?"

Such is the hold that culture can have over us. We come to act in regulated ways without really being aware that there are any regulations. When cultural norms are good for students, such as norms that say we never talk disrespectfully about children, we believe that all children can succeed, and we support professional learning, cultural norms can be positive. However, when cultural norms are not good for students, such as norms that say we blame the children and their parents for our unsuccessful students, we bully children, and we ridicule professional learning, then they can be very destructive.

One important leadership tactic, then, is for ICs to be sensitive to the cultural norms in a school and to work to change norms that are not good for students. By doing that, coaches function similarly to a group of leaders Debra Meyerson (2001) refers to as *tempered radicals*. "Tempered radicals are people who operate on a fault line. They are organizational insiders who contribute and succeed in their jobs. At the same time, they are treated as outsiders because they represent ideals or agendas that are somehow at odds with the dominant culture" (p. 5).

One of the most important ways in which ICs can lead is by shaping the kinds of conversations that take place in schools. A coach intent on changing school culture must be what Kegan and Lahey (2001) refer to as "a discourse-shaping language leader" (p. 20). That is, he or she must stand for a new kind of conversation while at the same time staying a part of the school culture. Deborah Kolb and Judith Williams (2000) suggest that we redirect conversation away from unhealthy topics, like gossip, by using communication maneuvers they call *responsive turns*. Responsive turns are communication tactics ICs can use to redirect potential unhealthy conversations. I've included four responsive turns suggested by Kolb and Williams, along with my definitions and some examples (see Table 14.1).

TACTIC 7: BEING AMBITIOUS AND HUMBLE

When the teachers at Jean Clark's middle school resisted her suggestions and criticized her methods, Jean was tempted to return to the classroom and a simpler life. "I've always got one foot out the door," Jean said. But Jean did not give in to the seductive promise of a less stressful life. Rather, she stayed the course with the partnership approach. Jean employed a wide variety of

Table 14.1 Responsive Turns

Tactic	What It Is	Example
Interrupt	Cutting off the negative conversation before it begins	"Oh crap, I'm late; I've gotta go."
Name	Describing what's going on so everyone can see it	"I just feel that if we keep complaining about kids, we're never going to come up with anything useful."
Correct	Clarifying a statement that is not true	"I was at the meeting, and Mr. Smith was actually opposed to the plan."
Divert	Moving the conversation in a different direction	"Speaking of Tom, when does the basketball season start this year?"

relationship-building and communication strategies. She took time to meet one-to-one with teachers, talked with her colleagues about their day-to-day lives inside and outside of school, and listened authentically and with empathy.

At the same time, Jean refused to drift into the background. She was determined and driven—she sought out opportunities to bring together collaborating teachers to do co-planning with her, focusing on teachers who had informal power in her school. Jean also worked with her principal to set up afterschool professional development sessions and to encourage him to apply pressure on some teachers whom she thought might particularly benefit from instructional support. And she was also a voracious learner—attending courses, reading articles and books, and learning as much as she could, as quickly as possible, so that she had valuable, up-to-date knowledge to share with teachers. In short, Jean took a partnership approach with her teachers, but at the same time, she was willful, deliberate, and driven as she led change at her school.

Jean's combination of leadership and partnership slowly began to pay off, and she started to see improvements in the way teachers taught and students learned in her school and in her district as a result of her efforts. Indeed, in a matter of months, Bo Manor Middle School began to attract the attention of educators throughout Cecil County, and the impact of Jean's willful and respectful approach began to extend across the county.

Jean's approach is one that I have seen employed consistently by effective coaches in schools across America. To really make change happen, ICs employ the respectful, patient, and dialogical methods of the partnership approach. At the same time, they are driven, almost obsessive, about making significant changes happen. In his book *Good to Great* (2001), Jim Collins has identified the same kind of paradoxical attributes in leaders of great organizations. When he looked for common traits among great companies, Collins explains, he was taken aback by what he found:

> We were surprised, shocked really, to discover the type of leadership required for turning a good company into a great one. Compared to high-profile leaders with big personalities who make headlines and become celebrities, the good-to-great leaders seem to have come from Mars. Self-effacing, quiet, reserved, even shy—these leaders are a paradoxical blend of personal humility and professional will. They are more like Lincoln and Socrates than Patton or Caesar. (p. 13)

Effective leaders, Collins reports, "are ambitious first and foremost for the cause, the movement, the mission, the work—not themselves—and they have the will to do whatever it takes . . . to make good on that ambition" (2005, p. 11). Much the same can be said about effective ICs—they are very ambitious, but their ambition is for improvements in instruction and in the experiences of children in schools. "Success," Jean reports, "brings success . . . and it's starting to stick. There's a bunch of us doing it; we're becoming partners."

TACTIC 8: TAKING CARE OF YOURSELF

Being a leader is emotionally challenging, and thousands of change agents have found it difficult to remain optimistic, energetic, and enthusiastic. When we are marginalized, attacked, or silenced, when our successes are downplayed and our contributions are overlooked, it is difficult to remain optimistic. As Heifetz and Linsky explain:

> When you lead people, you often begin with a desire to contribute to an organization or community, to help people resolve important issues, to improve the quality of their lives. Your heart is not entirely innocent, but you begin with hope and concern for people. Along the way, however, it becomes difficult to sustain those feelings when many people reject your aspirations as too unrealistic, challenging or disruptive. Results arrive slowly. You become hardened to the discouraging reality. Your heart closes up. (2002, p. 226)

Too frequently, as Table 14.2 suggests, professionals in schools find it too difficult to maintain their own innocence, curiosity, and compassion.

For ICs to remain emotionally healthy, given the challenges that can confront them in a school, they must take time to keep themselves healthy.

Table 14.2 Hope and Hopelessness When Leading Change

Quality of Heart	*Becomes*	*Dressed Up As*
Innocence	Cynicism	Realism
Curiosity	Arrogance	Authoritative knowledge
Compassion	Callousness	The thick skin of experience

SOURCE: Heifetz & Linsky (2002, p. 226).

Distinguish Your Role From Your Self

Frequently, the kind of people who choose to become ICs are precisely those who are deeply invested in their role. Thus, coaches may tie their own sense of worth directly to their success or failure with teachers in school. When a teacher chooses to use a new practice that helps students be successful, these ICs may have a momentary blissful sense that they are competent, making a difference, and living a life that counts. Then, when teachers stop implementing change, resist change, or attack interventions or, even worse, ICs may feel a deep despair, questioning whether or not their work, or even their life, matters. Such profound emotional upswings and downturns can take a real toll on a coaches' well-being.

Heifetz and Linsky (2002) explain that leaders need to be careful to separate their "role" from their selves: "when you lead, people don't love you or hate you. Mostly they don't even know you. They love or hate the position you represent" (p. 198). To remain healthy, coaches need to remember this.

Find Confidants

Finding someone or a group of people to confide in is a positive way ICs can protect themselves and remain healthy. ICs, by virtue of their role, are often on their own in a school. They are often unable to immerse themselves completely in a school, simply because they are always trying to change it. Coaches are in the school, but not of the school. As a result, they sometimes find themselves on the outside of the in-group, when the in-group is intent on gossiping, complaining, or blaming. For that reason, finding someone to confide in outside the school can be very helpful.

When Jean Clark was considering going back to her first love—the classroom—what kept her committed to being an IC was the development of a collaborative friendship with Sherry Eichinger, a special education teacher at Bohemia Manor Middle School. As the vignette below illustrates, Jean became an emotional and intellectual partner with Sherry. As is the case with true partnerships, Jean, the coach, gained from collaborating with Sherry as much or more as Sherry, the teacher, gained from Jean.

Faith

In the years previous, I was training to be a professional developer. But I had this fear that maybe I don't have good people skills, perhaps I shouldn't be doing this. I kept running into these adults who were getting really ticked off at me. I kept thinking, "Well, you know, I'm just getting more and more awkward here as I'm aging and I'm not able to get these folks to work with me as I used to." So I was just about ready to get out of this field and go back to the classroom.

But what I've been discovering is that I can do this really, really well as long as I have partners. I see that when I have a partner like Sherry. She was a Christi McCollum scholar. She has a master's in special ed and in transitions, and she will not back off for those kids—she will do lots of work. I gained a great deal to suddenly be around someone who works like that. She started coming to me and asking, "Well, how would you teach a kid that really didn't understand how to read?" and "I don't understand how to do this," and every time she asked me a question, I had to think about it, and as soon as I started to think about it, I started thinking about how I learned.

The two of us work so well together. We disagree with one another at times, but we're both working for the same thing; we're both working for the kids and an understanding with the kids. I can't do it by myself, and I see that she can't do it by herself. We support one another. She supports me emotionally when I'm really depressed; she tries to keep me up. And when she's really depressed, thinking, "OK, I'm not going to do this another year, everybody's at my throat," I talk to her about it and remind her how far we've come. So we support one another both cognitively and emotionally. Because it's hard to do this work without a partner.

Being a change agent, you can weather it, you can weather what happens to you if you have enough folks talking to you—not just talking to you, but giving you things to think about, and letting you see their growth, like I've seen her growth. Having her there, it has given me faith.

Find Sanctuary

The need to build in a time and place to recharge your batteries is not a new idea. In as ancient a document as Genesis in the Bible, we were advised to ensure that we take one day off from all of our work. Researchers studying top athletes have found that that biblical advice still holds true for active athletes. Loehr and Schwartz (2003), for example, have conducted studies of the attributes of great athletes. When they compared great athletes with good athletes, they found that great athletes don't try any harder or, in many cases, aren't any more skilled than good athletes, but they are much better at building variety into their training routine.

I believe that ICs can take a page from the great athletes that Loehr and Schwartz describe. Coaches, like athletes, need to be sure to build in opportunities to relax, refresh, and recharge. Jean Clark reports that she's fully aware that she does need to take care of herself, and she has her ways to relax and renew herself that work best for her. "I'm a writer; I write constantly. I read all the time, I go to counseling. I'm in 12-step meetings, you name it . . . I go to church . . . I do everything to stay emotionally healthy."

One simple way to recharge is to find a place where you are able to relax and cool your heels, so to speak. Your own personal sanctuary might be your favorite coffee shop downtown, a park bench, a quiet out-of-the-way corner in the library, or the swing on your front porch. What matters is that you find a place where you feel free to relax and let your mind stand at ease for an hour or two. I don't own a condo by the ocean or a cabin by a mountain stream, but I have found my own way to find sanctuary. In Lawrence, Kansas, where I live, there is a five-mile concrete trail that provides bikers, runners, and Rollerbladers with a quick route out of town and into a beautiful, wide prairie meadow. My sanctuary is to tie up my old pair of Rollerblades, program my iPod to play whatever music suits me on a given day, and roll out into the valley. For an hour or so with my Rollerblades, music, and the nature trail, I'm able to put the pressing deadlines and other challenges I face on hold, and simply rest and relax. Indeed, many of the ideas that have found their way into this book first flew into my consciousness when I was far away from my computer, blading through the valley just outside of Lawrence.

THE FINAL WORD ON JEAN CLARK AND BOHEMIA MANOR MIDDLE SCHOOL

During the last weeks of Jean's first year at Bo Manor, I was sitting in my office at the University of Kansas. When my phone rang, I picked it up and heard the voice of Joe Buckley, Jean's principal, on the other end of the line. Joe had never called me; in fact, I had never given him my telephone number, but he told me that he had gone out of his way to get it from Jean. "Jim," he said, "we've just gotten our test scores, and let me read some of them to you." Joe quickly rattled off some scores that, I learned, showed that in each grade, the number of students who were proficient in math and reading had doubled. Bohemia Manor School, it turns out, was the only school in Cecil County in which a majority of students were proficient in all subjects and all grade levels. The results, were, as Joe said, "amazing." "Jim," he concluded, "I just had to call you to thank you for your work supporting Jean. These scores just show how important she is to this school. She's done an awesome job this year."

Throughout that year, I had worked with Jean, and I knew what struggles she had gone through to win over her school and to make meaningful improvements in instruction to take root. When I heard how genuinely grateful and excited her principal was, I felt a deep sense of satisfaction. Jean had stuck it out, weathered the attacks, and led her school forward, and in the end, her school's students were clearly better for her work. Working as an IC, Jean had had an unmistakable, positive impact on the teachers in her school, and consequently, the students in her school were learning more and performing better. What could be better than that?[1]

GOING DEEPER

Reading about leadership is a bit like reading about surfing, I imagine. Books might help, but you really have to dive in and get wet to truly benefit from your readings. Most readers of this book, I suspect, are already confronting leadership challenges. In that case, the following sources should prove helpful.

Michael Fullan's books are a great starting point for the study of leadership.

Heifetz and Linsky's *Leadership on the Line: Staying Alive Through the Dangers of Leadership* (2002), accurately summarizes many of the emotionally taxing challenges a leader might face and offers practical strategies people can use to overcome those challenges. Heifetz and Linsky also explain how and why leaders should distinguish between technical and adaptive challenges.

Goleman, Boyatzis, and McKee's *Primal Leadership: Learning to Lead With Emotional Intelligence* (2002) applies the concept of emotional intelligence, first introduced by Daniel Goleman, to leadership. The authors contend that a leader's most important task, the primal task, is to address the emotional needs of those being led. Leaders who are astute enough to guide their teams to experience positive emotions are referred to as *resonant leaders*. The model of leadership they propose is consistent with the partnership principles, and the book's description of the relationship-building skills, leadership styles, and strategies necessary to create resonant leadership are very useful. The book also contains some excellent non-examples.

When I heard Dennis Sparks speak in 2005, he held up a copy of *Primal Leadership* and said, "If there is one book on leadership that educators should read, this is it." Some might make a claim that the same could be said for his book, *Leading for Results: Transforming Teaching, Learning, and Relationships in Schools* (2005). This is a remarkably concise work that contains 25 strategies people can employ to refine their leadership skills. Sparks's visionary *and* practical strategies include a variety of ways to clarify and achieve your goals, several suggestions for developing clear thinking, skills for improving authentic listening and encouraging dialogue, and other strategies leaders can employ to walk the talk as they lead.

Henry Cloud's *Integrity: The Courage to Meet the Demands of Reality* (2006) is a very readable but wise and useful book that describes six qualities that determine leadership success in business (I believe his suggestions also apply to the social sector). The six qualities are establishing trust, oriented toward truth, getting results, embracing the negative, oriented toward increase, and oriented toward transcendence.

Marcus Buckingham and Curt Coffman's *First, Break All the Rules: What the World's Greatest Managers Do Differently* (1999) introduces the Big Six Questions included in this chapter. Based on over 80,000 interviews conducted by the Gallup Organization, the book describes three basic strategies used by outstanding managers. First, in managing, leading, and "sustained individual success," the most productive leaders find the talents of people they work with and do not dwell on their negative aspects. Second, managers shape jobs to fit people, rather than shape people to fit jobs. Third, they are crystal clear in expectations and goals. Fourth, leaders choose employees for the talent they have, not just their expertise.

TO SUM UP

- Leadership is an unavoidable part of instructional coaching.
- There are eight tactics ICs can use to increase their effectiveness as leaders:
- *Stay detached:* Find ways to take the long view and keep yourself from being overly invested in each component of your coaching program.
- *Walk on solid ground:* Know what you stand for if you want others to stand with you.
- *Clarify your message:* Develop a deep understanding and clear way of communicating the ideas you have to share with others.
- *Be ambitious and humble:* Embody a paradoxical mix of ambition for students and personal humility.
- *Confront reality:* Ask questions that help you focus on the real situation in teachers' classrooms and in your school.
- *Understand school culture:* Recognize that behavior is often as much a product of organizational culture as it is of each individual's characteristics.
- *Manage change effectively:* Do all you can to ensure that your teachers know what is expected of them and have what they need to implement the teaching practices you share with them.
- *Take care of yourself:* If you want to lead change, you must protect and nourish yourself.

NOTE

1. At the end of Jean's second year, Bohemia Manor again showed more growth than any other middle school in Cecil County.

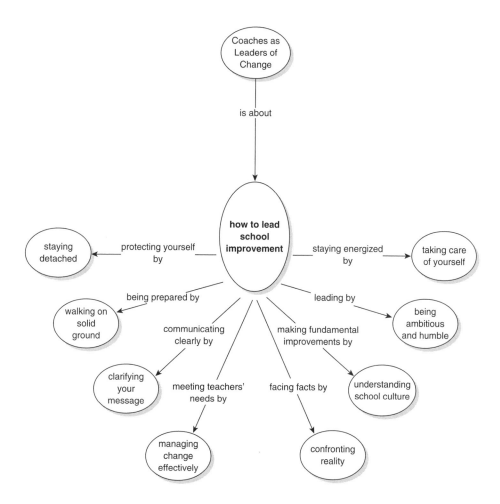

REFERENCES

Bossidy, L., & Charan, R. (2004). *Confronting reality: Doing what matters to get things right.* New York: Random.

Buckingham, M., & Coffman, C. (1999). *First, break all the rules: What the world's greatest managers do differently.* New York: Simon & Schuster.

Bulgren, J. A., Schumaker, J. B., & Deshler, D. D. (1993). *The concept mastery routine.* Lawrence, KS: Edge Enterprises.

Bulgren, J. A., & Lenz, B. K. (1996). Strategic instruction in the content areas. In D. D. Deshler, E. S. Ellis, & B. K. Lenz (Eds.), *Teaching adolescents with learning disabilities: Strategies and methods* (2nd ed., pp. 409–473). Denver, CO: Love Publishing.

Bulgren, J. A., Lenz, B. K., Deshler, D. D., & Schumaker, J. B. (2001). *Question exploration routine.* Lawrence, KS: Edge Enterprises.

Collins, J. (2001). *Good to great: Why some companies make the leap . . . and others don't.* New York: HarperCollins.

Collins, J. (2005). *Good to great and the social sector: A monograph to accompany Good to Great*. Boulder, CO: Collins.

Cloud, H. (2006). *Integrity: The courage to meet the demands of reality*. New York: HarperCollins.

Fullan, M. (1993). *Change forces: Probing the depths of educational reform*. New York: Falmer Press.

Fullan, M. (2001). *The new meaning of education change* (3rd ed.). New York: Teachers College Press.

Fullan, M. (2003). *Change forces with a vengeance*. New York: RoutledgeFalmer.

Goleman, D., Boyatzis, R., & McKee, A. (2002). *Primal leadership: Learning to lead with emotional intelligence*. Boston: Harvard Business School Press.

Greenleaf, R. K. (1998). *The power of servant-leadership*. San Francisco: Berrett-Koehler.

Heifetz, R., A., & Linsky, M. (2002). *Leadership on the line: Staying alive through the dangers of leading*. Boston: Harvard Business School Press.

Jensen, B. (2005). *What is your life's work? Answer the big questions about what really matters . . . and reawaken the passion for what you do*. New York: HarperCollins.

Kegan, R., & Lahey, L. (2001). *How the way we talk can change the way we learn*. San Francisco: Jossey-Bass.

Knight, J. (2006). Instructional coaching: Eight factors for realizing better classroom teaching through support, feedback and intensive, individualized professional learning. *The School Administrator, 63*(4), 36–40.

Kolb, D. M., & Williams, J. (2000). *The shadow negotiation: How women can master the hidden agendas that determine bargaining success*. New York: Simon & Schuster.

Lenz, B. K., Bulgren, J., Schumaker, J., Deshler, D. D., & Boudah, D. (1994). *The unit organizer routine*. Lawrence, KS: Edge Enterprises.

Loehr, J. S., & Schwartz, T. (2003). *The power of full engagement: Managing energy, not time, is the key to high performance and personal renewal*. New York: Free Press.

Meyerson, D. E. (2001). *Tempered radicals: How people use difference to inspire change at work*. Boston: Harvard Business School Press.

Rosenholtz, S. J. (1991). *Teacher's workplace: The social organization of schools*. New York: Teachers College Press.

Sparks, D. (2005). *Leading for results: Transforming teaching, learning, and relationships in schools*. Thousand Oaks, CA: Corwin Press.

Tichy, N. M. (with Cardwell, N.). (2002). *The cycle of leadership: How great leaders teach their companies to win*. New York: HarperBusiness.

Ury, W. (1985). *Beyond the hotline*. Boston: Houghton Mifflin.

Index

CORWIN
PRESS

The Corwin Press logo—a raven striding across an open book—represents the union of courage and learning. Corwin Press is committed to improving education for all learners by publishing books and other professional development resources for those serving the field of PreK–12 education. By providing practical, hands-on materials, Corwin Press continues to carry out the promise of its motto: **"Helping Educators Do Their Work Better."**